Assemble and Leap

In celebration of the 60th Anniversary of the S.O.B.H.D.

S.O.B.H.D.

World Governing Body
of Highland Dancing

Congratulations
I hope you enjoy the book
Good luck with your dancing
Sheall Russell

Assemble and Leap

In celebration of the 60th Anniversary of the S.O.B.H.D.

Published in 2010 by
The Scottish Official Board of Highland Dancing
Heritage House, 32 Grange Loan, Edinburgh EH9 2NR, Scotland

ISBN 978-0-9566206-0-6

Edited by Helen Ford

Printed by Astute Visual Communications

Index

Welcome to Assemble and Leap

Celebrating 60 years of the Scottish Official Board of Highland Dancing

Welcome to "Assemble and Leap", the 6oth Anniversary book of the Scottish Official Board of Highland Dancing – The World Governing Body of Highland Dancing.

This book highlights the vision of what this Board is all about, the dancer, Highland Dancing and the history of the people and organisations that have brought us all to where we are today. Throughout this book you will find names of people that should be remembered for their tireless hard work and dedication to Highland Dancing.

Dancers, Teachers, Examining Bodies, Affiliated Members, Organisations, Competitions and figureheads all have their own section. While reading through this book memories will be recalled, days will be reminisced, important events will be highlighted, dancers will be celebrated, past leaders and figureheads will be remembered, history will be retained, and our vision for the next sixty years will be revived.

In total there have been 7 chairmen during the past 60 years namely; Harry Fairley, Dr. Alistair C McLaren, Jack Muir, Brigadier A G L MacLean, Billy Forsyth MBE, Shendl Russell and Christine Lacey.

In the coming pages you will see or read about the earlier Chairmen either within the Inaugural Minutes of the Board or the extracts of the first couple of Board Minutes. You will then meet the current Office Bearers, Independent Members, Honorary Members, Director of Administration and past significant principal Ambassadors to whom we owe so much. And finally a section which I am sure will bring a smile to everyone's face, the photographs from a collection of old Cowal Programmes containing winners from the past to present from all over the world.

This book has been a tremendous amount of work from people throughout the world. From the gathering of information to the collecting of photographs and to the archiving of events, competitions and meetings, all have been very worthwhile exercises when you see the quality of the work within each section of the book. We owe so much to the leaders, teachers and figureheads of years past. Most if not all were dancers and had the vision to create a governing body that united the dancers of the day to the countries of the world through highland dancing. We also owe a huge debt of gratitude to all of our teachers from out with Scotland for keeping our heritage and traditions of Highland Dancing so very much alive, for this we are truly grateful.

Working together while moving forward, looking to the future while respecting and celebrating the past is an important ethos of my chairmanship. This project along with the DVD – "SOBHD - The Foundations of the Highland Technique" are ways which we will hopefully never forget the past or how we all got here. Knowing where we have been will help us all in getting to where we are going.

60 years ago the pioneers of our Board Assembled the highland dancers. It is now up to us, the future of this Board to work together, remembering the past and to keep Leaping towards a better tomorrow. Highland Dancers from all over the world, please join me in celebrating 60 years of The Scottish Official Board of Highland Dancing.

Christine Lacey
Chairman of the Scottish Official Board of Highland Dancing

Inaugural Meeting - 15th January 1950

Scottish Official Board of Highland Dancing - Inaugural Meeting

15th January 1950

Postal Headquarters 338 Duke Street Glasgow E.1.

1. The Inaugural meeting of the Scottish Official Board of Highland Dancing was held in the Plaza Ballroom, Stirling, on Sunday 15th January 1950 at 2.p.m.

2. Mr Jack Muir (SDTA) occupied the Chair and the following were present:

Representatives of Associations

a. Scottish Dance Teachers Alliance - J.L. McKenzie, J. Turpie, Miss N. Ross.
b. British Association of Teachers of Dancing - G. Walker, Miss Wallace, Miss Lindsay.
c. Scottish Country Dance Society - Miss Hadden, Mrs Brown.
d. United Kingdom Alliance - Miss H. Constable, J. Mowat, Mrs Ferguson, Miss McDonald
e. North British Ballrooms Association - H. Fairley. J.F. Stewart, F. Robertson, G. Jamieson.
f. British Ballet Organisation - Miss A. Calder.

Independent

Capt. Davidson, Capt. Gibson, Major Bourne, Mrs R. Watson, D.G. McLennan, Miss E. Thompson, Brig. Clark, Mr Purdon, Capt. Tait, Mr W.I. Russell, Capt. Bain, Mr. W. Christie. Mr Ross.

Apologies for inability to attend were intimated from the H.D.S.A and Mr. J. McConnachie.

3. The Chairman opened the meeting, by explaining his presence and the purpose of the meeting. He drew a comparison between the position of Highland Dancing today and that of Ballroom Dancing 21 years ago (i.e. pre Ballroom Official Board). He then invited discussion, the main point for consideration being “whether there existed a real need for an Official Control Board for Highland Dancing”.

The representatives of several Associations and many Independent Members spoke in favour of the project and a letter was read by Capt. Davidson from New Zealand Pipers’ and Dancers’ Association Inc. commending the venture and conveying their good wishes for its success.

It was unanimously decided that a Board of Control be formed, this body to be known as “The Scottish Official Board of Highland dancing”.

The Chairman then suggested that the best way to approach the forming of an Official Board was first of all to appoint an “Interim Committee” and give them the task of drawing up the Constitution, deciding upon some kind of proportionate representation and various other initial business. Their findings would require to be brought to another general meeting to be passed. This was agreed and Mr. Fairley proposed, seconded by Mr. Robertson that the Interim Committee should consist of: “2 Delegates from each of the seven Dancing Associations, 2 Delegates from each of 8 Games Committees and 8 Independent Members. This was carried unanimously”.

The Members of the Interim Committee are as follows:

S.D.T.A.	J.L. McKenzie and J. Turpie
B.A.T.D.	Miss Wallace and Miss Lindsay
S.C.D.S.	Miss Milligan and Mrs Brown
U.K.A.	Miss McDonald and Mrs Ferguson
N.B.B.A.	H. Fairley and J.F. Stewart
H.D.S.A.	(to be nominated by that body)
B.B.O.	Miss Calder and Miss Hopkins

Capt. Davidson, Miss Thompson, Colonel McLean, Major Bourne, Brig. Clark, Miss M. Aitken, Mr R. Watson, Mr J. McConnachie.

(Plus 16 Delegates from Games Committees - yet to be nominated).

The Chairman then suggested that a Chairman, Secretary and Treasurer of the Interim Committee should be elected. This was agreed and the following were elected:

Chairman	Mr. H. Fairley
Secretary	Miss Jean McLellan
Treasurer	Mr. J.F. Stewart

This being all the business, the meeting was terminated with a vote of thanks to Mr. Adam and his staff for their hospitality.

Scottish Official Board of Highland Dancing - Interim Meeting

15th January 1950

1. A short meeting of the Interim Committee was held immediately following the Inaugural Meeting with Harry Fairley in the Chair.

2. Invitation to Games Committees
It was decided to invite a representation on the Committee of two Delegates from each of the Games Committees as follows:

Aboyne, Braemar, Bridge of Allan, Cowal, Inverness, Luss, Lochaber, Oban and Thornton.

3. Annual Subscriptions
The Committee to suggest to the next General Meeting, that the Annual Subscription, payable to the Official Board when formed, should be:

Associations	5 gns
Games Committees	2 gns
Independent Members	1 gn (Altered to 10/6 at continuation of Inaugural Meeting)

4. Constitution
The Chairman suggested that the drawing up of the Constitution should be left over until next meeting of the Interim Committee to give the members the opportunity of preparing recommendations. This was agreed.

5. Representation of Scottish Official Board of Highland Dancing
After some discussion it was decided that the representation should be as follows:

Associations	2 Delegates from each.
Games Committees	2 Delegates from each. (as shown on map prepared by Capt. Davidson).
Independent Members	As already elected to the Interim Committee.

6. Date and Venue of next meeting:
The meeting accepted Mr Fairley's kind offer of his Victoria Halls, Leith Street, Edinburgh for the next meeting on Sunday 19th February and the time 2.30 pm.

Scottish Official Board of Highland Dancing - Interim Meeting

19th February 1950

Interim Committee

1. A meeting of the Interim Committee was held at 83 Leith Street, Edinburgh, on Sunday 19th February 1950, at 2.30 pm. (by kind permission of Mr. H. Fairley).

2. Mr. Fairley was in the Chair and those present were:

S.D.T.A.	Mr. J. Turpie
	Mr. J.L. McKenzie
B.A.T.D.	Miss Wallace
	Miss Lindsay
U.K.A.	Miss McDonald
	Mrs. Ferguson
B.B.O.	Miss Calder
H.D.S.A.	Mr. McDermid
	Mr. Sutherland
	Miss Tucker
	Miss Findlay
N.B.B.A.	Mr. J.F. Stewart
H.P.S.	Dr. A. McLaren
Cowal	J.S.Thompson

Independent Members
Major Bourne, Capt. Davidson, Mr. J. McConnachie, Miss M Aiken, Miss E. Thompson, Lt. Col. A. McLean.

Intimations of inability to attend where received from:

Brig. Clark, Mr J Watson, Mrs Brown, Miss J Milligan, Miss M Hopkins, Strathallan Meeting, Argyllshire Gathering, Braemar, Aboyne, Lochaber.

3. The minutes of the meeting held on 15th January 1950, having been circulated to members, was taken as read and confirmed.

Arising out of the Minutes
The Secretary stated that replies had been received from six of the Games Committees, but no acknowledgement had, as yet, been received from Inverness, Luss and Thornton Games Committees.

Also arising out of the minutes, it was decided not to use the zoning system in connection with the Games Committees Representation, but to have instead, one Representative from each Games Committee.

4. Correspondence

A letter was read from the Highland Pipers' Society asking for Representation on the Official Board and their representative was present at the meeting.

5. Byelaws

Draft suggestions for Byelaws governing the Official Board as prepared by the Chairman, were read and considered in great detail by the meeting and, with a few alterations, were passed for recommendation to the Board.

6. Any other Business

There followed a short discussion regarding the formation of a Technical Committee to act in an advisory capacity to the Board and it was suggested that not more than seven members should be elected.

Mr. Turpie recommended that each Dancing Association should appoint Technical Committee members.

Capt. Davidson said that he considered that just under 50% of the Technical Committee should consist of active teachers or dancers and the remainder should have retired from the profession.

The Chairman then asked the members to submit nominations in writing to the Secretary as soon as possible.

7. It was decided that the next meeting be held on Sunday 16th April at 2.30 pm. and that this should be a General Meeting. Mr. Fairley very kindly offered his premises for this purpose.
This being all the business, the meeting was terminated with a vote of thanks to Mr. Harry Fairley for his hospitality.

Note on Item 6

All nominations for the Technical Committee should reach the Secretary by Friday 24th March 1950.

Scottish Official Board of Highland Dancing - 1st Meeting

13th August 1950

Postal Headquarters 83 Leith Street Edinburgh

1. The first meeting of the Scottish Official Board of Highland Dancing was held at 83 Leith Street, Edinburgh, on Sunday 13th August 1950 at 2.30 p.m. (by kind permission of Mr. Harry Fairley).

2. Those present were:

Represented Member	**Delegates**
Scottish Dance Teachers Alliance	Mr Jack Muir
	Miss Jean McLellan
British Association of Teachers of Dancing	Miss E. Wallace
	Miss Mary Lindsay
United Kingdom Alliance of Professional	Mr James Turpie
Teachers of Dancing	Miss Peggy McDonald
Highland Dance Specialists Association	Miss C. Tucker
	Miss B. Findlay
British Ballet Organisation	Miss Adeline Calder
Scottish Country Dance Society	Mrs M.K. Brown
	Lord James Stewart Murray
North British Ballrooms Association	Mr. Harry Fairley
	Mr. J.F. Stewart
Highland Pipers' Society	Dr. A. McLaren
Cowal Highland Gathering	Mr. J.S. Thomson

Independent Members

Lt. Co. A. MacLean, Brig. Clark, Capt. T. Davidson, Mr R. Watson, Mr. J. McConnachie, Mr. D.G. McLennan.

Apologies for inability to attend were received from:
Miss E. Thomson, Major A.A. Bourne, Pipe Major G.D. Taylor and Miss Garland.

3. Mr. Muir opened the meeting, by proposing that the Chairman of the Interim Committee, Mr. Harry Fairley, should act as Chairman until such times as a Chairman of the Official Board was elected. This was Seconded by Col. MacLean and all agreed.

4. Minutes

The minutes of the continuation of the "Inaugural Meeting" having been circulated to members, were taken as read and confirmed.

5. Elections

Acting on the suggestion of Mr. Stewart, the meeting decided to give precedence to the election of members (No. 5 on the List of Elections) and the following were elected:

S.D.T.A. - proposed by Mr. Stewart and seconded by Mr. McConnachie
B.A.T.D. - proposed by Mr Muir and seconded by Miss McLellan
U.K.A. - Proposed by Miss Wallace and seconded by Miss Lindsay
H.D.S.A. - proposed by Mr. McConnachie and seconded by Miss McLellan
B.B.O. - proposed by Mr. Turpie and seconded by Miss McDonald
S.C.D.S. - proposed by Capt. Davidson and seconded by Dr. McLaren
H.P.S. - proposed by Capt Davidson and seconded by Mrs Brown
N.B.B.A. - proposed by Mr. Turpie and seconded by Col. MacLean
Cowal Games - proposed by Miss McLellan and seconded by Miss McDonald

Mr. Muir proposed that the eight Independent members of the Interim Committee, Brigadier H.J.D. Clark, Lieut-Col. A.G.L. McLean O.B.E., Major A.A. Bourne, T.D. Capt. T.S. Davidson, Messrs R. Watson, J. McConnachie, Miss E Thomson and Miss Mary Aiken, should be elected en bloc with the addition of Mr. D.G. McLennan. This was seconded by Mr Turpie and carried unanimously.

Mr. Muir, seconded by Miss McDonald, proposed that the position of Chairman should be dealt with next and this was agreed. Mr. Stewart, seconded by Mr. Muir, proposed that the voting should be by elimination. This was carried.

The following were nominees:

Mr. Harry Fairley - nominated by the U.K.A.
Mr. Jack Muir - nominated by the S.D.T.A.
Dr. McLaren - nominated by Capt. Davidson
Col. McLean - nominated by Brig. Clark
Brig. Clark - nominated by N.B.B.A.
Mrs M. K. Brown - nominated by N.B.B.A.

Both Brig. Clark and Mrs Brown withdrew their names and the result of the voting made Mr. Harry Fairley of Edinburgh, the first Chairman of the Board.

S.O.B.H.D.
World Governing Body of Highland Dancing

Election of Secretary

The following were nominees:

Miss J. McLellan – nominated by the U.K.A.
Miss Helen Constable – nominated by the U.K.A.
Miss E. Wallace – nominated by Miss Jean McLellan
Captain Davidson – nominated by Mr. Stewart
Col. MacLean – nominated by Mr. J. McConnachie

Miss McLellan and Miss Wallace withdrew their names and the result of the voting made Captain T. Davidson the first Secretary of the Scottish Official Board of Highland Dancing. Brig. Clark moved a warm vote of thanks to Miss Jean McLellan, who had undertaken the secretarial work during the eight months it had taken to form the Board. Miss McLellan thanked Brig. Clark and the members of the Board for the co-operation and courtesy they had shown to her and very much regretted the necessity to relinquish the secretarial duties owing to pressure of business.

Election of Treasurer

The following were nominated:

Mr. Thomson – nominated by Mr. Jack Muir
Mr. J.F. Stewart – nominated by Mrs Brown
On a vote being taken, Mr. Thomson became the first Treasurer of the Board

Election of Honorary President

The following were nominated:

Lord James Stewart Murray – nominated by Col. MacLean
Gen. Sir A.F. Christison – nominated by Brig. Clark
As a result of the voting, it was decided that the Board should approach Gen. Sir A.F. Christison, with a view to obtaining his consent to act in this capacity.

Election of Technical Committee

Mr. Muir, seconded by Mr. McConnachie, moved that the Technical Committee should be 20 in number and should be divided as follows:

2 Delegates from each of the Five Dancing Association Members (10) and the remainder (10) to be elected by the Board.
Mr. Stewart moved an amendment, that the Technical Committee should be 10 or 11 in number. On a vote being taken, the proposition carried by 12 votes to 7.

Mr Muir seconded by Miss McLellan, then moved that the election of Technical Committee be left on the table until the next meeting of the Board.

Mr. Stewart, seconded by Dr. McLaren, moved an amendment that the Independent Members of the Technical Committee be elected today.

On a vote being taken, the amendment carried.

Election of Independent Members of Technical Committee

1. D.G. McLennan
2. Col. A.G.L. McLean C.B.E.
3. Brig. Clark
4. J.L. McKenzie
5. A. McLaren M.B. Ch.B
6. J. McConnachie
7. Dr. A. Robertson
8. Sydney Black
9. Miss M. Aiken
10. Angus McPherson

The above were elected.

Scottish Official Board of Highland Dancing - 2nd Meeting

17th September 1950

1. The second meeting of the Scottish Official Board of Highland Dancing was held at 10 Calton Hill, Edinburgh, on Sunday 17th September, 1950 at 11.00 hours.

2. Those present were:

Represented or Affiliated Member	Delegates Names
British Association of Teachers of Dancing	Miss E. P. Wallace Miss M.F. Lindsay
British Ballet Organisation	Miss A.M. Calder Miss K.E. Garland
Cowal Highland Gathering	Mr. James S. Thomson
Highland Dancing Specialists Association	Miss Jessie Stewart Miss B. Findlay
Highland Pipers' Society	Dr. A. McLaren
North British Ballroom Association	Mr. Harry Fairley Mr. J.F. Stewart
Scottish Dance Teachers Alliance	Mr Jack Muir Miss Jean McLellan
United Kingdom Alliance of Professional	Mr James Turpie
Teachers of Dancing	Miss Peggy McDonald

Independent Members

Brigadier H.J.D. Clark, MC
Captain T.S. Davidson,
Lt. Colonel A.G.L. MacLean, CBE
Mr. D.G. McLennan.

Scottish Official Board of Highland Dancing - 1st Annual General Meeting

18th November 1951

The First Annual General Meeting of the Scottish official Board of Highland Dancing, was held at 83 Leith Street, Edinburgh, on Sunday November 18th, 1851, at 11:30am.

Those present were:

B.A.T.D.	Miss M.F. Findlay
B.B.O.	Miss K. Kirkland
	Miss A. Calder
Cowal Highland Gatering	Mr J.S. Thompson
H.D.S.A.	Cissie Tucker
H.P.S.	Miss J. Reynolds
N.B.B.A.	Mr J.F. Stewart
	Mr C. Wood
S.C.D.S.	The lord James Stewart Murray
S.D.T.A.	Mr J. Muir
	Mr R.H.J. Thomson
U.K.A.	Mrs J. Ferguson
	Miss P. MacDonald
Army	Lt. Col. A Gordon

Independent Members

Major A.A. Bourne
Mr D.G. McLennan
Lt. Col. A.G.L. MacLean
Brigadier H.J.D. Clark
Mr. R. Watson

Ex - Officio Members

Mr Harry Fairley
Miss C. Collie

Apologies for inability to attend were received from:

Mrs M. Brown
Dr. A Robertson
Dr A.C. McLaren
Mr Drummond
Miss J. McLellan

Elections

As no new nominations had been received, it was agreed that the present Office Bearers remain in office for a further year.

President	General Sir Philip A.E. Christison
Chairman	Mr Harry Fairley
Treasurer	Mr J.S. Thompson

Miss Collie agreed to remain in office until nominations for Secretary had been received from the Associations and Independent Members and had been placed on the Agenda for the next meeting.

Mr Muir proposed, seconded by Major Bourne, that the Represented Members be re-elected en bloc:

British Association of Teachers of Dancing
British Ballet Organisation
Cowal Highland Gathering
Highland Dancing Specialists Association
Highland Pipers' Society
North British Ballrooms Association
Royal Scottish Country Dancing Society
Scottish Dance Teachers Alliance
United Kingdom Alliance
Army

It was agreed that the present Independent Members be re-elected for a further year.
It was agreed that Lt. Col. A. Gordon, Mr J. Muir and Mr J.F. Stewart be appointed as auditors.

Official Highland Dancing Outfit

From the early 1950's

Betty Jessiman

Agnes Stewart

S.O.B.H.D.

World Governing Body of Highland Dancing

Millennium Champions Challenge

Atholl Clasp and Millennium Champions Challenge

In 1998 I attended the "Atholl Highlanders Ball" in the Ballroom of Blair Castle, Blair Atholl, Perthshire. Traditionally this is held the evening before the Atholl Gathering.

Christine Lacey was judging for me at the Gathering that year and we chatted about the Castle. Christine remembered the Atholl Dancing Festival was held in the Ballroom one year and thought it had a great atmosphere for Highland dancing. She also said to date nothing was arranged to celebrate the Board's 50th anniversary.

Through this conversation, the idea for Millennium Champions Challenge to celebrate the SOBHD's Golden Jubilee took seed. Firstly I had to convince my committee (the Atholl Dancing Association) then I had to convince Marjory Rowan, Billy Forsyth and the Board that we could make a success of the event. With Billy's help grant applications were successfully made so before long the event organisation was up and running!

The world-wide dancing community embraced the idea, as did residents in the Atholl area of Scotland, with many donations of all kinds offered.

Malcolm Appleby was one of those residents. Malcolm is now the foremost gun engraver in the United Kingdom, and his famous Raven Gun is housed in the Royal Armouries. His many commissions include the engraving of the orb on the Prince of Wales Coronet, King George VI and Queen Elizabeth Diamond Stakes Trophy for De Beers, the 500th anniversary silver cup for the London Assay Office and a major silver cup and cover for the Royal Museum of Scotland. Malcolm also made the seal for the Victoria and Albert Museum and was commissioned to make the silver centre piece for the New Scottish Parliament. He also has examples of his work in many collections throughout the world. We were obviously in good company!

It was Malcolm's suggestion that he design, produce and hand engrave a gold brooch and call it the Atholl Clasp. If we raffled the original then that would cover his cost. This we duly did.

He allowed his design to be used as the artwork for medals and created the silver gilt, silver and bronze clasps for the over-all winners. He also suggested that the Atholl Dancing Association use the art work as our logo.

Also at the event in 2000, Miss Jessie Stewart became the first recipient of the Atholl Clasp. The Atholl Dancing Association wanted the memory of this friendly event to live on through the presentation of "The Atholl Clasp".

To our delight the Board agreed and for the last 10 years, the award has been presented annually to people within the dancing community who have served their sport extremely well.

All the recipients have given their lives to Highland Dancing. Nominations are given to the Board each year and the Office-Bearers select the recipient.

A video/DVD was made of the 2000 event, the sales of which are still managing to fund the Clasp which Malcolm Appleby continues to make for us.

Jessie Stewart receiving Atholl Clasp in 2000, from Past President Billy Forsyth.

Malcolm Appleby's Drawing of the Atholl Clasp

This is Malcolm Appleby's line drawing of the Atholl Clasp. The design was used for all the medals presented in 2000.

Millennium Champions Challenge started exactly 10 years ago today - from Friday 24 March to Sunday 26 March 2000 with the competition taking place on Saturday 25 March 2000. This was one of sportscotland's Major Events for the Millennium. We even got mentioned in the New York Times – wow!

Past Recipients of the Award

2000	Jessie Stewart MBE	2005	Jean Ritchie
2001	Evelyn McLaren	2006	Heather Jolley
2002	Margaret Todd	2007	Sheena McDonald
2003	Marjory Rowan	2008	Wilma Tolmie
2004	Adeline Duncan	2009	Billy Forsyth MBE

Some of the Previous Office Bearers & Auditors

of the Scottish Official Board of Highland Dancing

From left: Dr Alistair MacLaren, Jack Muir, Harry Fairley, Lord James Stewart Murray, Adeline Calder, Harry Clark

BRIGADIER ALASDAIR MACLEAN OF PENNYCROSS

The Brigadier was Chairman and President of SOBHD for a number of years, Director and Producer of the Edinburgh Military Tattoo from its inception and a real character. He came from Lochbuie on the Island of Mull and served with the Queens Own Cameron Highlanders for 33 years. He was a good piper and excellent dancer, as witnessed by Willie Cuthbertson who danced with and competed against him on many occasions. According to an Adjutant at Edinburgh Castle he was above all an outstanding showman and commentator but totally unpredictable. This was confirmed by the Board Secretary, Marjory Rowan, who had to deal with him for many years during his Chairmanship of SOBHD.

For instance, we are told he phoned one evening to invite Marjory and her husband to Cocktails the following Sunday and on hearing of a problem over baby sitters said just bring the children. Big Mistake! When Marjory arrived complete with Baby and Carry Cot plus two children, Mrs MacLean (who had been taught dancing by Cissie Tucker and who had three children of her own), was unperturbed but the Brigadier was not amused. The instruction was 'put THAT in another room on a bed'. His lounge was a treasure trove of goodies with drums as tables all around the room. While her sons played and banged on all the drums her daughter went round lifting and examining all the other trophies. The visit did not last long.

A week before the Brigadier's death Marjory received a phone call from Mrs MacLean asking her to take a taxi round to the house. When she arrived Mrs MacLean was at the door with her coat on and said simply 'he's in that room and the best of luck'. There was no good morning greeting from the Brigadier in the bed just the instruction 'sort it', meaning the multitude of papers spread all over the bed. It took quite a few hours to 'sort it' into piles for the Army, the Tattoo, the SOBHD etc. When finished she was instructed to go to the stair and see if Mrs MacLean had returned. She had not so Marjory was instructed to go into the lounge and bring back a bottle of whisky and two glasses. Marjory didn't drink whisky and asked if he was allowed it. 'I don't give a Bugger, just go and get it' was the reply. She had a drink with him and when his wife returned he gave Marjory a hug and she left. He died five days later.

STEWART BELL

Mr. Bell was a Sheriff of the Court in Edinburgh and latterly in Glasgow.

He was connected to Highland Dancing through the H.P.S and the S.P.A. He became an Independent Member shortly after its inaugural meeting. During the early 60's he was one of the auditors for the Board's accounts, the other auditor being Miss Adeline Calder.

DR ALISTAIR MACLAREN

Dr MacLaren lived in Edinburgh and had a medical practice in Edinburgh He was involved in Highland Dancing through the Highland Pipers' Society and the Scottish Pipers' Association. His son Hamish also danced and played the pipes, being taught at Merchiston Castle School and privately by Miss Cissie Tucker. On the death of Brigadier, Dr. MacLaren was elected President of the Board. Prior to that he was Vice President of the Board.

In the early 1950's Marjory Rowan worked in a legal office and one day was told by the boss Mr Nightingale, to put on her "Shawl and Bonnet" and come with me in the car. She had no idea where she was going and her boss didn't speak in the car. They arrived at the house and the door was opened by Dr MacLaren. He greeted Mr Nightingale and then spotted Marjory.

Mr Nightingale was surprised that his client should know Marjory. On that day, Marjory was there to witness signatures on the papers before being dispatched to the car. On the return journey Mr Nightingale asked about Highland Dancing. Dr MacLaren had told him that Marjory shouldn't have to work on a Saturday as she was very good at this Highland Dancing and needed Saturdays to compete.

A few days later, he sent for Marjory and she was told to report to him every Monday about any competitions she had attended and if she needed the next Saturday off. Her boss became really interested in Highland Dancing, never having heard of it before Dr MacLaren mentioned it. Marjory rarely worked Saturdays after that day.

Some of the Previous Office Bearers & Auditors of the Scottish Official Board of Highland Dancing

WILLIAM MACNIVEN CUTHBERTSON

William MacNiven Cuthbertson or 'Willie' as he was fondly known , was one of the Highland Dancing GREATS! He was a Champion Dancer in his own right but my knowledge of this wonderful man relates to his expertise as a Teacher and Adjudicator of Highland Dance.

Many well known people in the 'Dancing World' were taught by this renowned teacher, Billy Forsyth MBE, Betty Turkington, Iain MacDonald to name but a few. With the exception of only one section, in 1961 his pupils won every Scottish Championship and two World Championship Titles at Cowal Highland Gathering.

I recall my first class at his house in Aitken Street, Glasgow, little did I realise, that this man was going to have a huge influence in my life. As the lesson progressed a few other dancers joined the class at various intervals. This was when I realised that these dancers were in a different league in fact 'Champion Dancers'.

During class we would dance on a wooden floor which was rolled out to cover the carpet. He would sit on a low seat and accompany us on a small set of bagpipes which I think are known as a quarter set. Blowing into the mouthpiece with one side of his mouth and shouting instructions from the other side. When working on correction work , he would whistle the tune, as to dance "out of time" was not an option. If you did not push your knees back a tap with his cane ensured that you complied. Praise was seldom given in class, "that's better" was as good as it got! He would demonstrate steps to his pupils and as a child I used to be fascinated by his small feet. My first introduction to Spread/Split High Cuts was being placed between the backs of two wooden chairs on which two pupils sat to stop the chairs from moving (no fancy barres in those days) Willie expertly demonstrated the high cuts and I thought, Oh my goodness! Will I ever be able to do these? He was also known for his expertise in teaching Sailor's Hornpipe and Irish Jig. Perfecting the correct rhythm for these dances was a requirement instilled in his pupils. Throughout the years I learned he had a great sense of humour. There was the time we were all going to a Highland Games to compete and he told some of the older pupils "don't come back without a trophy". Well no one won the trophy !! Undaunted they purchased a small cup from Woolworth and written on the front was "To The World's Biggest Charlie!" He thought this was hilarious and propped it up pride of place on the mantelpiece.

His expertise as an S.O.B.H.D. Adjudicator was much sought after and he travelled extensively both at home and abroad with his wife "Cissie Tucker" to adjudicate at major Championships. I have so many happy memories of my time at the "Cuthbertson School" His supreme ability as a teacher is legendary and I am eternally grateful for the knowledge I gained from him. In 2009 my pupil won the William MacNiven Cuthbertson Trophy at the Commonwealth Championships. I shed a little tear as I was so delighted and I know he would have been too!

William MacNiven Cuthbertson left a legacy that has had a huge influence on to-days Highland Dancers who all benefit from the "JOY OF HIGHLAND DANCE"

This brief reminiscence of Willie was written by Irene McKechnie and endorsed wholeheartedly by Betty Turkington, Billy Forsyth and Iain Macdonald all of whom had the same great experiences of Willie's wit, technical knowledge and perhaps most importantly his stories of dancing everywhere from Glasgow Music Halls to Highland Gatherings throughout Scotland, particularly the Islands during the 1920s and 30s.

Some of the Previous Office Bearers & Auditors of the Scottish Official Board of Highland Dancing

ADELINE CALDER

Miss Calder was the Principal of the Madam Ada School of Dancing which she ran in Edinburgh, with her partner, Miss Moyra Ronald. Miss Calder represented the B.B.O. which was a Member of the Board from its inception. She wrote the syllabus for Highland Dancing for the B.B.O. Australasian Branch, which eventually became the Australian Board of Highland Dancing. Miss Calder and Miss Ronald drove ambulances during the war and decided to go into business together after the war.

Miss Calder taught the dancing, Miss Ronald ran the business, although she had a great interest in Highland Dancing, being an Honorary Member of the B.B.O. and the U.K.A. She was also the Highland Branch Secretary for the U.K.A. for many years.

Miss Calder came from a dancing family in Edinburgh and Miss Ronald came from Glasgow and her brother was a very famous author.

MARJORY ROWAN

Marjory Rowan (Mrs MacLeod) lives and for many years taught in Edinburgh. The daughter of Cissie Tucker, she was closely involved with SOBHD from its early days, in fact before she ever became a delegate to SOBHD she says as a teenager she often acted as Babysitter for children of SOBHD Committee members during their discussions. Her first position with SOBHD was as delegate for the Victoria (Australia) Scottish Highland Dancing Association.

She was appointed Secretary/Treasurer of SOBHD (following Elspeth Strathern) and served the Board in that capacity and eventually as Director of Administration for over 50 years. She was a hard taskmaster and acted strictly to the rules and regulations of the Board. Her replies and decisions did not always suit those writing or phoning to SOBHD but while her manner could be brusque she always acted fairly and to the letter of the rules and constitution. For many years she virtually ran SOBHD single handed from one of the bedrooms of her home in Bruntsfield, Edinburgh. Only after the introduction of the Registration Schemes did she agree to take on a part time assistant but even then due to the high standards she required of anyone working alongside her, she often found herself once again doing everything herself when the assistants decided to call it a day.

Marjory herself was a major Championship and competition winner and over the years taught many Champions including World Champions. Until recently, and as her SOBHD duties allowed, Marjory was in demand as a judge and examiner and travelled extensively throughout the United Kingdom, North America and Europe. Marjory started and has been the only organiser of the Commonwealth Championship, now in its 40th year, one of the oldest of the SOBHD recognised Championships held in Scotland.

Some of the Previous Office Bearers & Auditors of the Scottish Official Board of Highland Dancing

BILLY FORSYTH MBE

Twice winner of the World Highland Dancing Championship, Billy has extensive experience as performer, manager and director of stage, arena, television and cabaret shows in Scotland and around the world. He has adjudicated at Dance Championships on every continent, toured and performed throughout Canada and the United States, demonstrated and lectured in such diverse locations as Tokyo, Japan, Quito in Ecuador and Karachi, Pakistan and performed regularly in cabaret at venues such as Gleneagles Hotel and Dunblane Hydro Hotel, both near his base in Central Scotland. For many years he performed on television and in stage shows with Scotland's leading entertainers.

For almost 20 years he has been Highland Dance Director for the world famous Royal Edinburgh Military Tattoo and in recent years his Edinburgh Tattoo Highland Ceilidh Dancers team has performed in the Amsterdam Arena, in the London Palladium, the Nova Scotia International Tattoo, the Netherlands National Tattoo and both the Basel Tattoo and Aventicum Festival in Switzerland in addition to many other events in Continental Europe. In 2004 his Tattoo team took part in the Royal Celebrations to mark the opening of the new Scottish Parliament Building at Holyrood in Edinburgh by H.M. the Queen and in 2009 the team performed at the Royal Windsor Castle Tattoo with members of the Royal Family, including the Queen and the Duke of Edinburgh, attending every show. The team has performed regularly in Edinburgh Castle at military ceremonies including the 'Installation of the Governor of the Castle' and 'Beating the Retreat'

In 2005 he was responsible for the dance component of "The Edinburgh Military Tattoo, A Salute to Australia" in Sydney NSW, and this followed his similar responsibility at the Millennium Year "Edinburgh Tattoo in New Zealand". Almost 200 dancers were involved in each of those events. In February 2010 he was in Australia with the Edinburgh Military Tattoo and over the last year his Tattoo team has performed at Tattoos in the Netherlands and Germany as well as at many events in the United Kingdom. In the spring of 2010 he was asked to organise a team of 100 Highland Dancers to perform as part of the pre-match entertainment at the Scotland v England Rugby International in Murrayfield Stadium Edinburgh. Over the years he has given opportunities to hundreds of overseas dancers to perform in Scotland at the Edinburgh Military Tattoo in association with the Tattoo Dance team.

After almost 25 years as Chairman of the Scottish Official Board of Highland Dancing, the World Governing Body, Billy was elected for a further 12 years as Honorary President of SOBHD, which co-ordinates a network of over 60 independent associations and organisations around the world, representing over 50,000 Scottish Highland Dancers.

Billy is a founder Member and Director of the Scottish Traditions of Dance Trust, the only organisation charged with the remit to research, collect, conserve, foster and promote all of Scotland's Heritage of Music and Dance. He also markets his own design of Highland and Scottish Country dance shoes, selling to retailers, instructors and dancers all over the world.

During a long professional career he was Financial Controller and then Chief Executive with the Scottish Youth Hostels Association, the largest provider of accommodation for young people travelling around Scotland and part of the Hostelling International network. In that position he travelled extensively throughout Europe and around the World attending meetings and conferences on student travel and exchanges and coordinating standards for international projects He thus continued his connections with organisations providing opportunities for travel and cultural exchange for young people.

In June 2007 Billy was awarded an MBE (Member of the Order of the British Empire) in the Queen's Birthday Honours List and was presented with it by Prince Charles at an investiture in Buckingham Palace, London.

Billy's wife, Denise, is Team Manager and Medical Supervisor for the Tattoo Dancers.

Current Office Bearers

of the Scottish Official Board of Highland Dancing

PRESIDENT - SHENDL RUSSELL

Shendl was born and raised in Ayr, Scotland where she studied Highland Dance under world renowned teachers May Falconer, Willie Cuthbertson and Elspeth Strathern. She is a former Scottish Champion and 1st runner up in the World Championship. As a teacher herself, Shendl's achievements have included training the 2004 Adult World Champion.

She is a Member of the World Wide Judges' Panel of the Scottish Official Board of Highland Dancing; a Fellow member and Examiner with the Scottish Dance Teachers' Alliance. After serving as Chairman for 10 years, Shendl currently holds the position of President of the Scottish Official Board of Highland Dancing, the World Governing Body.

Shendl continues to teach, adjudicate and conduct workshops throughout Scotland, Canada, United States, Australia, South Africa and New Zealand. Shendl is the Head Teacher at Barassie Primary in Troon, Scotland and an associate government inspector of schools.

VICE PRESIDENT - JESSIE STEWART – HAGGARTY MBE

When Jessie was six years old, her Dad, who was Pipe Major in the Vale of Leven Pipe Band, wanted Jessie to have a violin lessons, her Mum preferred piano lessons, however, they compromised and sent her to dance lessons. Her teacher, Sam Gladsby lived and taught in Alexandria, Jessie's home town.

As she progressed with her dancing, she transferred to Alec Massey, a well known and respected teacher in Clydebank. Jessie was very successful in competitions due to her hard work and dedication.

Jessie started teaching at fourteen years of age, first with a neighbour's daughter and from there, a few more students, until the Stewart School of Dancing in Alexandria was formed.

Her students have been very successful in Examinations and Competitions winning every major Championship in Highland Dancing throughout the U.K. Jessie has also trained students in Canada, U.S.A., Australia, Tasmania and many other countries.

The Scottish School of Arts in Banner Elk, North Carolina, was a teaching ground for twelve years and many of today's teachers were trained by Jessie at this annual event.

Jessie was one of the pioneers in the formation of the Scottish Official Board of Highland Dancing and is the only surviving member of the original Board. She has given her knowledge freely, to raise the standard of Highland Dancing, both at home and abroad.

She was also an Adjudicator of the Scottish Official Board of Highland Dancing and an Examiner of the British Association of Teachers of Dancing.

A truly dedicated teacher and lecturer, continually striving for perfection and helping other teachers and dancers gives her great pleasure. Jessie is very highly respected around the world with all the teachers and students she has had the pleasure of working.

Jessie is also the recipient of the Atholl Clasp, two Carl Alan Awards and many more tributes throughout the years.

Current Office Bearers of the Scottish Official Board of Highland Dancing

CHAIRMAN - CHRISTINE LACEY

Christine was elected Chairman of the Scottish Official Board of Highland Dancing in November of 2006. Christine is also a Fellow, Examiner of the B.A.T.D. as well as an International Adjudicator on the S.O.B.H.D.

Among Christine's credits are, six times World Highland Dancing Champion.

Although well renowned in the world of Highland Dancing, Christine has also achieved recognition in both Tap and Ballet. She has held the titles of British Senior Ballet Champion; Scottish Junior and Senior Ballet Champion; Scottish Junior and Senior Tap Champion. Collectively, in all three disciplines she has accumulated over 250 Championship Titles.

She is always in great demand lecturing, examining and adjudicating all over the world.

Christine was trained at the Stewart School of Dancing in Alexandria, Scotland and is still currently teaching there.

Christine's teachers at The Stewart School of Dancing were Jessie Stewart - Haggarty MBE, Agnes Stewart and Nancy Haggarty - Gibbons.

Christine is most indebted to all three ladies for giving her the skills and the passion for Dance. At present she is in Senior Management with the Bank of Scotland and is happily married to Donald MacPhee who is also well known throughout the world for his bagpiping skills.

Christine is pictured above with all 3 of her teachers at Mrs Haggarty's luncheon celebration in the Glasgow Piping Centre.

HELEN FORD

Helen Ford was born and bred in Glasgow, Scotland. From an early age she attended the Sadie Simpson School of Dancing, where she trained in all Theatre Branches, including Highland.Having qualified as a teacher, she continued her training with Miss Elizabeth P. Wallace, Miss Jean Ritchie, Agnes Stewart and Jessie Stewart-Haggarty MBE, with Miss Simpson and Miss Wallace being wonderful mentors. It was a privilege to have such knowledgeable and highly respected teachers all of whom became friends in later life.

Helen is a Past President of the British Association of Teachers of Dancing 1991 - 1995, a member of their Executive Council, Chairman of the Stage and Ballet Committee, Chairman of the Majorette Committee and a member of the Association's Highland Committee. She was their Overseas Administrator for 10 years, developing and promoting all disciplines of dance in the Theatre Branches throughout Canada and America where she was instrumental in the setting up of the Sadie Simpson Highland Scholarship in North America. Helen is also a Fellow and Examiner of the Association.

Current Office Bearers of the Scottish Official Board of Highland Dancing

Helen danced professionally in both the King's and the Pavilion Theatres in Glasgow and also ran a very successful School of Dancing, with many of her students continuing in the profession both in the Theatre and in Teaching. Helen is married to Joe, a Marine Engineer, who is constantly travelling the world with his job. She has had the opportunity to travel with him on many occasions seeing some very beautiful and exotic countries.

Now working as Director of Administration with the Scottish Official Board of Highland Dancing, she is very busy and enjoying the challenge of this new position. She is delighted that the Board has launched a DVD, "Foundation of S.O.B.H.D. Technique", in celebration of their 60th Anniversary.

Independent Members

of the Scottish Official Board of Highland Dancing

CHRISTINE E. AITKEN

Christine started dancing at the age of three and studied Highland, Tap, Ballet and Modern Dance. Her first Highland teacher was Nancy Dickson and later Miss Jessie Stewart _ Haggarty MBE. Effie Drummond was her instructor for Tap, Ballet and Modern Dance.

She competed regularly in Highland Dancing and Stage Festivals and won the 10 years Championship at the Cowal Highland Games in 1957 and was successful in many other competitions.

Christine has been principal of her dancing school for 47 years, teaching all subjects. Her pupils compete regularly at Highland Competitions and are very successful. She is a Fellow and Examiner with the British Association of Teachers of Dancing, a past Vice – President, Member of the Executive Council, Chairman of the Association's Highland Committee and a Member of the B.A.T.D. Stage and Ballet Committee.

At present Christine is Convenor of the S.O.B.H.D. Judges Committee and was until her election as an Independent member, Convenor of the S.O.B.H.D. Technical Committee. She was also a Delegate for the B.A.T.D. on the S.O.B.H.D. for around 30 years.

Christine is most grateful to her dancing teachers, because without their wealth of knowledge, she would not be where she is today in the Dancing World.

SHEENA McDONALD

Sheena McDonald started dancing from an early age, learning Ballet, Tap and Highland.

Her Ballet and Tap education was at the Glasgow Ballet school and her Highland was with her sister Anne. Anne trained Sheena to win numerous Championships including four World Championships.

As a Fellow Examiner with the Scottish Dance Teachers' Alliance, she has travelled worldwide, including America, Australia, Canada, Holland, Japan and South Africa.

Sheena was President of the S.D.T.A. for five years.

With the Scottish Official Board of Highland Dancing, she is a judge, an Independent Member and has been a member of the Technical and Judges Committee for many years.

Sheena was also the recipient of the Atholl Clasp for her dedication to Highland Dancing.

IRENE MCKECHNIE

At the age of 12years I joined the dance school of the late great William MacNiven Cuthbertson. He ignited in me, a lifelong passion called "Highland Dancing". Entirely due to this great Dancing Master's superb teaching skill I won Juvenile, Junior & Adult World Championship Titles. I loved every minute of my time in the competitive field and have so many happy memories of days at the Highland Games with my mum and dad.

My life as a professional dancer then followed. T.V. Shows and tours with Jimmy Shand and the White Heather Club provided me with an opportunity to earn an income doing something I loved!

I have been very fortunate to see my pupils win all Major Championships in the U.K. My love of teaching has never waned since the first class I taught. The thrill of nurturing a young child from their first dance steps right through to winning a Championship Title is wonderful. To my absolute delight my daughter 'Nadine' also a Juvenile World Championship Winner was also bitten by the bug of Highland Dancing and now teaches with me.

I consider it a great honour to be an Independent Member of the S.O.B.H.D. And have been privileged to be a Member of Technical and Judges Committees for more years than I care to admit. When first joining the Technical Committee other members were:- Mrs Jessie Stewart-Haggerty MBE, Miss Sadie Simpson, Miss Evelyn McLaren, Miss Cissie Tucker, Miss Jean Ritchie, Mrs Margaret Todd. Some of whom were responsible for the First Edition of the S.O.B.H.D. Text Book. Elite company indeed! As a new Member to the Committee I was very much in awe of their expertise and knowledge and their absolute commitment to Highland Dancing.

Lifelong friends have been made because we share the same passion. It is in our hearts and souls "THE LOVE OF HIGHLAND DANCING".

CELIA ORR

Celia started dancing at three years of age with a local dance teacher Isobel Orr, at the age of seven, she had won two Third Placings at Cowal.

Progressing on to the Highland World with the Tucker-Rowan School, Edinburgh, better known as Cissie Tucker and Marjory Rowan, who remained Celia's Highland Dancing teachers her entire dancing days. At the same time Celia attended the Scottish Ballet School in Edinburgh, under the direction of Marjory Middleton MBE.

At 11 years of age, Celia won her first Championship, the Land O' Burns Championship, which was held annually at Butlin's in Ayr. This was followed by winning many Championships throughout her Highland career from Juvenile to Adult.

After completing full time training at the Scottish Ballet School in 1972, Celia opened a full time Dance school in Lanark. In 1987 moved to 33 Hope Street, Lanark, providing a private Registered dance school for children in a 20 mile area. Celia teaches Ballet, Highland, Tap and Jazz to over 200 children each week.

1976 was a big year, she passed her Judges Test, retired as a competitive dancer and took over from Billy Forsyth MBE as rep for Southern California H.D.A. on the Board.

She has been an Independent Member of the S.O.B.H.D. for nearly 20 years and is at present a member of the Board's Technical, Judges, Registration and Disciplinary Committees.

In remission from Breast Cancer, she works harder than ever both in her Dance school and for the Board. Pupils have won many open and closed Championships and is delighted that he pupil Leigh-Ann Plenderleith now represents New Zealand on the Board and is also on the Website and Quality Assurance Committee's and until this year was on the Finance Committee. The good work carries on.

Dancing highlights were many, here are a few:

1. Winning the World Juvenile Championship 1964
2. Oscar Winner – 1966 age 14 years
3. Dancing and being presented to the Queen at Holyrood Palace in 1968.
4. Judging all over the world and meeting many old and new friends in Canada, U.S.A. and South Africa.
5. Attending the magical night at Edinburgh Castle for the Board's 50th Anniversary
6. Winning T.V. Come Dancing 'Off Beat' section with fellow students at Scottish Ballet School.
7. Passing Membership examination with the U.K.A. aged 18 years with Miss Adeline Calder as the examiner.
8. Passing R.A.D. Advanced Ballet Examination aged 20 years with Miss Louise Brown as the examiner.

It seems a long time since, as a wee girl aged 9 years, she would get a lift on the milk lorry at 8 am on a Saturday morning and travel 15 miles to Mid-Calder and then wait at the road corner for another family to collect her to take her to the Ballet School in Edinburgh, returning from West Calder at 2pm in the afternoon. During the week, her Dad would drive her to Edinburgh for her Highland class, doing her homework on the way and on arriving home, her Dad would still have to do the milking!!

Love of dance comes from within and you have to do it for yourself. Some would say competitive highland is an illness and after 55 years, she still has not found a cure. It is with grateful thanks to her excellent teachers and dedicated parents, that Celia was able to fulfil her dreams.

She would like to congratulate the past and present Top Table for their fantastic work at home and worldwide. Bringing the S.O.B.H.D. into the 21st century has made Highland Dancing instantly available no matter where you live in the world.

Having been at the 25th, 40th and 50th Anniversary Celebrations, she is now looking forward to the 60th in August.

Celia would like to wish the S.O.B.H.D. a fantastic 60th Anniversary year and especially to our Vice-President Mrs Jessie Stewart – Haggarty MBE aged 97 years who has been the back bone from the start.

FRANCES PATERSON

Frances started dancing at the age of three, attending the Madame Ada School (Adeline Calder) in Regent Terrace, Edinburgh where she was introduced to tap and ballet. Later teachers were Maureen McMahon who introduced her to Highland Dancing, then Jean Carnie whose school also had a pipe band where Frances learned to play the bagpipes. Her final teacher was Jeanette Jamieson. Frances was extremely grateful to all her teachers who in their different ways increased her love of dance in all its forms. As a youngster she also fitted in Piano Lessons (at 8 o'clock in the morning), Swimming Lessons and Piping Lessons.

Professionally, Frances first qualified with the UKA and is now a Fellow in Highland and National, a Member in Tap and Ballet and an Examiner. Other qualifications include a Fellowship in Highland with the BATD, and a Membership with the SDTA, and Adjudicator of the SOBHD World Wide Judges Panel.

At the age of sixteen, Frances started her dance school; her first pupil was her next door neighbours five year old. For a few years classes were held in her mother's front room until increasing numbers caused the classes to move to church halls and the local YMCA.

Over the years Frances has been fortunate to have many fine, hard working young people attend classes. Many of them have been successful competitive dancers winning Championships at home and abroad including two winners of the world Championship. Her students have gone on to become teachers and judges and some have achieved successes on the professional stage.

In 1969 Frances took over the organising of the International Festival of Dancing which hosts the British Open Championship, and two events – The British Overseas Championship confined to competitors from out with the UK and The Scottish Boys Championship confined to Boys under 16 years of age. Both events are unique in that there are no comparable events anywhere else in the world. Many members will remember the beautiful Music Halls in George Street Edinburgh where events were staged for many years. Over the years the Festival presented Stage, Accordion, Ballroom, Disco, Verse Speaking, Traditional Irish, Scottish Country Dancing and International Folk Dancing Competitions. Today financial restraints make it possible to present only Highland, Stage and Choreography events in venues in Musselburgh.

The Festival joined the SOBHD as a Competition Organisation; its first representatives were Councillor Frank Stewart till his death in a plane crash and Tony Fusco of Edinburgh. Frances took over in 1969 and has been attending meetings ever since. Years later Frances was honoured with an Independent Membership of the Board. For the last few years Frances has worked in the SOBHD Headquarters as Competitors Registration Organiser for the UK. As a member of the Technical Committee and the Judges Committee Frances keeps her knowledge of Highland Dancing finely tuned.

In her non dancing life, Frances was a Primary School Teacher, teaching first in West Lothian and finally as a Peripatetic Teacher in Music in Edinburgh Primary Schools. Now retired, Frances does not know how she managed to fit in so many things. Today there doesn't seem to be enough hours in the day.

Independent Members of the Scottish Official Board of Highland Dancing

BETTY SUTHERLAND

Betty Sutherland started Dance class at 3 years of age in her hometown of Alexandria, Scotland under the tutelage of Mrs. Haggarty (Jessie Stewart), one of the founder members of the S.O.B.H.D.

She presently teaches with her daughter Jan, in their own studios in Alexandria, where they teach a full range of subjects.

Their students are regular prize-winners at Competitions and Championships both in Highland and Stage Dance. Their successes include Scottish, British, North American and World Championships. Betty is a regular visitor to Canada, America and South Africa as a Lecturer and Adjudicator, she also travels extensively as a Fellow and Examiner with the Scottish Dance Teachers' Alliance.

She is a Past President of the Scottish Dance Teachers' Alliance Ltd. (2000 – 2003) and was their delegate on the SOBHD for many years.

In 2007 she was privileged to be made an Independent Member of the SOBHD.

BETTY TURKINGTON

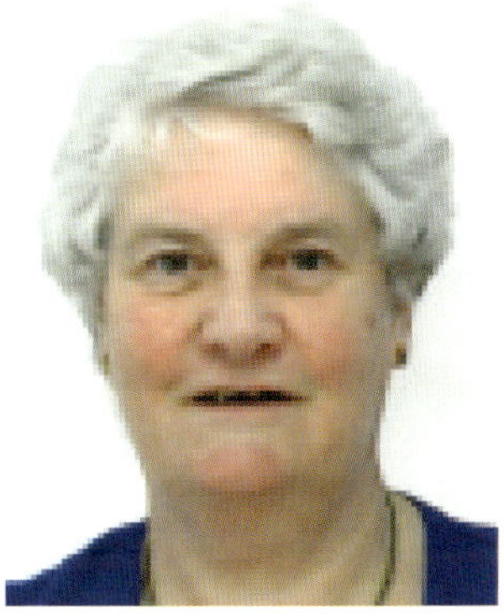

Betty started dancing at the age of four and was taught by Elspeth Strathern.

During her competitive career, Betty had various teachers and while a student of Willie Cuthbertson, she was the First Winner of the World Junior Championship at The Cowal Highland Gathering.

Betty's competitive career was completed under the guidance of Elspeth Strathern and during that time, became a Fellow of the British Association of Teachers of Dancing.

"A Tribute to J.L. McKenzie" was choreographed by Elspeth Strathern and Betty was chosen to be the first dancer to perform this piece.

Honorary Members
of the Scottish Official Board of Highland Dancing

VALERIE GEDDES

As a Highland Dancer Val was taught by Mr Jack McConachie and progressed through all the medal tests, continuing with Professional Examinations. Val joined the BATD as an Associate in 1960 then gained her full Membership and went onto pass her Fellowship examination before being appointed a BATD examiner. Val is now a Life Member of the BATD and a qualified dance teacher with the RSCDS.

As a teacher of dancing, Val enjoyed success with her own school for over 30 years with students participating in all levels of examination including Professional examinations. Her students were invited to perform at many Festivals of Dance all over Europe including the Europeade.

It was Miss Jessie Stewart and Miss Jean Ritchie who encouraged Val to take the SOBHD judges test in 1969 and on passing this exam, Val has been fortunate enough to judge at many competitions and Championships including the World Championship at Cowal on a number of occasions.

Val feels very honoured to have been an examiner of the BATD for 35 years even travelling to Canada and America on three overseas tours. Val represented the BATD as a delegate on the SOBHD for nearly 30 years and was a member of the Highland Committee of the BATD.

Throughout her career, Val has always encouraged dancers from both the UK and overseas to take Professional Exams to further themselves and of course to ultimately sit the judges exam. Val has always been a constant advocate of the SOBHD promoting its mission and persuading those with different ideas, that the Board was the way forward.

Since 1973 Val has organised competitions under the SOBHD and has also run workshops and Championship lectures. It was Val who was instrumental in the formation of the HDTAE and of course it's Membership to the SOBHD and she still is the treasurer.

Val has dedicated her life to Highland Dancing with a passion and she feels she comes alive in its midst. Val's husband was a highland dancer and that is how they met and none of her "dancing life" would have been possible without his unparalleled support.

Val was absolutely thrilled to have been nominated for the position of Honorary Member of the SOBHD by the BATD and even more so being elected and being the first from England. Such a great honour.

NANCY HAGGARTY – GIBBONS

Dancing has always been part of Nancy's life. She started dancing at a very young age, her mother, Jessie Stewart – Haggarty and her two aunts Catherine Stewart and Agnes Stewart were her instructresses.

Nancy was very successful in Highland Dancing, due to her hard work and determination.

At 16 years of age, she became an Associate of the British Association of Teachers of Dancing and is now a Life member and Examiner of the B.A.T.D.

Nancy taught at the Stewart School of Dancing for many years along with her mother, their students were very successful, winning numerous Championships throughout the U.K. including the World Junior, Juvenile and Adult titles.

She is also an adjudicator of the Scottish Official Board of Highland Dancing and an Honorary Member. Nancy represented the British Association of Teachers of Dancing at the Technical meetings of the Scottish Official Board of Highland Dancing.

In 1981, Nancy moved with her family, to Fox Creek in Alberta, Canada and is still involved with teaching, workshops, adjudicating and examining, always enjoying working with children and young adults.

Iain on the right with his good friend Alex Martin.

IAIN C MACDONALD

Iain started Highland Dancing with his Mothers teacher's son to see if he would be any good.

He did very well and started taking lessons with the World famous Bobby Cuthbertson who he remained with until Bobby moved to the East of Scotland and Andy Sutherland and Jacky Grant took over Bobby's classes.

After a short period of time Iain became a student of Bobby's half brother , Willie Cuthbertson, he again was an excellent teacher to many World Champions and Iain and Willie remained personal friends until Willie's death.

Iain competed successfully on the Games and Competition circuit and in 1962 was runner up in the Worlds Championships to Sandra Bald (Jones).

Iain sat his Professional Examinations with The British Association of Teachers of Dancing and with the Scottish Dance Teachers Alliance and then became a Member of the International Panel of the "Scottish Official Board of Highland Dancing" for many years.

Iain has had the pleasure of Adjudicating Highland Dance Championships and Competitions both home and abroad, in the United States, Canada, South Africa and Japan.

As is well known, Iain is also an excellent Piper to Highland Dancers and in 1999 was appointed "Director of Piping" for the World Championships at Cowal Highland Gathering. He was also made an "Honorary Life Member" by the Directors of "The Cowal Highland Gathering" in recognition of over 30 Years of service.

In 2009 Iain was appointed as an "Honorary Member" of "The Scottish Official Board of Highland Dancing"

MRS MARGARET PATERSON OAM.

Although she wasn't born in Scotland, Margaret Paterson has plenty of Scottish blood in her veins. Her grandfather hailed from Stonehaven and her grandmother, who emigrated from the island of Islay, was a highland dancing teacher. Margaret's mother, Mrs Elsie Innes Barker, now in her 91st year and an Honorary Adjudicator with the Australian Board of Highland Dancing Inc., carried on the tradition and is a well respected personality in Australian Highland Dancing circles. Margaret, who trained in highland, ballet, jazz, tap, Irish and ballroom dancing,

was taught highland dancing initially by her mother and later trained with Mrs Pearl Neilson (deceased) and finally with Miss Jan Roach. In 1962 & 1963 Margaret won the first registered Open Queensland Highland Dancing Championships and in the same year won the Open Queensland Irish Dancing Championships.

The Thistle Highland dancing Studio was established by Margaret and her mother and sister in Brisbane -1968 and since then Margaret has trained dancers for examinations, competitions and performance work. She has been a guest teacher at workshops and seminars throughout Australia and in New Zealand and in addition to her very thorough work in SOBHD technique she is highly skilled and very well respected choreographer. For her service to highland dancing she was recently appointed a Fellow Member of the National Dancing Association of Australia.

As a member of the ABHDI Judges Panel and World Wide Judges Panel SOBHD, Margaret has judged competitions and Championships throughout Australia and overseas. Margaret has made several visits to Scotland to enrich her knowledge of correct SOBHD technique and she has produced numerous champion dancers who have competed throughout Australia and in New Zealand, Scotland, America and Canada achieving excellent results.

Margaret held the position of President of the Australian Board from 1995 until 1997 and then again for five years from 2000 until 2005. In 2006 Margaret was awarded the Medal of the Order of Australia in the general division for service to Highland Dancing as a teacher and adjudicator and she also holds a Celtic Honour, Duine Urramach (Noble Person), in recognition of service to the dancing community and the State of Queensland. In 2008 she was delighted to be accepted as an Honorary Member of the SOBHD.

JEAN RITCHIE

Jean Ritchie has always been a very dedicated member of the BATD. She takes great pride in bringing a Beginner dancer to a Championship winner. Also very involved in making sure all aspects of Highland Dance are fair, and a true supporter of the SOBHD, she is never afraid to speak her mind in a truthful way, which sometimes was unpopular. Nevertheless if it needed said, Jean Ritchie said it!

Many of her dancers have won Championship titles including World Champion, Lorraine Brown.

In 1969, she was one of the first Highland Examiners to conduct an Examining tour of the United States and Canada. Many teachers have wonderful memories of her teaching at Grandfather Mountain at the School of Scottish Arts with Jessie Stewart training young teachers to become judges of the SOBHD.

As with all the "Grande Dames" of Highland Dance, Jean Ritchie was always there to help many teachers. She always thought the best way to improve dancing technique was to be willing to share her vast expertise with anyone who wanted help.

Now almost 88 years young, she is retired and still living in Renfrew with her son Stewart. Her daughter, Elizabeth, now lives and teaches Highland Dance in Spokane, Washington State, USA.

AGNES STEWART

Miss Agnes Stewart started dancing at an early age and had considerable success around the games. After World War II Agnes went into the Adults and was a consistent prize winning competitor. Some of her success' include BATD Members Trophy twice, 3rd place in the World's at Cowal behind the Winner Margaret Samson and runner up May Falconer (Agnes received a silver plated biscuit barrel which is still in her possession today!) and in 1953 and 1954 Agnes won The British Open Championships. Agnes became active in the SOBHD when Miss Elizabeth Wallace retired as the BATD representative and Agnes took over as BATD delegate. She then was asked by Butlin's main man Wilfred Orange to organise Butlin's Dance Festival and represent Butlin's on the Board, which she did for many years. Agnes then became an Honorary Member.

Agnes started teaching at the age of 12 as her one sister Catherine Stewart went into the Services during the War and her other sister Jessie Stewart was having her family. Agnes was trained in all dancing disciplines. She was the youngest member of the BATD Executive Council at the age of 18 as well as an Examiner; Life Member of the BATD and conducted many North American tours. Agnes is also a Life Member of the British Ballet Organisation and has been a member for over 60 years. She still leads an active teaching schedule with many champions to her credit. As a matter of note, Agnes Stewart is one of the 2 Ladies dancing in the new SOBHD DVD – "Foundations of SOBHD Technique".

MARGARET TODD

Margaret Todd was trained in Highland Dancing by Isa Russell and in Stage, by Jack Muir.

Mrs Todd joined the Scottish Dance Teachers' Alliance in 1947 and was made an examiner in 1965. In 1970, she was asked to examine in Canada and America, which she did, making many friends for the Alliance. She served for seven years as Highland Branch Convenor, was on the Executive Council and was Vice-President for ten years.

Mrs Todd is also a Life Member of the British Association of Teachers of Dancing.

In 1981 she was made an Independent Member of the Scottish Official Board of Highland Dancing and from 1983, she was a member of the Technical and Judges Committees, serving from then until 2004 without a break of service.

In 1993, Mrs Todd was awarded Citizen of the Year in recognition of her work for charity. She has donated thousands of pounds throughout the years. There is a plaque to commemorate this work in the Beatson Hospital, Glasgow, with Livingston School of Dance appearing on a Gold Bar Plaque.

Her Dance school has been established now for 50 + years and has trained many successful students to Championship level.

In 2003 Mrs Todd was thrilled to receive the Athol I Clasp from the S.O.B.H.D. Membership.

A life which has, by anyone's standards, been totally dedicated to Highland Dancing.

WILMA TOLMIE

Wilma commenced Highland Dancing at the late age in today's terms of thirteen, and received lessons from the well known Dundee teacher, Alice Fox, and latterly Edith Bell.

She developed a love for dance, and was soon out competing initially as a junior at the Highland Games in the East of Scotland, and as an adult around Scotland as a whole, with a particular affinity for the North and North-East. Her pinnacle in competing was to gain the adult World Championship at Cowal in 1965.

She started teaching in Dundee when she was 16 years. Her hard work resulted in the class becoming renowned throughout the world, with students gaining almost every award attainable, with pride of place to her four World Champions.

Not content with just teaching, she took an active part initially in the BATD becoming an Examiner, and Life Member and making many friends in Scotland and overseas, and was for 21 years Chairman of the East of Scotland Branch. In addition, she has taken an active part in the administration of the SOBHD through attending as a delegate, Independent Member, and now as an Honorary Member. She was a member of both the Technical and Judges Committees of the Board, and was for many years Convenor of these committees.

At local level, she was instrumental in founding the Dundee Highland Association and the Tayside Highland Dancing Association.

She recognised that through a common love of dance, young people from around the world could meet and share each other's culture in coming together at international events under the auspices of the CIOFF, an offshoot of UNESCO. Her answer was to help found the Tayfolk Dance and Music group and travel with them throughout Europe taking part in International Dance Festivals.

Her dedication to Highland Dancing was recognised in her being awarded the Atholl Clasp by the SOBHD in 2008.

ROBERT MACNIVEN CUTHBERTSON

My recollections of this great dancing master: by Victor Wesley

Formally known to all in the Highland Dancing World as Bobby, He was born in Springburn Glasgow Scotland in the district of Provan and in the early 20th century became noted for his prowess as a highland dancer of outstanding ability.

There have been many articles written on his career and rightly so, as he was truly an expert exponent of highland dancing and of teaching, and had the ability to put his personal indelible stamp of greatness on all that were fortunate to study with him or even to get close enough know him.

In his youth he won the World Juvenile Championship at Cowal Gathering in 1910, 11, 12, and 13, he went on to compete as an adult professional at the highland games from 1914 only to be interrupted with the start of World War I. He served in the Argyll and Southern Highlanders and then in the Gordon Highlanders, and while in the army he won many accolades and Championship medals for his dancing.

Bobby trained both with Neil Cameron and Willie McLean in Glasgow. He was regarded in his day as the greatest exponent of highland dancing. He had great strength and meticulous regard to precision coupled with a grace and fluidity, that was in those day's unquestionably remarkable, he was noted for his extended high cutting and entrechat's as well as his characterisations of dances such as hornpipes and jigs, and latterly became noted as a master teacher and a judge, and too, earning a reputation as one of highland dancing's truely great characters.

In the early part of the 20th century it was predominately male dancers who competed at the games, with a break through ladies started to grace the platform and in some cases compete directly with the males. On one occasion Bobby confided in me that his most respected rivals were two dancers, one by the name of Jean Telfer from Port Glasgow and in his words the greatest lady dancer ever to grace the dancing platform the other was a gentleman by the name of Sydney Black from Edinburgh who he felt was very worthy of his acknowledgement and approval. As a teacher Bobby trained many great competitive dancers who went on to pass this knowledge to their students and many who are part of this dancing world today.

Bobby Cuthbertson was part of the original meeting in 1950 to set up the SOBHD; he was the founder of the HDSA, Highland Dancing Specialists Association with many of its membership now involved and active within the SOBHD. He also founded the original HDA in Edinburgh.

His character was most evident when he judged, as he would call out the amount of steps to the dancers when they were on the platform and direct them only by surname in the steps to be danced and in certain order, and you had better been prepared. Fling 8 steps always with two backsteps, Sword 5&1, S/Trubihas 6 or 8 & 2 quick with an entrechat step and entrechat ending, a full Reel, and Hornpipes usually 7 and a H/cut, Jig 7 and 1 but more often many more steps. On one occasion he asked for 14 steps in the jig. Bobby Cuthbertson was larger than life both on the platform, in his teaching and judging he left us all with a great legacy. And to this is most deserving of recognition.

JANET GARDNER GALLACHER

Janet's contribution to dance began in 1935 when she was aged just 4. She competed regularly for 35 years at all levels and gained much success as a Juvenile Champion and at highland games the length and breadth of the country. The final five years of her competing career saw her dance on the same board as her daughter Fiona, and the family has many photographs of them both wearing their Kilt or Jig and Hornpipe outfits. And of course the games in the North have a particular fondness for Janet as this is where she was courted by her husband Danny, who was a very successful athlete. Indeed, at Cowal in 2009, they both were applauded by the crowd for reaching 50 years of married bliss!!

Janet taught from the age of 11 – initially under the guidance of her mother – and continued until she retired due to ill health in 2005.

Many hundreds of young dancers benefitted from her teaching skills – and indeed she has always been a bit of a celebrity in the Levenmouth area as nearly every family can boast at least one generation as a "Janet Gardner dancer", and many fondly remember her cycling to her classes all over Fife with her record player strapped to the back of her bike.

Janet joined the U.K.A. in 1960 and became an examiner in 1980 – travelling extensively with this. She was recently awarded the Lifetime Achievement Award at the Highland Gathering of the U.K.A. and it is proudly displayed on what is known as the 'wall of fame' in her home.

Her dynasty will continue through her daughter and her grand-daughter, Kirstin Stewart. And of course, she is still travelling to Championships and competitions whenever health allows as Kirstin's number one supporter.

Together, the three generations of this dancing family would like to congratulate the SOBHD on 60 glorious years.

ISOBEL ST. JOHN

Isobel was a Cowal Junior Champion twice, the Daily Record Highland and National Champion and also the Isle of Man Champion.

She started learning to dance at the age of four and a half with Miss Lilly Meldrum of Motherwell and after a couple of years Lilly advised Isobel's mother to take her to Bobby Cuthbertson, who Isobel thought was a fantastic teacher. Unfortunately her parents found the travel to and fro quite difficult, so Bobby advised that they take Isobel to Miss Isa Russell in Hamilton, who was one of Bobby's star pupils.

After the War Isobel started teaching Highland Dancing and Tap Dancing, the St. John School of Dancing. Sometime later, she began judging, including the Cowal Games and various Competitions up and down the country. Her judging also took her to Australia twice this was done while visiting her daughters who lived there.

Isobel also ran monthly Competitions in Motherwell and Ferniagair.

BETTY HAGGART - PRINCIPAL ELIZABETH ANN SCHOOL OF DANCE

The Elizabeth Ann School of Dance, was established in Kirkcaldy in the 1940's Miss Haggart also had a Ballroom where Saturday night dances were held until 1955, then she taught in the Masonic Hall until she retired in the 1960's

Her sister Mary played the piano for all classes but when the Sailors' Hornpipe was danced Miss Haggart always took over the Piano and played for that dance.

Miss Haggart was an examiner in all branches of Dance and was involved with the formation of the SOBHD when she was a delegate for the SDTA.

Miss Haggart was an amazing teacher in many aspects of Dance. Her students were successful in Ballroom, Stage and Highland Competitions, and in RAD Ballet exams. There was something special about her, that made you want to do your very best in every class. She was always well groomed, with perfect makeup and hair, and when in the same room as her, one felt that they must not slouch!!

ELIZABETH ANN SCHOOL OF DANCE

Students included: Back row, from left: Evelyn Steele (Clarke), Alison Walker, Joyce Milne, Elizabeth Farmer (McLauchlan), Marjory Grieg , Sandra Bald (Jones), Sylvia Henderson.

Front: Celia Pate, Margaret Farmer. Margo Stevenson - Miss Betty Haggart (Far Right)

Nixon Charity Action Group Paisley

This was formed around 1978

The catalyst for the formation of the group was the fact that my brother William who suffered from cerebral palsy and who was a well known figure around the dancing circuit would have benefitted from an electric wheelchair. Any of you who knew my mother will testify to the fact that her "raison d'etre" was to ensure that William would have the most comfortable journey through the life which had been destined to be harder than most. To this end and with the encouragement of, in particular, Mrs Haggarty, Agnes Stewart and my dance pupil Maryanne McCreadie. In the first instance, the idea of harnessing the goodwill and camaraderie of the participants in the Highland Dancing circuit emerged. A group of parents in my own dance school and other willing participants formed the Nixon Action Group which organised the first of what was to become many annual charity competitions to raise thousands and thousands of pounds over the years for various charities through the caring and amazing response and involvement of the Highland Dancing fraternity. That first year not only did William get his electric wheelchair (in which he subsequently terrorised all drivers by regularly driving it up the middle of Paisley High Street) but there was an excess of funds! Again anyone who knew my mother will know that she could be VERY persuasive. Everyone participating in these events from the volunteers on the door to judges, pipers, stewards (notably Frances Paterson and May Falconer) etc gave their services for no charge. She spent the whole year planning from event to event. The minute one was over she would be on the phone to butchers, bakers and anyone and everyone who would provide raffle prizes, food for the judges, trophies, medals or indeed anything at all which would enhance the cause. I have to make special mention of the fact that three judges set the record of having judged free of charge at every single event since its conception. A special recognition must go to Shendl Russell, Ritchie Gibson and Kay Alexander. For the pipers and particularly Iain MacDonald, Alex Martin and Stewart Bowman, it became over the years an annual forum where tempos and other piping related matters could be aired. After the first year and indeed until she died at the age of 82 in 2001 she delighted in the fact that the Nixon Action Group had made a difference to so many worthwhile causes.

Sadly none of us at that point could devote as much time to the cause as she did and the last event took place in 2004 .However and to conclude, as Christine Lacey stated at a recent SOBHD meeting "There will be a wee woman up there who will be looking down with delight on the new generation of Highland Dancing related charity events."

D G MACLENNAN

(Member of Executive and Technical Committees, Royal Academy of Dancing), whose "Guide to Teachers, Dancers, and Judges" was adopted as "Standard" at a Conference held in Edinburgh, 1925, and since followed by the best dancers and professionals throughout the country. Awarded La Palme d'Or (R/F) pour Encouragement Public (Ligue Francaise d' Entr'aide Sociale) 1934.

Highland and Traditional Dances by D G MacLennan.

REFLECTIONS ON HIGHLAND DANCING

By Marguerite Reid

To describe in a few words the exhilarating experiences of Highland Dancing and to compress in a few short paragraphs a history of how it was developed over the centuries is just about impossible.

From roughly 9:00 am to 5:00 pm today, you will witness dances which will take at the most, three or four minutes to perform. Yet the actual time it has taken these dancers to prepare themselves has been years- years of training, dedication, study, joy, tears, sore muscles, pulled tendons and a competitive spirit which makes each dancer want to be the best in his or her class in whatever dance they are performing. It is not a matter of just moving your feet to music, for the feet sing what the piper plays. When all your knowledge, training, and love for what you are doing combine favorably, it is difficult to subdue the feeling which comes from deep within yourself. Highland Dancing is an incredible adventure!!

For spectators to thoroughly enjoy the dancing events, they should acquaint themselves with what the dancers on the platform are trying to accomplish. It is one thing for a dancer to put on a nice outfit and look like a competitor; quite another to put into the dance all of the details the teacher has, over the years, tried to impart, and be a competitor.

To have been a Highland dancer, teacher, judge (and that is the usual progression) we all had to be exposed at a very young age to this contagious disorder called "Highland Dancing." Once the sickness takes root in your very body and soul, there is no relief, no cure. Consider the facts. How many people in their right mind would spend years of time in lessons and practice, and then put on a kilt, hose, jacket, tight shoes- all the appropriate costume- and go out in the sun when the temperature is often 90+ degrees, dance their legs off all day, repeat the process a week or two later, do this for the whole competition season, and call it FUN?

There is a great amount of history in all of the dances that we, as teachers, are trying to preserve. Of all the legends surrounding the Highland Fling, the most acceptable is that the dancer is imitating a deer on the Scottish hillside. The arm movements certainly look like the caberfeidh (deer antlers). The Sword Dance has long been titled "Gillie Callum (the servant of God Columba). Columba, who brought Christianity to Scotland and established the Culdee Church with its heart on the beautiful isle of Iona, was later canonized. The Sword Dance represents the triumph of good over evil, with the sword of the victor, held in the right hand, placed over the Sword of the vanquished, held in the left. The Seann Triubhas, Sailors Hornpipe, and Irish Jig all show similarities to each other. All have circular patterns and brush and shuffle movements common to each, although there is a slight different treatment of a brush and a shuffle in the first. The interlacing pattern of the Celts, symbolic of everlasting life, is preserved on the great stone Ionian crosses in Scotland, and these patterns are also apparent in the Strathspey and Highland Reel. The everlasting chain, the one beginning and one end, is also seen in Celtic art patterns and can be noted in the spirals in the Reel of Tulloch.

Between the lines of history, the breathtaking beauty of the country, the absolutely swelling pride one feels the minute the piper starts, and the deep love from within of this thing called Highland Dancing, this indeed incredible adventure is one not soon forgotten.

ANDREW SUTHERLAND

Andrew *with his good friend Jackie Grant.*

A proud young man with a fine array of trophies.

CISSIE TUCKER

Cissie Tucker was a well known dance teacher and adjudicator in Edinburgh for over 50 years.

She was taught by Sydney Black, a recognised exponent of highland dancing in the early 1920s and continued to visit with him until his death.

She was a member of SOBHD from its inception, first of all representing the Highland Dancing Specialists Association then the United Kingdom Alliance (she was an Examiner for both organisations) and finally she was elected and Independent member. She was also a member of the Technical and the Judges Committees for many years and a member of the Judges Panel. Miss Tucker was one of the very early members of SOBHD who helped to set up the Constitution and Rules for all those who followed.

She travelled a lot in the UK and in North America judging and conducting Judges Test. There is a story of Miss Tucker and Miss Jessie Stewart in an attempted mugging by two youths in the USA outside a restaurant after an evening meal. Although dragged along the ground holding tight to her handbag the two ladies between them managed to fight off the youths. They were kept overnight in a local hospital and it's probable after that experience the youths thought twice about attacking two Scots Ladies again. After all it was explained, the passports and all their money was in the handbag and no way were they taking it off them.

Cissie Tucker later married Willie Cuthbertson and set up home in Glasgow combining their two dance schools.

IAN WILSON

Ian Wilson was a member the SOBHD for many years as representing Butlin's Dance Festival. Ian came from a Ballroom dance background of which he taught with his much beloved wife Agnes Stewart. He co-organised Butlin's Dance Festival as well as Balloch and Luss for many years. Ian was responsible for the project of creating the Beginners, Novice, and Intermediate registration categories for the Board, the system that is still in use today. After serving in the Royal Navy, Ian was a member of the Vale of Leven Scottish Junior Cup winning side in 1952/3 and then became a professional football player for Aberdeen and Gillingham.

ELIZABETH P. WALLACE

Elizabeth P. Wallace was affectionately known as Betty and was born in Ayrshire into a dancing family, her father Joseph Wallace originated from Kilmarnock.

Miss Wallace was qualified in all branches of dance, Highland, Stage and Ballet and also Ballroom. She was a true professional in every sense of the word, mentoring her students throughout their dancing careers. Her life was devoted to dance.

She was a Fellow and Examiner in the British Association of Teachers of Dancing, a very knowledgeable lady who was highly respected and admired by her colleagues.

Betty was always promoting dance and encouraging young Associates to further their knowledge and learn all that they could about dance.

She was a keen advocate of the Scottish Official Board of Highland Dancing and was in attendance at the inaugural meeting in September 1950 and was the B.A.T.D. Technical Delegate to the Board's Technical Committee from its conception in October 1950. She was also an Independent Member of the Board.

Cowal Highland Gathering
and the Scottish Official Board of Highland Dancing

Cowal Highland Gathering and the S.O.B.H.D.

Although the first Cowal Highland Gathering was held in 1894 it was not until 1902 that a Juvenile Highland Dancing Competition was added to the programme. The first Juvenile World Championship was then held in 1932.

The first Adult World Championship was held in 1948, preceding the SOBHD by two years. The first reference to the SOBHD in the Gathering minutes is in a report of a meeting held on 6th April 1951 when our own Mr. J. S. Thompson reported on the work of the SOBHD and confirmed he had been appointed Hon. Treasurer of the new organisation. He went on to confirm that the Cowal rules of Highland Dancing had been adopted by the SOBHD and that the SOBHD had recognised that the World Championships belonged to Cowal and at no time would be held elsewhere.

In those early years it appears that the relationship between the two organisations was strained with the Cowal Committee refusing to pay a fee to the SOBHD for the right to hold "Championships" at Cowal. In Cowal's opinion the World Championships were Cowal's Championships. There are references in the committee minutes to an exchange of letters and various meetings which were held throughout the 1950s regarding this issue. In 1960 the SOBHD offered to provide a legal document which would recognise the rights of Cowal as "owner" of the world Championships and confirm that the Championships would remain at Cowal "in perpetuity".

Things worked well on this basis until the mid sixties when there were complaints from one dancing organisation that, unlike other Championships, Cowal was neither paying its fees nor applying for its Championships. There were several meetings where Cowal stated its case and defended its position but in 1968 the Cowal Committee received a letter from the SOBHD which notified the committee that the Board did not intend to recognise the Cowal Championships that year. Cowal took the decision to fight this boycott of its Championships and, after subsequent meetings, decided to withdraw its representation from the SOBHD and continue to hold the World Championships that year.

The Cowal minutes confirm that the SOBHD held its own World Championships in Gourock in 1969 whilst Cowal maintained its position and held its own World Championships the same year. It was early 1970 before an agreement was reached whereby Cowal agreed to recognise the Board's rules and introduce the practice of using only SOBHD appointed judges over the coming two years and, in return, the SOBHD recognised Cowal's right to hold the World Championships in perpetuity.

Thankfully therefore, the relationship between the two organisations began to improve and has continued to do so to this day with both organisations working closely together for the mutual benefit of competitors and teachers alike.

Cowal is a very different event now, with greatly improved facilities for both the dancer and spectator. The Board of Directors at Cowal are very much aware of the great importance of the World Highland Dancing Championships to many dancers throughout the world and have embarked on a programme of improvements which has seen an upgrading of the infrastructure and the organisation of the Championships.

In recent years, Cowal has held meetings with all the overseas organisations and all the teaching bodies in order to share ideas and listen to feedback with a view in furthering the Championships. Cowal is delighted that all of the teaching organisations and some of the overseas bodies have supported Cowal financially through various means of sponsorship.

Highland Dancing is so important to Scottish culture and Cowal Highland Gathering will continue to uphold the great traditions of this art form and work closely with the SOBHD to promote Highland Dancing throughout the world.

Cowal Highland Gathering

Programmes from the past

Picture Gallery of Merit

WINNERS OF CHAMPIONSHIPS at COWAL GATHERING, 1932

Isabella St. John, Bellshill.
Champion Highland Dancer under 7, 1932.
(J. B. M'Ewen Challenge Trophy.)

Ila Anderson, Kirn.
Champion Highland Dancer under 9, 1932.
(Urquhart and A. D. Cameron Challenge Trophies.)

Margaret Fisher, Glasgow.
Champion Highland and Best Dressed Dancer under 11, 1932.
(Campbell and Yare Challenge Trophies.)

William K. Campbell, Bishopbriggs.
Champion Highland Dancer under 13, 1932.
(Cowal Challenge Trophy.)

Jean Murray, Dunoon.
Champion Local Dancer under 15, 1932.

Gladys Bruce, Largs.
World's Champion Highland Dancer, 1932.
(Lawrie Challenge Trophy.)

Dorothy J. Bruce, Liverp
Best Dressed High
Dancer under 15, 193
(Gordon Challenge Trop

Picture Gallery of Merit

WINNERS OF CHAMPIONSHIPS at COWAL GATHERING, 1930

Elizabeth Fisher, Govanhill.
Champion Highland Dancer, under 7, 1930.
(J. B. M'Ewen Challenge Trophy).

Emma Cargill, Kirkcaldy.
Champion Highland Dancer, under 9, 1930.
(Urquhart Challenge Trophy).

Wm. K. Campbell, Bishopbriggs.
Champion Highland Dancer and Best Dressed Dancer, under 11, 1930
(Campbell and Yare Trophies).

Connie Chalmers, Aberdeen.
Champion Highland Dancer, under 13, 1930.
(Cowal Challenge Trophy).

Jessie A. K. Duncan, Perth.
Champion Highland Dancer, under 15, 1930.
(Lawrie Challenge Trophy).

Sadie Simpson, Glasgow.
B:st Dressed Dancer in Highland Costume, under 15, 1930.
(Gordon Challenge Trophy).

Mairi M'Callum, Innellan.
Champion Local Dancer, under 15, 1930.
(Forrest Challenge Trophy).

45

Picture Gallery of Merit

WINNERS OF CHAMPIONSHIPS at COWAL GATHERING, 1933

Pearl Kilgour, Thornliebank.
Champion Highland Dancer under 7 years, 1933.
(J. B. M'Ewen Challenge Trophy.)

Mary M'Callum, Campbeltown.
Champion County Dancer under 15 years, 1933.
(Forrest Challenge Trophy.)

Ila Anderson, Kirn.
Champion Highland Dancer under 9 years, 1933.
(Urquhart, Cameron and Yare Challenge Trophies, Victory Cup Winner)

Winnie Mann, Stevenston.
World's Champion Highland Dancer, 1933.
(Lawrie Challenge Trophy.)

Margaret Fisher, Glasgow.
Champion Highland Dancer under 11 years, 1933.
(Campbell Challenge Trophy, Victory Cup Winner.)

Anna M'F. Moore, Blackpool.
Champion Highland Dancer under 13 years, 1933.
(Cowal Challenge Trophy.)

Stella Vickers, Rochdale, Lancs.
Best Dressed Highland Dancer under 15 years, 1933.
(Gordon Challenge Trophy.)

31

Picture Gallery of Merit

WINNERS OF CHAMPIONSHIPS at COWAL GATHERING, 1928

Elizabeth Anderson, Stirling.
Champion Highland Dancer under 7, 1928.
(J. B. M'Ewen Challenge Trophy).

Ruby Murray, Newmains.
Champion Highland Dancer, under 9, 1928.
(Urquhart Challenge Trophy).

Connie Chalmers, Aberdeen.
Champion Highland Dancer, under 11, 1928.
(Campbell Challenge Trophy).

Helen Wright, Dennistoun.
Champion Highland Dancer, under 13, 1928.
(Cowal Challenge Trophy).

Isa Russel, Hamilton.
Champion Highland Dancer, under 15, 1928.
(Lawrie Challenge Trophy).

Edna M. C. M'Farlane, Stirling.
Best Dressed Dancer in Highland Costume, under 15, 1928.
(Gordon Challenge Trophy).

Cathie MacGregor, Dunoon.
Champion Local Dancer, under 15, 1928.
(Forrest Challenge Trophy).

Elsie Aitken, Leven.
Best Dressed Dancer in Highland Costume, under 11, 1928.
(Yare Challenge Trophy).

39

Picture Gallery of Merit

WINNERS OF CHAMPIONSHIPS at COWAL GATHERING, 1927

Greta Purdue, Port-Glasgow. Champion Highland Dancer under 7, 1927. (J. B. M'Ewen Challenge Trophy).

Elsie Aitken, Leven. Champion Highland Dancer under 9, 1927. (Urquhart Challenge Trophy).

Gladys Bruce, Glasgow. Champion Highland Dancer under 11, 1927. (Campbell Challenge Trophy).

Annie Hallyburton, Springburn. Champion Highland Dancer under 13, 1927. (Cowal Challenge Trophy).

Peggy Shaw, Denny. Champion Highland Dancer under 15, 1927. (Lawrie Challenge Trophy).

Isa Russel, Hamilton. Best Dressed Dancer in Highland Costume, under 15, 1927. (...lan Challenge Trophy).

Cathie MacGregor, Dunoon. Champion Local Dancer under 15, 1927. (Forrest Challenge Trophy).

Jeanie Rice, West Kilb... Best Dressed Dancer in Highland Costume, und... 1927. (Yare Challenge Tro...

Picture Gallery of Merit

WINNERS OF CHAMPIONSHIPS at COWAL GATHERING, 1935.

Buntie Downie. ("M'Niven Cuthbertson" Trophy, 1935.)

Nancy Gilmour. ("Castle Toward" Trophy, 1935.)

Ila Anderson, Wrexham. ("Yare" Challenge Trophy and "Elkington" Challenge Trophy, 1935.)

Dorothy Jean Bruce. World's Champion Highland Dancer, 1935. ("Lawrie" Trophy.)

Betty Rox. Scottish Champion, 1935 (under 9 years). (The "Gray" Challenge Troph...

Picture Gallery of Merit

WINNERS OF CHAMPIONSHIPS at COWAL GATHERING, 1936.

Cathie Stewart. ("M'Niven Cuthbertson" Trophy, 1936.)

Chrissie Cameron. ("Yare" Challenge Trophy, 1936.)

Bunty Downie. World's Champion Highland Dancer, 1936. ("Lawrie" and "Forrest" Challenge Trophies.)

Grace Sorrie. ("A. D. Cameron" Trophy, 1936.)

Ila Anderson, Wrexham. ("Castle Toward" and "Margaret Fisher" Trophies, 1936.)

Nettie Wilson. ("J. B. M'Ewan" Shield, 1936.)

C

33

Picture Gallery of Merit

WINNERS OF CHAMPIONSHIPS at COWAL GATHERING, 1937.

Isobel St. John ("M'Niven Cuthbertson" Trophy, 1937.)

Margaret H. Muir ("Yare" Challenge Trophy, 1937.)

Bunty Thomson World's Champion Highland Dancer, 1937. ("Lawrie" Trophy, 1937.)

William Macdonald ("A. D. Cameron" Trophy, 1937.)

May G. Falconer ("Castle Toward" and "Margaret Fisher" Trophies, 1937.)

Catherine Armour ("J. B. M'Ewan" Shield, 1937.)

C

33

Picture Gallery of Merit

WINNERS OF CHAMPIONSHIPS AT COWAL GATHERING 1954

★

CATRIONA BUCHANAN (Stirling) World's Champion Adult Highland Dancer "Scott Cameron" Trophy 1954

LOUISE GALBRAITH (Greenock) World's Champion Juvenile Highland Dancer "Lawrie" Trophy 1954

GLORIA D. THOMSON (Perth) "Gray" Trophy 1954

HELEN McPHEE (Dunoon) "A. D. Cameron" Trophy 1954

ENA WARDEN (Dundee) "J. B. McEwan" Trophy 1954

Picture Gallery of Merit

WINNERS OF CHAMPIONSHIPS AT COWAL GATHERING 1956

★

SHEENA McDONALD (Thornliebank) World's Champion Adult Highland Dancer "Scott Cameron" Trophy 1956

ANNE McILROY (Rothesay) World's Champion Juvenile Highland Dancer "Lawrie" and "Agnes Campbell" Trophies 1956

ANNE BEVERIDGE (New York) "Gray" Trophy 1956

IRENE GALLOWAY (Kirn) "A. D. Cameron" Trophy 1956

WILMA McGOWAN (Motherwell) "J. B. McEwan" T

Picture Gallery of Merit

★

WINNERS OF CHAMPIONSHIPS AT COWAL GATHERING 1957

SHEENA McDONALD (Thornliebank) World's Champion Adult Highland Dancer "Scott Cameron" Trophy 1957

SANDRA BALD (Kircaldy) World's Champion Juvenile Highland Dancer 1957

EVAN C. MacKAY (Glasgow) "Lamont" Shield 1957

BILLY MURRAY (Alexandria) "Gray" Trophy 1957

IRENE GALLOWAY (Kirn) "A. D. Cameron" Trophy 1957

ELAINE DISHINGTON (Edinburgh) "J. B. McEwan" Trophy 1957

40

CHRISTINE AITKEN (Paisley) "Elkington" Trophy 1957

SYLVIA HENDERSON (Crossgates) 'Margaret Fisher" Trophy 1957

CATH. M. STEWART (Inveraray) "J. C. Forrest" Trophy 1957

AGNES McCALLUM (Inveraray) "Margaret Tait" Trophy 1957

P./M. R. MacCallum (8th A. & S. H.) "Glen Caladh" Trophy 1957

HUGH A. McCALLUM (Campbeltown) "Inverchapel" Trophy 1957

41

Picture Gallery of Merit

★

WINNERS OF CHAMPIONSHIPS AT COWAL GATHERING 1961

BETTY JESSIMAN (Huntly) World's Champion Adult Highland Dancer "Scott Cameron" Trophy 1961

IRENE McKECHNIE (Grangemouth) World's Champion Juvenile Highland Dancer "Lawrie" Trophy, 1961

JOHN A. FORD (Kirn) "J. C. Forrest" Trophy, 1961

MARLYN BOWIE (Chryston) "Margaret Fisher" Trophy 1961

FIONA GRAHAM (Haggs) "Elkington" Trophy, 1961

DOREEN ALLISON (Kirn) "A. D. Cameron" Trophy 1961

36

BETTY A. TURKINGTON (Glasgow) World's Champion Junior Highland Dancer "Argyllshire Standard" Trophy, 1961

CECILIA PATE (Cardenden) "Agnes Campbell" Trophy 1961

FIONA PERRY (Glasgow) 'J. B. McEwan" Trophy, 1961

DOROTHY RAE (Edinburgh) "Gray" Trophy, 1961

ARCHIE MACTAGGART (Islay) Burgh Cup, 1961

R. A. BARRON (St. Andrews) "Glen Caladh" Trophy, 1961

37

Picture Gallery of Merit

★

WINNERS OF CHAMPIONSHIPS AT COWAL GATHERING 1960

FLORA S. GRUBB (Newcastle, N.S.W.) World's Champion Adult Highland Dancer 'Scott Cameron" Trophy 1960

CECILIA PATE (Cardenden) World's Champion Juvenile Highland Dancer and "Agnes Campbell" Trophy 1960

MARTIN WILSON (Dunoon) Burgh Cup, 1960

BILLY MURRAY (Alexandria) "Margaret Fisher" Trophy 1960

MAUREEN C. SUTHERLAND (Abernethy) "Elkington" Trophy 1960

DOREEN ALLISON (Kirn) "A. D. Cameron" Trophy 1960

36

GRACE LINDSAY (Kirn) "J. C. Forrest" Trophy 1960

FIONA GRAHAM (Haggs) "Gray" Trophy, 1960

DOROTHY RAE (Edinburgh) "J. B. McEwan" Trophy 1960

MAUREEN FORD (Kirn) "Margaret Tait" Trophy, 1960

JAMES JACKSON (Balloch) "Inverchapel" Trophy, 1960

DONALD MACPHERSON (Glasgow) "Brymay" and "Glen Caladh" Trophies, 1960

37

Picture Gallery of Merit

★

WINNERS OF CHAMPIONSHIPS AT COWAL GATHERING 1958

SHEENA McDONALD (Thornliebank) World's Champion Adult Highland Dancer "Scott Cameron" Trophy 1958

SYLVIA HENDERSON (Crossgates) World's Champion Juvenile Highland Dancer and "Margaret Fisher" Trophy 1958

RODERICK McDONALD (Kirn) Burgh Cup 1958

ANNE WARDEN (Dundee) "Gray" Trophy, 1958

SALLY HIGGINS (Dunoon) "A. D. Cameron" Trophy 1958

ELSPETH A. PERRY (Glasgow) "J. B. McEwan" Trophy 1958

38

Picture Gallery of Merit

★

WINNERS OF CHAMPIONSHIPS AT COWAL GATHERING 1967

IRENE McKECHNIE (Grangemouth) World's Champion Adult Highland Dancer 'Scott Cameron' Trophy 1967

CHRISTINE CROW (Edinburgh) World's Champion Juvenile Highland Dancer 'Lawrie' Trophy, 1967

ANN C. SIMMONS (Dunoon) 'J. C. Forrest' Trophy, 1967

GRACE D. HIGGINS (Kirn) 'Agnes Campbell' Trophy Castle Toward & J. C. Forrest 1967

MAUREEN BARR (Kirkcaldy) 'Margaret Fisher' Trophy 1967

JANICE MURRAY Dunlop 'Gray Trophy', 1967

LYNN ERBRICK (Cornwell's Heights, USA) World's Champion Junior Highland Dancer 'Argyllshire Standard' Trophy, 1967

JAMES McC. McCORKINDALE (Campbeltown) 'Margaret Tait' Trophy, 1967

SANDRA KENNEDY (Bearsden) Elkington Challenge Trophy 1967

ANNE MILNE (Alexandria) 'J. B. McEwan' Trophy 1967

PETER C. McCALLUM (Campbeltown) Dunoon Burgh Cup

HECTOR MacFADYEN (Pennyghael) Glen Caladh, Brymay, McLellan and McCallum

37

Picture Gallery of Merit

LINDA RANKIN (Prestwick) World's Adult Champion 'Scott Cameron' Memorial Challenge Trophy

CHRISTINE A. LACEY (Alexandria) World and Scottish Champion Juvenile Highland Dancer 'Lawrie' Trophy and 'Agnes Campbell' Trophy

SANDRA KENNEDY (Bearsden) World's Champion Junior Highland Dancer 'Argyllshire Standard' Trophy

WINNERS OF CHAMPIONSHIPS AT COWAL GATHERING 1975

KATHLEEN B. MACKENZIE (Ontario) 'Margaret Fisher Challenge' Trophy

ELIZABETH OLIPHANT (Kirn) 'J. C. Forrest' Challenge Trophy

40

SANDRA M. ABERDEIN
(Keith)
World's Champion
Junior Highland Dancer
'Argyllshire Standard'
Trophy, 1966

GRACE D. HIGGINS
(Kirn)
'Margaret Tait' Trophy,
1966

FIONA PERRY
(Glasgow)
Elkington Challenge Trophy
1966

JACQUELINE HARVEY
(Kilwinning)
'J. B. McEwan' Trophy
1966

GEORGE JOHNSTON
Piper, Scots Guards
Dunoon Burgh Cup

HECTOR MacFADYEN
(Pennyghael)
Brymay, McLellan and
McCallum

Picture Gallery of Merit

VICTOR WESLEY
(Glasgow)
World's Champion
Adult Highland Dancer
'Scott Cameron' Trophy
1968

ROSEMARY McGUIRE
(Banknock)
World's Champion
Junior Highland Dancer
'Argyllshire Standard'
Trophy, 1968

GRACE HIGGINS
(Kirn)
World's Champion
Juvenile Highland
Dancer
'Agnes Campbell'
Trophy and 'J. C.
Forrest' Trophy
1968

WINNERS OF CHAMPIONSHIPS AT COWAL GATHERING

SHENDL RUSSELL
(Ayr)
'Margaret Fisher' and
'Castle Toward' Trophy
1968

CHRISTINE SIMMONS
(Paisley)

JANICE SLAVEN
(Mossend)
Elkington Challenge
Trophy, 1968

JAMES McC. McCORKINDALE
(Campbeltown)
'Margaret Tait' Trophy
1968

HECTOR MacFADYEN
(Pennyghael)
Glen Caladh, Brymay
McLellan & McCallum

ALASDAIR ROSS
(Glasgow)
Dunoon Burgh Cup

CHRISTINA A. MacDONALD
(Kirn)
'A. D. Cameron' Trophy
1968

35

NANCY L. HAYS
(Alberto, Canada)
World's Champion
Junior Highland Dancer
"Argyllshire Standard"
Trophy, 19 65

GRACE D. HIGGINS
(Kirn)
"Margaret Tait" Trophy,
1965

FIONA PERRY
(Glasgow)
Elkington Challenge Trophy
1965

MARY NEILL
(Whitburn)
"J. B. McEwan" Trophy
1965

A. J. WILSON
(Campbeltown)
Dunoon Burgh Cup

HECTOR MacFADYEN
(Pennyghael)
Brymay, McLellan and
McCallum

37

Picture Gallery of Merit

LYNNE DICKSON
(Sydney, Australia)
World's Champion
Adult Highland Dancer
'Scott Cameron' Trophy

SANDRA SCAFATE
(Ohio, U.S.A.)
World's Champion
Junior Highland Dancer
'Argyllshire Standard'
Trophy

FIONA PERRY
(Glasgow)
World's Champion
Juvenile Highland
Dancer
Lawrie Trophy

SANDRA KENNEDY
(Bearsden)
'Margaret Fisher' and
Castle Toward

WINNERS OF CHAMPIONSHIPS AT COWAL GATHERING 1970

ANNE C. SIMMONS
(Dunoon)
'Margaret Tait' Trophy

BOBBY CRANSTON
(Stirling)
Elkington Challenge
Trophy

LESLEY E. BOWMAN
(Dundee)
Gray Challenge Trophy

RONALD LAWRIE
(Glasgow)
Brymay, John McLennan
and McCallum

JAMES McC. McCORKINDALE
(Campbeltown)
'J. C. Forrest' Trophy

CAROL PONSONBY
(Port Glasgow)
J. B. McEwan Shield

Picture Gallery of Merit

VICTOR W. WESLEY
(Glasgow)
World's Champion
Adult Highland Dancer
'Scott Cameron' Trophy

AILEEN ROBERTSON
(Ayr)
World's Champion
Junior Highland Dancer
'Argyllshire Standard'
Trophy

SANDRA KENNEDY
(Bearsden)
World's Champion
Juvenile Highland
Dancer
'Lawrie' Trophy

MARY NEIL
(Whitburn)
'Agnes Campbell' and
'Ballimore' Trophies

WINNERS OF CHAMPIONSHIPS AT COWAL GATHERING 1972

CHRISTINA A. MACDONALD
(Kirn)
'Margaret Tait' Trophy

32

CAROL JAMIESON
(West Calder)
'Elkington'
Challenge Trophy

ELIZABETH ANGUS
(Kirn)
'A. D. Cameron' Trophy

P./M. J. McGregor
(Perth)
'Glen Caladh,' 'Brymay,'
'John McLennan,'
'McCallum' and
'Walter Scott' Trophies

LORRAINE W. HASTINGS
(Dumfries)
'Gray' Challenge Trophy

TRUDIE J. POTTHAST
(Clydebank)
'J. B. McEwan' Shield

33

Picture Gallery of Merit

HUGH D. BIGNEY
(Lynnfield U.S.A.)
World's Champion
Adult Highland Dancer
'Scott Cameron' Trophy

LINDA RANKIN
(Prestwick)
World's Champion
Junior Highland Dancer
'Argyllshire Standard'
Trophy

SANDRA KENNEDY
(Bearsden)
World and Scottish
Champion
Juvenile Highland
Dancer
'Lawrie' Trophy and
'Agnes Campbell' Trophy

CHRISTINE A. LACEY
(Alexandria)
'Margaret Fisher'
Challenge Trophy

WINNERS OF CHAMPIONSHIPS AT COWAL GATHERING 1973

CHRISTINA A. MACDONALD
(Kirn)
'J. C. Forrest'
Challenge Trophy

LEAH BOUNDS
(Innellan)
'Margaret Tait'
Challenge Trophy

ELIZABETH ANGUS
(Kirn)
'A. D. Cameron' Trophy

P./M. J. McGregor
(Perth)
'Glen Caladh', 'Brymay',
and 'Walter Scott' Trophies

LORRAINE W. HASTINGS
(Dumfries)
'Gray' Challenge Trophy

GILLIAN K. GREIG
(Kirkcaldy)
'J. B. McEwan' Shield

DONNA J. GRAHAM
(Haggs)
"Elkington" Trophy 1959

JUNE LESLIE
(Kirkcaldy)
"Gray" Trophy 1959

KATHLEEN DRUMMOND
(Dundee)
"J. B. McEwan" Trophy 1959

MAIRI MACKERRELL
"Bowmore"
"Margaret Tait" Trophy 1959

KENNETH MACDONALD
(Glasgow)
"Glen Caladh" Trophy
1959

RONALD LAWRIE (Oban)
"Brymay" and
"McCallum" Trophies
1959

37

COWAL HIGHLAND GATHERING
Highland Dancing Trophy Winners 1984

ANNE MILNE
(Canada)
WORLD JUVENILE CHAMPION
Lawrie Challenge Trophy
and
William Inglis Trophy

GREGOR BOWMAN
(Dundee)
WORLD JUNIOR CHAMPION
Argyllshire Standard Trophy

LESLEY F. BOWMAN
(Dundee)
WORLD ADULT CHAMPION
Scott Cameron
Memorial Challenge
Trophy

EILIDH MacINNES
(Oban)
ARGYLL CHAMPION
J. C. Forrest
Challenge Trophy
and
Gladys MacDonald
Challenge Trophy

TANIA CRAWFORD
(Harthill)
SCOTTISH CHAMPION
Agnes Campbell
Trophy
Castle Toward Trophy

Picture Gallery of Merit

50

BILLY MURRAY (Alexandria) "Elkington" Trophy 1958

MOIRA GRAHAM (Haggs) "Agnes Campbell" Trophy 1958

CATH. M. STEWART (Inveraray) "J. C. Forrest" Trophy 1958

AGNES McCALLUM (Inveraray) 'Margaret Tait' Trophy 1958

THOMAS PEARSTON (Glasgow) "Glen Caladh" Trophy 1958

RONALD LAWRIE (Oban) "Brymay", "McLennan", "McCallum" Trophies 1958

39

SANDRA McGILP (Ardrishaig) 'Margaret Tait' Challenge Trophy

LOUISE DODDS (Edinburgh) 'Elkington' Challenge Trophy

RODERICK J. B. McCOURT (Bathgate) 'Lamont' Shield

STEWART GAUDIN (Glasgow) 'Inverchapel' Challenge Trophy

PIPE MAJOR JAMES L. HENDERSON (Dunoon) Dunoon Burgh Cup

ARTHUR H. FAIRFULL (Carrick Castle) 'Warner' Challenge Trophy

GILLIAN GREIG (Kirkcaldy) 'Gray' Challenge Trophy

MANDY JANE PAIRMAN (Jamestown) 'J. B. McEwan' Shield

41

Picture Gallery of Merit

★

WINNERS OF CHAMPIONSHIPS AT COWAL GATHERING 1959

GORDON F. YEATS (Tarves) World's Champion Adult Highland Dancer 'Scott Cameron" Trophy 1959

SYLVIA HENDERSON (Crossgates) World's Champion Juvenile Highland Dancer and "Agnes Campbell" Trophy 1959

HUGH A. McCALLUM (Campbeltown) Burgh Cup and Inverchapel Trophy 1959

CECILIA PATE (Cardenden) "Margaret Fisher" Trophy 1959

CATHERINE M. McLEAN (Dunoon) "A. D. Cameron" Trophy 1959

AGNES M. McCALLUM (Inveraray) "J. C. Forrest" Trophy 1959

36

★

Picture Gallery of Merit

★

WINNERS OF CHAMPIONSHIPS AT COWAL GATHERING 1976

★

AILEEN ROBERTSON (Ayr) World's Adult Champion 'Scott Cameron' Memorial Challenge Trophy

MARY NEILL (Whitburn) World's Champion Junior Highland Dancer 'Argyllshire Standard' Trophy

AVRIL SMITH (Kelso) 'Margaret Fisher Challenge' Trophy

SCOTT PATERSON (Lochgilphead) 'J. C. Forrest' Challenge Trophy

41

Cowal Highland Gathering

Programmes from the past

★ Picture Gallery of Merit ★

WINNERS OF CHAMPIONSHIPS AT COWAL GATHERING 1977 ★

LINDA RANKIN
(Prestwick)
World Adult Champion
'Scott Cameron' Memorial Challenge Trophy

AILSA SIMPSON
(Barrhead)
World Champion
Juvenile Highland Dancer 'Lawrie' Challenge Trophy

ELAINE DUNCAN
(Hamilton)
'Margaret Fisher' and 'Ballimore' Challenge

ELIZABETH ANGUS
(Kirn)
'J. C. Forrest' Challenge Trophy

CHRISTINE A. LACEY
(Alexandria)
World Junior Champion
Argyllshire Standard Challenge Trophy

AILSA SIMPSON
(Barrhead)
World Champion
Juvenile Highland Dancer 'Lawrie' Challenge Trophy
Scottish Champion (14-16)
'Agnes Campbell' Trophy

SANDRA KENNEDY
(Bearsden)
World Adult Champion
'Scott Cameron' Memorial Challenge Trophy

ELAINE DUNCAN
(Hamilton)
'Margaret Fisher' Challenge Trophy

SCOTT PATERSON
(Lochgare)
'J. C. Forrest' Challenge Trophy

MARGARET McLEOD
(Kirn)
'Margaret Tait' Challenge Trophy

SHARON TAYLOR
(Dunoon)
'Chris Cameron' and 'Margaret Ford' Challenge Trophies

GILLIAN K. GREIG
(Kirkcaldy)
'Elkington' Challenge Trophy

JANEY LEADINGHAM
(Arbroath)
Yare Challenge Trophy.

KAREN FAIRBAIRN
(Cockburnspath)
'Gray' Challenge Trophy

M. M. MAWDSLEY
(Edinburgh)
"Gordon" Challenge Trophy

43

CATHERINE CHALMERS
(Greenock)
World's Champion Junior Highland Dancer "Argyllshire Standard" Trophy, 1964

★

GRACE D. HIGGINS
(Kirn)
"Margaret Tait" Trophy, 1964

★

FIONA PERRY
(Glasgow)
"Gray" Challenge Trophy 1964

★

ALISON HAMILTON
(Dundee)
"J. B. McEwan" Trophy 1964

JOHN MacDONALD
Dunoon Burgh Cup

★

HECTOR MacFADYEN
Glen Caladh McCallum and Brymay

37

Trophy Winners 1982

JENNIFER LINDSAY
(Canada)
World Junior
Champion
Argyllshire Standard
Trophy

GILLIAN K. GREIG
(Dysart)
World Juvenile
Champion
Lawrie Challenge
Trophy

CHRISTINE A. LACEY
World Adult
Champion
Scott Cameron
Memorial Challenge
Trophy

KRISTA TRONNES
(Canada)
Margaret Fisher
Challenge Trophy
and McNiven

MARGARET McLEOD
(Kirn)
J. C. Forrest
Challenge Trophy

Trophy Winners 1982

ALISON J. MacGREGOR
(Laurencekirk)
Gray Challenge
Trophy

NICOLA GRANT
(Kirriemuir)
Elkington Challenge
Trophy

LYNN SKELTON
(Dunoon)
Chris Cameron
Challenge Trophy

EILIDH MacINNES
(Oban)
Gladys MacDonald
Challenge Trophy &
Rita Ford

MICHELLE S. BAIRD
(Canada)
Agnes Campbell
Trophy &
Castle Toward
Trophy

FIONA C. McIVER
(Tiree)
Margaret Tait

Picture Gallery of Merit

JENNIFER LINDSAY
(Canada)
World Junior
Champion
Argyllshire Standard
Trophy

GREGOR BOWMAN
(Dundee)
World Juvenile
Champion
Lawrie Challenge
Trophy

AILSA SIMPSON
(Barrhead)
World Adult
Champion
Scott Cameron
Memorial Challenge
Trophy

KIM KERR
(Canada)
Margaret Fisher
Challenge Trophy

MARGARET McLEOD
(Kirn)
J. C. Forrest
Challenge Trophy

42

SUSAN A. ADAMS
(Dundee)
Gray Challenge
Trophy

ANNE MILNE
(Canada)
Elkington Challenge
Trophy

ALISON BAWN
(Southend)
Chris Cameron
Challenge Trophy

FIONA MacNEIL
(Houston)
Agnes Campbell
Trophy &
Balliemore Shield

EILIDH MacINNES
(Oban)
Gladys MacDonald
Challenge Trophy &
Margaret Tait
Challenge Trophy

NADINE McKENZIE
(Polmont)
J. B. McEwan
Challenge Trophy

43

Cowal Highland Gathering

Programmes from the past

COWAL HIGHLAND GATHERING
Highland Dancing Trophy Winners 1983

ANN MILNE
(Canada)
WORLD JUVENILE CHAMPION
Lawrie Challenge Trophy
and
Margaret Fisher Trophy

GREGOR BOWMAN
(Dundee)
WORLD JUNIOR CHAMPION
Argyllshire Standard Trophy

HELEN FITZPATRICK
(Stenhousemuir)
WORLD ADULT CHAMPION
Scott Cameron Memorial Challenge Trophy

EILIDH MacINNES
(Oban)
ARGYLL CHAMPION
J. C. Forrest Challenge Trophy
and
Gladys MacDonald Challenge Trophy

NATALIE GRAY
(Canada)
SCOTTISH CHAMPION
Agnes Campbell Trophy
Castle Toward Trophy

Picture Gallery of Merit

50

Picture Gallery of Merit

★

WINNERS OF CHAMPIONSHIPS AT COWAL GATHERING 1966

SANDRA WRIGHT
(New Zealand)
World's Champion Adult Highland Dancer
'Scott Cameron' Trophy
1966

ROSEMARY McGUIRE
(Banknock)
World's Champion Juvenile Highland Dancer
'Lawrie' Trophy, 1966

ELSPETH B. CAMPBELL
(Campbeltown)
J. C. Forrest' Trophy, 1966

ANNE COCHRANE
(Paisley)
'Agnes Campbell' Trophy
McNiven Cuthbertson Cup
1966

BETTY MONTGOMERY
(Dundee)
Margaret Fisher Trophy,
1966

ALISON HAMILTON
(Dundee)
'Gray Trophy', 1966

36

COWAL HIGHLAND GATHERING
Highland Dancing Trophy Winners 1983

JOHN KERR
(Campbeltown)
Margaret Tait Challenge Trophy

NICOLA GRANT
(Kirriemuir)
Elkington Challenge Trophy

DEBORAH KELLY
(Erskine)
Wm. Inglis Memorial Trophy

JULIE McLEAN
(Hunter's Quay)
Chris Cameron Trophy

DERYCK MITCHELSON
(Monifieth)
Isobel St. John Trophy

ALISON MacGREGOR
(Laurencekirk)
Gray Challenge Trophy

Picture Gallery of Merit

51

Picture Gallery of Merit

★

WINNERS OF CHAMPIONSHIPS AT COWAL GATHERING 1964

BILLY FORSYTH
(Bridge of Allan)
World's Champion Adult Highland Dancer
"Scott Cameron" Trophy
1964

CECILIA ORR
(Forth)
World's Champion Juvenile Highland Dancer
"Lawrie" Trophy, 1964

ANNE L. MACRAE
(Kirn)
"J. C. Forrest" Trophy, 1964

ANNE CRAIG
(Edinburgh)
"Agnes Campbell" Trophy,
1964

FIONA GRAHAM
(Haggs)
Gordon, Margaret Fisher and Mary McNeill trophies

JAMES McCORKINDALE
(Campbeltown)
"A. D. Cameron" Trophy
1964

36

PICTURE GALLERY OF MERIT

WINNERS OF CHAMPIONSHIPS AT COWAL GATHERING 1979

AILSA SIMPSOM (Barrhead) World Junior Champion Argyllshire Standard Challenge Trophy

ELAINE DUNCAN (Hamilton) World Champion Juvenile Highland Dancer Lawrie Challenge Trophy Agnes Campbell Trophy

CHRISTINE A. LACEY (Alexandria) World Adult Champion Scott Cameron Memorial Challenge Trophy

GREGOR S. A. BOWMAN (Dundee) Margaret Fisher Challenge Trophy

ELIZABETH ANGUS (Kirn) J. C. Forrest Challenge Trophy & Gladys McDonald Challenge Trophy

41

SANDRA McGILP (Ardrishaig) 'Margaret Tait' Challenge Trophy

KATHRYN GILL (Dunoon) A. D. Cameron Challenge Trophy

T. SPEIRS (Edinburgh) John MacLellan Challenge Trophy

BRIAN WAITES (Kilwinning) 'Gray' Challenge Trophy

HEATHER BAKER (Bearsden) 'J. B. McEwan' Shield

39

Picture Gallery of Merit

JOHN L. GRAHAM (Avonbridge) McCallum Challenge Trophy

KATIE ROWAN (Ayr) World's Champion Junior Highland Dancer 'Argyllshire Standard' Trophy

CHRISTINE A. LACEY (Alexandria) World and Scottish Champion Juvenile Highland Dancer 'Lawrie' Trophy and 'Agnes Campbell' Trophy

KATHLEEN B. MACKENZIE (Ontario) Elkington Challenge Trophy

WINNERS OF CHAMPIONSHIPS AT COWAL GATHERING 1974

CHRISTINA A. MACDONALD (Kirn) 'J. C. Forrest' Challenge Trophy

38

Picture Gallery of Merit

★

WINNERS OF CHAMPIONSHIPS AT COWAL GATHERING 1965

WILMA TOLMIE (Dundee) World's Champion Adult Highland Dancer "Scott Cameron" Trophy 1965

ROSEMARY McGUIRE (Banknock) World's Champion Juvenile Highland Dancer 'Lawrie' Trophy, 1965

MARGARET LAUDER (Kirn) "J. C. Forrest" Trophy, 1965

ANNE COCHRANE (Paisley) "Agnes Campbell" Trophy 1965

CHRISTINE CROWE (Edinburgh) Margaret Fisher trophy

JAMES McCORKINDALE (Campbeltown) "A. D. Cameron" Trophy 1965

36

Cowal Highland Gathering

Programmes from the past

Picture Gallery of Merit

WINNERS OF CHAMPIONSHIPS at COWAL GATHERING, 1934

Isabella St. John, Motherwell. Champion Highland Dancer (under 9 years), 1934 (Urquhart Trophy.)

May F. Alexander, Glasgow. Champion Highland Dancer (under 7 years), 1934. (J. B. M'Ewan Shield.)

Ila Anderson, Kirn. Champion Highland Dancer (under 11 years), 1934. (A. D. Cameron and Elkington Trophies.)

Thos. D. M'Ivor, Dundee. Best Dressed Dancer in Highland Costume (under 11 years) 1934. (Yare Trophy.)

Elspeth Strathern, Cathcart. Best Dressed Dancer in Highland Costume (under 15 years), and World's Champion Highland Dancer, 1934. (Gordon and Lawrie Trophies)

Joan Blair, Tarbert. Champion County Dancer (under 15 years), 1934. (Forrest Trophy.)

Margaret Fisher, Glasgow. Champion Highland Dancer (under 13 years), 1934. (Gray Challenge Trophy.)

COWAL HIGHLAND GATHERING
Highland Dancing Trophy Winners 1984

JOHN KERR (Campbeltown) Margaret Tait Challenge Trophy

NICOLA GRANT (Kirriemuir) Isobel St. John Trophy

ALISON J. MacGREGOR (Laurencekirk) Elkington Challenge Trophy

JULIE McLEAN (Hunter's Quay) Chris Cameron Trophy

DERYCK MITCHELSON (Monifieth) Margaret Fisher Trophy and McNiven Cuthbertson Cup

DAWN FRASER (Glenrothes) Gray Challenge Trophy

Picture Gallery of Merit

COWAL HIGHLAND GATHERING
Highland Dancing Trophy Winners 1989

KATRINA MARTIN (Dunoon) ARGYLL CHAMPIONSHIP Margaret Tait Challenge Trophy

JULIE McLEAN (Dunoon) ARGYLL CHAMPIONSHIP J C Forrest Challenge Trophy Gladys MacDonald Challenge Trophy

JACQUELINE SMITH (Ontario) WORLD JUNIOR CHAMPIONSHIP Argyllshire Standard Challenge Trophy

GARETH MITCHELSON (Monifieth) WORLD ADULT CHAMPIONSHIP Scott Cameron Memorial Challenge Trophy

Picture Gallery of Merit

44

COWAL HIGHLAND GATHERING
Highland Dancing Trophy Winners 1990

SHARON McCREADY (Dunoon) Argyll Trophy The Chris Cameron Trophy

EMMA STEPHEN (Fraserburgh) SCOTTISH CHAMPIONSHIP The J.B. McEwan Shield

KATRINA MARTIN (Dunoon) SCOTTISH CHAMPIONSHIP The Gray Challenge Trophy Argyll Championship The Margaret Tait Trophy The Gladys MacDonald Challenge Trophy

CAROLINE REID (Dalry) SCOTTISH CHAMPIONSHIP The Milton Trophy

Picture Gallery of Merit

43

Cowal Highland Gathering

Programmes from the past

COWAL HIGHLAND GATHERING
Highland Dancing Trophy Winners 1986

DERYCK J. MITCHELSON (Monifieth) WORLD JUVENILE CHAMPION Lawrie Challenge Trophy and Agnes Campbell Trophy

GREGOR S.A. BOWMAN (Dundee) WORLD ADULT CHAMPION Scott Cameron Memorial Challenge Trophy

ANN MILNE (Canada) WORLD JUNIOR CHAMPION Argyllshire Standard Trophy

JOHN KERR (Campbeltown) ARGYLL CHAMPION J.C. Forrest Challenge Trophy

ALISON J. MacGREGOR (Laurencekirk) Isobel St. John Trophy

NICOLA D. GRANT (Kirriemuir) WILLIAM INGLIS Memorial Trophy

Picture Gallery of Merit

COWAL HIGHLAND GATHERING
Highland Dancing Trophy Winners 1988

JULIE MacLEAN (Dunoon) ARGYLL CHAMPIONSHIP Margaret Tait Challenge Trophy Gladys MacDonald Challenge Trophy

JOHN KERR (Campbeltown) ARGYLL CHAMPIONSHIP J.C. Forrest Challenge Trophy

DERYCK MITCHELSON (Monifieth) WORLD JUNIOR CHAMPIONSHIP Argyllshire Standard Challenge Trophy

GARETH MITCHELSON (Monifieth) WORLD ADULT CHAMPIONSHIP Scott Cameron Memorial Challenge Trophy

Picture Gallery of Merit

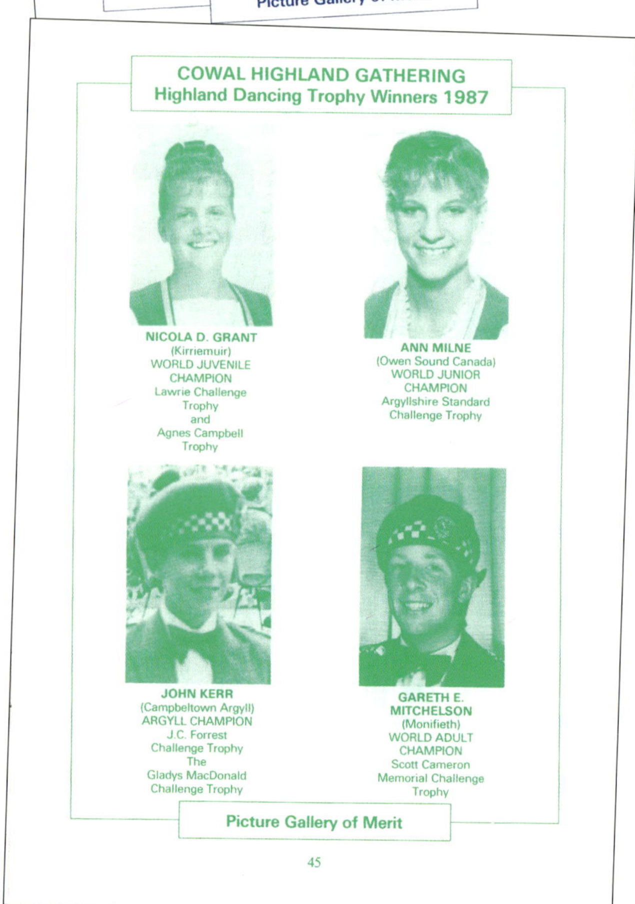
COWAL HIGHLAND GATHERING
Highland Dancing Trophy Winners 1987

NICOLA D. GRANT (Kirriemuir) WORLD JUVENILE CHAMPION Lawrie Challenge Trophy and Agnes Campbell Trophy

ANN MILNE (Owen Sound Canada) WORLD JUNIOR CHAMPION Argyllshire Standard Challenge Trophy

JOHN KERR (Campbeltown Argyll) ARGYLL CHAMPION J.C. Forrest Challenge Trophy The Gladys MacDonald Challenge Trophy

GARETH E. MITCHELSON (Monifieth) WORLD ADULT CHAMPION Scott Cameron Memorial Challenge Trophy

Picture Gallery of Merit

45

COWAL HIGHLAND GATHERING
Highland Dancing Trophy Winners 1986

AILEEN A. McALLISTER (Campbeltown) Margaret Tait Challenge Trophy

HELEN GALBRAITH (Dunoon) Gladys MacDonald Challenge Trophy

NADINE McKENZIE (Polmont) Elkington Challenge Trophy

DONNA L. FERGUSON (Campbeltown) Chris Cameron Trophy

SHIRLEY I. FRASER (Alford) Margaret Fisher Trophy

KAREN McKNIGHT (Hamilton) Gray Challenge Trophy

Picture Gallery of Merit

47

Cowal Highland Gathering Champions

Picture left to right: ***David Wilton, Rachel McLean, Tony Cargill at the Tay Bridge in 2004***

Cowal Highland Gathering Champions 2007

Fiona Lee
World Junior Champion 2007

Morgan Bramford
World Juvenile Champion 2007

Some Cowal Highland Gathering Champions

David Wilton
World Junior Champion 2006

Coleen Rintamaki
World Adult Champion 2005

Rachel McLean
World Junior Champion 2004

Tony Cargill
World Adult Champion 2004

Cowal Highland Gathering
Adult World Dancing Champions

YEAR	NAME	ORIGIN
1948	May Falconer	Motherwell
1949	Margaret Samson	Stirling
1950	Margaret Samson	Stirling
1951	J L McKenzie	Aberdeen
1952	J L McKenzie	Aberdeen
1953	J L McKenzie	Aberdeen
1954	Catriona Buchanan	Stirling
1955	Catriona Buchanan	Stirling
1956	Sheena McDonald	Thornliebank
1957	Sheena McDonald	Thornliebank
1958	Sheena McDonald	Thornliebank
1959	Gordon Yeats	Tarves
1960	Flora Stuart Grubb	Australia
1961	Betty Jessiman	Huntly
1962	Sandra Bald	Kirkcaldy
1963	Billy Forsyth	Bridge of Allan
1964	Billy Forsyth	Bridge of Allan
1965	Wilma Tolmie	Dundee
1966	Sandra Wright	New Zealand
1967	Irene McKechnie	Grangemouth
1968	Victor Wesley	Glasgow
1969	Victor Wesley	Glasgow
1970	Lynn Dickson	Australia
1971	Rosemary McGuire	Banknock
1972	Victor Wesley	Glasgow
1973	Hugh Bigney	USA
1974	Aileen Robertson	Ayr
1975	Linda Rankin	Prestwick
1976	Aileen Robertson	Ayr
1977	Linda Rankin	Prestwick
1978	Sandra Kennedy	Bearsden

YEAR	NAME	ORIGIN
1979	Christine Lacey	Alexandria
1980	Christine Lacey	Alexandria
1981	Ailsa Simpson	Barrhead
1982	Christine Lacey	Alexandria
1983	Helen Fitzpatrick	Stenhousemuir
1984	Lesley E Bowman	Dundee
1985	Gareth Mitchelson	Monifieth
1986	Gregor Bowman	Dundee
1987	Gareth Mitchelson	Monifieth
1988	Gareth Mitchelson	Monifieth
1989	Gareth Mitchelson	Monifieth
1990	Gregor Bowman	Dundee
1991	Deryck Mitchelson	Monifieth
1992	Gregor Bowman	Dundee
1993	Jacqueline Smith	Ontario
1994	Deryck Mitchelson	Monifieth
1995	Deryck Mitchelson	Monifieth
1996	Jacqueline Smith	Ontario
1997	Gregor Bowman	Dundee
1998	Gregor Bowman	Dundee
1999	Colleen Rintamaki	Ontario
2000	Colleen Rintamaki	Ontario
2001	Colleen Rintamaki	Ontario
2002	Colleen Rintamaki	Ontario
2003	Colleen Rintamaki	Ontario
2004	Tony Cargill	Forfar
2005	Colleen Rintamaki	Ontario
2006	Erin Rose	Ontario
2007	David Wilton	Forfar
2008	David Wilton	Forfar
2009	David Wilton	Forfar

Cowal Highland Gathering
Junior World Dancing Champions

YEAR	NAME	ORIGIN
1961	Betty Turkington	Glasgow
1962	Cecilia Pate	Cardenden
1963	Irene McKechnie	Grangemouth
1964	Catherine Chalmers	Greenock
1965	Nancy Hays	Alberta
1966	Sandra Aberdein	Keith
1967	Lynn Erbrick	Cornwell's Heights
1968	Rosemary McGuire	Banknock
1969	Rosemary McGuire	Banknock
1970	Sandra Scafate	Ohio
1971	Noreen Keros	Michigan
1972	Aileen Robertson	Ayr
1973	Linda Rankin	Prestwick
1974	Katie Rowan	Ayr
1975	Sandra Kennedy	Bearsden
1976	Mary Neill	Whitburn
1977	Mary Beth Miller	Kansas
1978	Christine Lacey	Alexandria
1979	Ailsa Simpson	Barrhead
1980	Fiona E Nash	California
1981	Jennifer Lindsay	British Columbia
1982	Jennifer Lindsay	British Columbia
1983	Gregor Bowman	Dundee
1984	Gregor Bowman	Dundee
1985	Tania Crawford	Harthill
1986	Ann Milne	Ontario
1987	Ann Milne	Ontario
1988	Deryck Mitchelson	Monifieth
1989	Jacqueline Smith	Ontario
1990	Dawn Brennan	Ontario
1991	Lorraine Brown	Kilbirnie
1992	Estelle Clewes	British Columbia
1993	Natalie Quick	Ontario
1994	Natalie Quick	Ontario
1995	Natalie Hall	Ontario
1996	Lyndsay Reid	Stirling
1997	Colleen Rintamaki	Ontario
1998	Colleen Rintamaki	Ontario
1999	Tony Cargill	Arbroath
2000	Tony Cargill	Arbroath
2001	Kimberlee Couper	Ontario
2002	Rachel McLagan	Blairgowrie
2003	Laura Cafferty	Ontario
2004	Rachel McLean	Dundee
2005	David Wilton	Forfar
2006	David Wilton	Forfar
2007	Fiona Lee	British Columbia
2008	Alexandra Matthews	Ontario
2009	Morgan Bamford	New Plymouth

Congratulations! Wishing you many happy years of dancing! Rachel McLagan.

Cowal Highland Gathering
Juvenile World Dancing Champions

YEAR	NAME	ORIGIN
1932	Gladys S Bruce	Largs
1933	Winnie H Mann	Stevenston
1934	Elspeth Strathern	Glasgow
1935	Dorothy J Bruce	Liverpool
1936	Bunty Downie	Dunoon
1937	Bunty Thomson	Glasgow
1938	Bunty Thomson	Glasgow
1939	May G Falconer	Motherwell
1946	Maureen C McMahon	Edinburgh
1947	Margaret Blyth Samson	Stirling
1948	Fay Innes	Dunfermline
1949	Catriona Buchanan	Stirling
1950	Catriona Buchanan	Stirling
1951	Sheena McDonald	Thornliebank
1952	Morag McKenzie	Stirling
1953	Ann Convery	Troon
1954	Louise Galbraith	Greenock
1955	Ann Convery	Troon
1956	Ann McIlroy	Rothesay
1957	Sandra Bald	Kirkcaldy
1958	Sylvia Henderson	Crossgates
1959	Sylvia Henderson	Crossgates
1960	Cecilia Pate	Cardenden
1961	Irene McKechnie	Grangemouth
1962	Kathleen M Scott	Musselburgh
1963	Rosemary McGuire	Banknock
1964	Cecilia Orr	Forth
1965	Rosemary McGuire	Banknock
1966	Rosemary McGuire	Banknock
1967	Christine Crowe	Edinburgh
1968	Grace D Higgins	Kirn

YEAR	NAME	ORIGIN
1969	Veronica Langton	Newarthill
1970	Fiona Perry	Glasgow
1971	Sandra Kennedy	Bearsden
1972	Sandra Kennedy	Bearsden
1973	Sandra Kennedy	Bearsden
1974	Christine Lacey	Alexandria
1975	Christine Lacey	Alexandria
1976	Mary Beth Miller	USA
1977	Ailsa Simpson	Barrhead
1978	Ailsa Simpson	Barrhead
1979	Elaine Duncan	Hamilton
1980	Elaine Duncan	Hamilton
1981	Gregor Bowman	Dundee
1982	Gillian Greig	Dysart
1983	Ann Milne	Canada
1984	Ann Milne	Canada
1985	Deryck Mitchelson	Monifieth
1986	Deryck Mitchelson	Monifieth
1987	Nicola Grant	Kirriemuir
1988	Jacqueline Smith	Canada
1989	Alison MacGregor	Laurencekirk
1990	Nadine McKenzie	Polmont
1991	Natalie Quick	Ontario
1992	Carleigh Leighton	Ontario
1993	Natalie-Anne Hall	Ontario
1994	Jacqueline Deeney	Port Glasgow
1995	Colleen Rintamaki	Ontario
1996	Colleen Rintamaki	Ontario
1997	Michelle Cumagun	Texas
1998	Tony Cargill	Arbroath
1999	Ashley Knox	Michigan

JUVENILE WORLD CHAMPIONS CONTINUED...

YEAR	NAME	ORIGIN
2000	Gillian O'Leary	Natal
2001	Gillian O'Leary	Natal
2002	Joanna Buchan	Peterhead
2003	Marielle Lesperance	Ontario
2004	David Wilton	Forfar
2005	Morgan Bamford	New Plymouth
2006	Morgan Bamford	New Plymouth
2007	Morgan Bamford	New Plymouth
2008	Morgan Bamford	New Plymouth
2009	Robyn Hart-Winks	Kirriemuir

The Dunoon Herald and Cowal Advertiser

Mr James Murchison, photographer, Dunoon, was busy with his camera at the Cowal Highland Gathering. The photo, top left, shows Lady Maclean of Duart, presenting the band awards; top right, the finalists in the World Adult Highland Dancing Championship including, fourth from left, Sheena McDonald, Thornliebank, the winner; Jackie Johnston, Maxweltown, runner-up, second from right; and Lelah Nicholson, Melbourne, Australia, extreme left, who was third; photo, bottom left, two wrestlers hard at it, and bottom right, the 8th Argyll and Sutherland Highlanders looking very "braw" in their new uniforms proudly lead the march past. They are led by Drum-Major Alex. Black and the salute is being taken by Sir Charles Maclean. Inset, Anne McIlroy, Rothesay, the World Juvenile Highland Dancing champion.

Cowal Highland Gathering

Memories of Cowal

Carl Allan Award Winners

1993

Sadie Simpson & Helen Ford
(President B.A.T.D.)

2010

Christine Lacey (Chairman of SOBHD)
& Jessie Stewart - Haggarty MBE

The British Association of Teachers of Dancing

2010 marks the 118th anniversary of the formation of the British Association of Teachers of Dancing (BATD). Founded in 1892, the BATD was the very first association formed for professional teachers of dancing and remained the only one for a decade until the formation of the UKA in 1902.

Registered as a Friendly Society in 1896, the BATD remains the only dance organisation to have been registered as such. The Association has grown from strength to strength, from a small beginning of around twenty-four founder members in 1892, to a current membership approaching 4,000. The British was originally formed to encourage dance professionals to work together to improve and develop the art of dancing in all its forms, an aim carried through to the present time and on into the future.

During the past 118 years many changes have taken place. Originally occupying some office space in Uptons Academy, a small dance studio in London, the BATD Head Office has over the years been situated in various locations, including two different locations in Glasgow, Cumberland Street and then Marywood Square, where it remained until its move in 2009 to its current location in Govan Road.

The Executive Council of the Association comprises: President, 2 Vice Presidents, 3 Trustees, Treasurer and 9 Executive Council Members. Nominees for the various positions are put forward by the various Regions of the Association and all positions are elected by the membership at Conference, as are the members of the various committees. Currently there are eight Regions in Scotland and England, eight in Canada and America, one in Malta and one in Belarus.

It is at Regional level that members are able to become more involved and seek office, beginning with Regional positions, such as Chairman, Vice-Chairman, Secretary or Treasurer, then, if they wish to progress to a national level, seek nomination for Executive Council or one of the technical committees. Regional meetings are a very important part of the function of the BATD, with propositions for changes to Rules or Byelaws also being put forward by the Regions.

The income of the BATD, as with most other organisations, comes from subscriptions, sales of books/badges, medal test and examination fees. Most dance styles are covered, such as Ballroom, Latin, Stage, Ballet, Highland, Theatre, Jazz, Street Dance, Hip Hop, Cheer Pom, Salsa and Merengue. The BATD uses syllabi and technique books written by various knowledgeable technical experts in the various dance styles, many of them written by BATD technical committee members. For Ballroom the Guy Howard technique book has been adopted and for Latin American, the Walter Laird technique book. The Association uses the Salsa/Merengue/Mambo syllabus written by Paul Harris.

The first Conference was held in May 1892 at the Uptons Academy in London, where Head Office resided, chaired by the first President, Mr. F. Wyatt. Our first Scottish President was Mr J. B. McEwan in 1901. Having been based in Scotland for a large number of years, the British Association of Teachers of Dancing is sometimes thought to be a Scottish Association but that is far from true as Members come from North, South, East and West of Great Britain, as well as countries overseas, including a large membership in North America.

By 1905 membership had grown to 119. The growth of the Association was slow, due in part to the fact that only full-time dance teachers who had passed an extremely testing professional examination to qualify, were admitted. A number of other dance organisations had also started to spring up in competition by this time giving the professionals a choice.

Formation of other Districts of the Association commenced in 1905 with the introduction of the Glasgow, Leeds and Manchester Districts. These were in addition to London District which was where Head Office was located. In 1919/1920 a further two Districts were formed, however by 1928 the districts returned to three in number and remained so for around 12 years.

Over the years many professionals have moved from other organisations to the BATD and vice versa. In 1916, F.C. Barlow became President of the NATD, but records show that he joined the BATD in 1920 and became a member of the Executive Council in 1924 and 1925. Mr M. Munro joined the Association in 1923 having been credited with being the Founder of the Allied Dancing Association in 1922. When the Imperial Society formed its Ballroom branch in 1924 the General Secretary was Mr F. C. Leslie, thought to be the F. C. Leslie who had become President of the BATD in 1911, having first served as an Executive Council member and Vice President. The British Association of Teachers of Dancing has therefore been an integral part of dance development throughout the years.

1918 introduced the first Lady President, Mrs N. Leslie. By this time membership of the Association had risen to 200.

During the early years of the Association the principal style of dance covered was Old Time or Sequence dance. Branches of dance other than Sequence were not mentioned until 1927 when a Miss E. P. Wallace received her Operatic Certificate.

Professionals were all full-time in those days, unlike today. In order to become a professional one had to be employed by an established professional as an assistant teacher. Once it was considered that the candidate was capable, he or she would be entered into the Association as a Probationer before being able to take the Membership examination. The Association badge and certificate could only be obtained if all other work was relinquished and the candidate became a full-time teacher of dance. If at any time the candidate left the profession the badge and certificate had to be returned. Probationers were semi-professional and were expected to attend all District meetings and have a sound knowledge of the Association Rules. Being a Probationer allowed the candidate to become a full Member at the age of eighteen instead of waiting until twenty-one. An Associate examination could also be taken at eighteen.

Unfortunately many of the old records have been lost during the various moves Head Office made over the years. It can, however, be established that the Ballroom branch was first started around 1926. Records show that in 1931 the first 'Display' certificate was issued and this certificate was issued until around 1936 after which there is no mention of it. From 1936 there is the first mention of Stage certificates and it is thought possible that 'Display' was the precursor of Stage. In 1937, the first lady to receive a certificate for Tap was recorded, although no starting date for the Tap branch is mentioned in the records. During the same period the BATD used to issue a Health and Keep Fit certificate, although it is not known what the examination entailed. The first of these certificates was issued in 1937.

One of the most important additions to the income of the various dancing organisations was the introduction of Medal Tests. First introduced to the dancing world in 1932 by Mr E. F. Newton, a Past President of the NATD, the awarding of medals of proficiency has made a significant financial difference to all dance teaching organisations.

By the 1930s the public had found a keen interest in dancing and a number of different organisations had been formed, along with various dance clubs, which were extremely popular. Dancing also played a part in the war effort as, with the help of the various organizations and dancers in general, the 'Dancers Victory Fund' was started, sponsored by the Official Board of Ballroom Dancing from an original proposition from the ISTD.

This fund, which closed in 1945, raised over £11,000 for the purchase of a Mosquito and a Procter Training Aircraft for the Royal Air Force.

Around 1937 Phonographic Performance Licences and Performing Rights Society licences were first introduced requiring dance teachers to pay fees to these bodies for using music.

BATD Membership had been rising steadily over the years and by 1939 had reached 824.

At the beginning of the 1940s dancing was in a very buoyant state with large increases in the medallist business, leading to many changes being seen in the British Association of Teachers of Dancing. In 1941, Districts of the Association were increased to five covering large areas of the country: London, Scotland, Yorkshire, Lancashire and Northern. This position continued until 1949 when three more were added_ Midland, Bristol (later to become Western District) and South Africa, possibly the first overseas District for the BATD.

In 1945 two annual conferences were held at the same time due to the 1944 Conference having been cancelled following an order from the Government. Conference in those days ran from Sunday to Friday rather than Friday evening to Sunday evening as it is now.

There was a large influx of new members and associates during 1946, over 1,000 children's examinations and around 2,000 amateur tests. At Conference the syllabus of the Stage and Tap sections were amalgamated forming one branch. The BATD had also sadly lost two of the three trustees who passed away during the preceding year and the third retired from his post, leaving all three trustee positions to be elected. This must have been quite a daunting position for the Association to be in but the three new Trustees successfully managed to take the Association forward, one of them serving for the following four years, one until 1961 and the third until 1977.

By Conference 1947 the Association had specialists in all branches of dance and issued 22 certificates to Professional and Amateur candidates in Highland, Ballroom, Operatic, Tap and Stage.

In 1948 the Lord Provost of Edinburgh received the British Association of Teachers of Dancing as a professional body on the Tuesday evening of Conference - possibly the first Civic Reception held in Scotland. This was also the year in which the Latin American section was first set up.

In the late 1940s and 1950s Latin American dancing became popular and enjoyed its formative years in the UK, although dance history records that the first time that Rumba entered Great Britain was around 1934. Many experts including Dimitri Petrides, Monsieur Pierre and Lyndon Wainwright and Felicia wrote books on the subject. In 1949/1950 Come Dancing appeared on the television, the Official Board of Ballroom Dancing began its Annual Inventive Dance competition and the International Council of Ballroom Dancing was formed.

The BATD President visited Paris in 1949 and brought back a number of applications for membership of the Association. Three Honorary memberships were granted and 11 applications for membership approved. South Africa was also showing great interest in the 'English style' of dancing at that time and two BATD members were employed to demonstrate, lecture and teach there, the tour helping to increase the 'British connection' in that country.

Delegates from the BATD joined the new Official Board Old Time sub-committee in 1947 and worked extremely hard in the development of the Old Time branch of the Association. A few years previously part-time teachers had been permitted to join the Association, but only full-time teachers were permitted to take a Fellowship examination. Associates, Members and Fellows then paid different subscription fees, whereas today only students pay a reduced amount.

The registered office of the BATD by 1949 was the Howard Hotel, The Strand, London, with business being run from Manchester. During this time the British Association also had many young members who were making a great impression on the competition scene. An amateur and professional syllabus in the Latin American dances had been added to the repertoire of the BATD, constructed by the Latin American committee. This work enabled the Association to hold examinations in that style of dance.

1951 Conference saw the acceptance of an EC proposition that no member be permitted to join any Ballroom Dancing Association not affiliated to the Official Board. It was also the year in which the decision was taken that two examiners were necessary for a Fellowship examination. By the following Conference membership had risen to over 1,000 and the decision was taken that the Executive Council be reduced from 24 members to nine members, not counting the officers. This remains the current structure of the Association today.

Stage and Highland Dancing were very successful disciplines for BATD members by this time. At the International Festival of Stage and Highland Dancing in Edinburgh in 1953, 3,000 competitors from Scotland,

England, South Africa, Australia, Canada and the USA took part. In the Coronation Highland Dancing Championship open to the World, with competitors from six countries, BATD members took the first three places. In addition BATD teacher, Miss Ella Hardy, who has since held many high offices in the Association, won the International Festival Trophy for the school gaining the most points in all sections of the Stage division. Her school also won the Gamba Trophy For Ballet, the Ryvita Trophy for Tap, the Blue Blanket Trophy for Nationals, the David Sharp Trophy for the best Class A and the David Sharp Cup for the best Class C. Miss Agnes Stewart also won the Challenge Cup for the competitor gaining the highest points in all sections and the Senior Highland Championship, with her school winning the Dorothy Glendinning Broadswords Cup and the Class A Jig and Hornpipes Cup. It was obviously a most successful year for the BATD!

During the 1950s many different Ballroom Championships were introduced and received a great response. By 1955 Rock and Roll had hit the scene, with such popularity that the BATD, and most dance teacher organisations, included a Rock and Roll section in their medal test system.

The foundation of the Canadian and American Districts of the British Association of Teachers of Dancing came along in 1957 and the first examinations were held 'across the pond'. This was closely followed by a 'Canadian Tour', with the BATD Overseas Administrator of the time, Miss Sadie Simpson, travelling to Toronto to undertake a seven-week tour and an extremely full schedule of examinations, competitions and meetings in both Highland and Stage. This very successful trip covered Toronto, Ontario, Niagara, Long Island and Connecticut where Miss Simpson adjudicated at the Rounhill Highland Games. Following the games she continued to New York, Pittsburgh, North Carolina, Hamilton, Buffalo, Alexandria, Montreal and Ottawa. Quite a gruelling schedule! During this tour 31 new members were enrolled. The Tour continues to this day.

From 1892 until 1963 the BATD employed the services of a Musical Director or Musical Advisor. Sixteen persons with great musical knowledge held this position over those years. Most notable of these was Mr Harry Davidson, famous for a radio programme 'Those were the Days', who held the position for sixteen years. Mr Davidson saw the advantage of the media coverage given by the BBC Old Time music programmes, which helped to bring Old Time dancing back into the public eye. Two other BATD members were also connected with these programmes, Mr A. J. Latimer, President of 1932, and later Mr Charles Craythorne.

The inception of the Teacher's Shield award began around 1964. This was awarded to teachers who supported the medal test system in the various branches. With the growth of the Highland and Ballet sections of the Association it soon became more and more difficult to select winners for the Teacher's Shield as the standard of teaching was so high.

During the mid-sixties the great response to the many Ballroom Championships began to show signs of slowing but the advertising value of these events made up for any shortfall in the financial balances. Other areas of the business were expanding, such as the medal test income, mainly due to the increase in Stage branch activities and the success of the Canadian and American business. In the earlier periods the Association had been dominated by the Ballroom branches but this situation changed as other branches developed and began to dominate the scene.

Examiners from Great Britain were conducting tours of Canada and America and it was decided that resident examiners should be engaged to provide continuity to the Business, primarily in the Highland and Stage branches. New at that time was the Association's Ballet work for both home and overseas. The 1965 Tour had resulted in a new Territory being opened up in America, whilst at home the children's one-dance medal tests and Ballet and Stage tests were continuing to increase at a phenomenal rate. The Stage, Ballet, National and Highland Festivals were also becoming extremely successful. The BATD was slowly but surely making progress under the financial guidance of Mr S. Atack. He, along with others of that era, built a firm financial foundation for the BATD that has been the envy of many Associations during our long history.

Conference 1967 saw the introduction of important new rules: 1) that the President of the Association shall be a full-time teacher or administrator of dancing - which remained in operation until 2007, and 2) that there be created a position of Senior Vice-President, being the Vice-President having the longer consecutive period as Vice-President. 1967 also saw dancing legends Anthony Hurley and Fay Saxton giving the demonstration and ballroom lectures at Conference, reported in the Conference Report Bulletin to be one of the best ever demonstrations seen at BATD Conference.

At the end of the 1960s members were keen to cut costs and the EC began giving consideration to a different format for Conference. It was thought that if the number of days was reduced it might encourage more members to attend. This would reduce the cost of attending Conference, often the major concern of many of the younger dance teachers. During 1970 Conference the decision was taken to hold future Conferences in Scotland, Blackpool and London, although this was amended in 1976 to be Scotland, Blackpool and the London area. 1970 Conference was particularly memorable having the very highly regarded Peter Eggleton and the late Brenda Winslade, winners of the World Professional Modern Championships on several occasions, giving a wonderful exhibition of Ballroom dancing. The exhibitions given by true icons of dance are always in the forefront of the memory.

For the first time the Conference Report listed the examiners of the Association in 1971. At the time there were 59 in Scotland and England and six in Canada and North America. Scottish examiners made up nearly half of the total, due mainly to the amount of business received from north of the border, especially in the Highland and Stage branches. 1971 also saw, for the first time since 1956, the inclusion of advertising material from dance schools and dance wear centres.

The early 1970s were financially good years for all dancing organisations, especially the BATD, although things did become more difficult by the middle of the decade. For the first time a Ballroom Scholarship was introduced to try to give incentive to the younger generation. New publications of the Association were brought out including a new Glossary in the Ballet section and a new book covering the set dances in Tap. The Association Treasurer, Mr Stan Atack was honoured in 1973 by becoming the Chairman of the Official Board of Ballroom Dancing (now known as the BDC, British Dance Council). This was a busy year as the Northern District held their first Stage Festival, which was a resounding success at Hartlepool Town Hall. In addition a new sequence trophy, The President's Trophy, was awarded in the Latin American section to accompany the existing Worrall Trophy (Old Time) and Chester Trophy (Modern) awarded at the BATD Annual Inventive Dance Competition.

The introduction of the BATD Ballet Scholarships came in 1975. During this year, due to the success of the examinations and tests held in Canada and America, the first Overseas Administrator was appointed. The Overseas Administrator was to be responsible for the smooth running and coordination of all aspects of the business overseas.

A change occurred in 1976 when members from the East of Scotland were encouraged to form their own area, which they did. This Region is now known as Scottish East and North. 1976 also saw BATD members Robin and Rita Short being presented with a Carl Alan Award. Robin Short also received a further Carl Alan Award in 1994 and 1998. Robin Short is a Past President, many times former EC member and represented the Association many times on the Board of Directors of the Official Board of Ballroom Dancing (British Dance Council). He is now an Honorary Member of the BDC. Other high ranking members of the BATD who have been honoured by receiving a Carl Alan Award include: Mr Frank Venables 1973 and 1996, Miss Sadie Simpson 1993, Mr. Eric Higgins in 1977, Mrs Jessie Stewart-Haggarty MBE in 1995 and 2010, Miss Bonnie Barr in1995 and 2010, Mr Freddie Boultwood in 1993, 1998, 1999 and 2004, Mr Ian McLeod in 1998, Miss Barbara Woff in 2001, Miss Gillian Anderson in 2001 and 2009, Mr Tony Curley in 2003, Miss Freda Compton in 2008, Mr & Mrs Warren and Jayne Bullock in 2009 and Miss Elma Whyte in 2010. This list is, however, not exhaustive.

The BATD have been running the prestigious English Championships for ballroom and Latin American competitors for many years, since the late 1940s or early 1950s. Held over the years in various venues, it was not until l976, when it was organized by Mr. Freddie Boultwood at the Hammersmith Palais for the second time, that it really made its mark on the competitive calendar and became one of the more prestigious events. In more recent years the English Championships have been held at Earls Court International, at Watford Coliseum and at the Lakeside Leisure Complex at Frimley Green, its current venue.

The Majorette branch also came into fruition in 1976 and started to become an important part of the Association.

1977 saw the introduction of the new modern technique book, the Guy Howard 'Technique of Ballroom Dancing'. Guy Howard was invited to attend Conference and give a seminar on his technique. The 1970s also saw the introduction of a new Disco Dance test in an effort to encourage and develop Disco Dance classes. Rock 'n' Roll was added to the Disco section during 1993 to keep abreast of the changes in popular dance styles.

The Queen also reached her Silver Jubilee year in 1977 and many dance related organisations held Jubilee events. A Dancers' Jubilee Fund was initiated and raised £10,000 towards the appeal, which was to encourage service by young people to their local communities. The 'Queen's Silver Jubilee Championships' were presented by the Official Board of Ballroom Dancing and organised by Eric Morley on behalf of Mecca Promotions. This event had television coverage, celebrity prize presenters and gave a boost to the dancing profession with all associations and organisations working together.

In January 1981 at Head Office, Marywood Square, Glasgow the inaugural meeting of the BATD Highland Committee took place. This committee remains in place today, giving support and encouragement to this highly successful branch of the Association.

During the 1980s another landmark in the BATD history was reached. The General Secretary, Mr Peter Cuthbert, decided to retire having served as General Secretary since 1953. Mr Cuthbert had given loyal service to the Association in this capacity for thirty years.

On January 1st, 1984 Mr Terry Fielden took over the reins until 1989, followed by our current General Secretary, Mrs Katrina Allan, who moved into the position in 1990. Mrs Allan guided the Association through its Centenary and then on into the twenty first century - and may she continue to lead it for many years to come.

BATD President Shelagh Connolly with seven Past Presidents in the visitors waiting area at Govan Road.

Back row: Roy Sharpe, Bryan Isaac, Freddie Boultwood, Helen Ford, Diane Barro Barron
Front row: President Shelagh Connolly, Bobby Barr, Margaret Smith

The 1980s also saw the purchase of new Head Office premises at 23 Marywood Square, Glasgow, which remained Head Office until the move to new premises in 2009. The reference to 'new' premises with regard to Marywood Square might be a little inaccurate due to the vast amount of unforeseen major renovation it required!

The Highland branch, by 1986, had been one of the most prominent within the BATD for many years and had teachers who were responsible for training great Canadian, Scottish, American and World Highland Dance Champions.

A new dance craze hit the scenes in 1987 with the release of the film Dirty Dancing. Lectures were given at District meetings and at Conference by two EC members experienced in the dance style - generally known as Mambo at that time - in the hope that it would develop into a lucrative business opportunity. Although slow to take-off this dance form gradually became very popular, along with Merengue and the now very popular Salsa, grouped together now under the BATD Club Latino syllabus.

An important development in 1987 was the introduction of new BATD areas in Canada and America. These were: California, British Columbia and North West States, Alberta, Ontario-Toronto, Western Ontario, USA Atlantic Seaboard, Maritime Provinces and Eastern Ontario-Ottawa. The re-organisation this involved was tremendous, with each new area having to have its own administration set up.

A year later, in 1988, professional and amateur examinations were conducted in Germany, Malta, Australia, Spain and Italy. Enquiries for the BATD examination facilities were also received that year from Norway, Belgium, Switzerland, Sri Lanka and Korea. This was a very busy year for the British as it was also the first time that the BATD Highland, Ballet and Stage Festival was held in Western Ontario.

Official opening the new BATD Head Office in Govan Road.

Mr Freddie Boultwood and Mr Bobby Barr - Past Presidents of the BATD

Mr Freddie Boultwood, who had been President for four years, decided in 1990 that he would not stand for re-election due to having been awarded the honour of the position of President of the Official Board of Ballroom Dancing (now known as the British Dance Council), a position he held until 2004.

The British Association of Teachers of Dancing reached its Centenary in 1992, the first dance teacher organisation to celebrate 100 years. Mr Bryan Isaac, then one of the BATD Vice Presidents, took the opportunity of writing a book 'Centenary - A Brief Review of One Hundred Years', charting the birth and rise of the British during its 100 year history, along with a brief account of memorable historical world wide events occurring along the way. This book was used for much of the information contained in this article up to this point. Centenary Conference hotel was the Moat House International, Glasgow, situated on the banks of the Clyde and now known as the Crowne Plaza Hotel.

During the 1990s business expanded with professional examinations being taken additionally in Latvia, Ukraine and Belarus. Inaugural evenings were held and attended by representatives from many countries including Russia, Estonia, Lithuania, Poland, Ukraine, Finland and England. These were very successful evenings leading to increased business for the BATD.

The Millennium arrived and Conference was held at the Carrington House Hotel, Bournemouth. This was the year that saw our first overseas member being voted onto the Executive Council, Miss

Shelagh Connolly, closely followed in 2001 by our second overseas EC member, Mr Joseph Wallin. 2001 also saw a proposition being passed that Conference would be held in a central location, although this was superseded in 2004 when it was passed that Conference would be held wherever the EC recommended, with Scotland being the venue every third year.

During the early 2000s the political scene throughout the dance world had begun to change and there was more movement of members between organisations. The BATD agreed that approved members from other dance teacher organisations could be accepted into the Association at Associate or Membership level without the need for an examination. Fellows would only be admitted at Membership level and would have to take the BATD Fellowship examination to obtain recognition as a Fellow of the Association.

Canadian and American business continued to grow and in 2003 the British saw its first overseas EC member become a Vice President. The following couple of years were very busy for the various Association committees, their work culminating in the introduction in 2005 of new syllabi in Stage Grades, Associate Grades, Professional Latin American, Professional Club Latino, Modern Ballroom, Sequence, amateur Ballroom and amateur and professional Freestyle. This was closely followed the following year by the decision being taken to delete the Student Teacher examination.

2007 Conference voted to lift the restriction on members of the Association having to be full-time teachers of dance in order to become officers of the Association. Fewer members were running full-time dance schools resulting in less being eligible to take up office. Around this time the BATD rulebook was overhauled and updated to take it into the twenty-first century. The second North American Vice President was also appointed.

This brings the brief résumé of the BATD up to 2008, an important year, especially for overseas members as our first North American President was voted in, Miss Shelagh Connolly, who stands as our President today in her second term - our current First Lady.

With a new decade swiftly approaching, the BATD in 2009 introduced the first Junior and Senior Freestyle Scholarship. This was a very successful event that will be taken on into the future.

At the beginning of 2009 the General Secretary and Head Office staff moved to the prestigious purpose built Watermark Business Park on the banks of the Clyde in Glasgow. These offices are bright and airy and present the staff with a very comfortable and modern working environment, very different from the previous premises. We look forward to our General Secretary, Mrs Katrina Allan, continuing to lead the way through 2010 and taking the BATD onwards through the next decade.

SADIE SIMPSON

Sadie Simpson was the daughter of a Wigtownshire dairy farmer and commenced her dancing studies at a very early age and throughout the years, became one of the most outstanding teachers in the dancing profession.

In her lifetime she was connected with very many charity organisations, providing hospital beds and donations to worthwhile causes. To help brighten their lives, she entertained the less fortunate and during the last war, she organised performances for the war wounded and also the German prisoners of war. Sadie Simpson was known for her outstanding work both in this country and overseas.

Sadie was a Past President and a Fellow Member, an Examiner and also a former Trustee of the British Association of Teachers of Dancing. She was Chairlady of the Association's Highland and Stage and Ballet Committees, devoting much personal time to the progress of dance. She was an Honorary Member of the World Governing Body, The Scottish Official Board of Highland Dancing. Sadie, a former Lady World Highland Dancing Champion was invited and honoured by the Professional Scottish Arts Conference in Las Vegas, Nevada in 1986 and honoured by the famous St. Thomas School in Houston for services to dance in the state of Texas. Due to her outstanding work in this country, Canada and America, she became the first Scottish lady to be inducted into the American Dancing Hall of Fame in 1984. She was so highly regarded by her colleagues in Britain, that in 1988 they held a banquet in her honour – and what a day that was.

Sadie received the famous 'Carl Alan Award' for outstanding services to the world of dance; this presentation was made by Angela Rippon in 1993.

Throughout Sadie Simpson's outstanding career in dance, she continued to fight cancer, having undergone major surgery three times. Her personal cure for this dreadful condition was very positive thinking and positive faith. She kept up a letter service, giving comfort and advice to so many people with the same illness. To Sadie, fighting cancer was a most serious dedication.

Throughout her busy and sometimes traumatic life, she never lost her wonderful sense of humour or her ability to make one feel "extra special".

A magnificent woman in every sense of the word, she was a teacher, a mentor and a very dear friend. She will always be the most generous, loving and caring lady many have had the privilege of knowing.

MARY FRASER LINDSAY

Miss Lindsay was trained at the McEwan School in Glasgow. She began the Lindsay School of Dancing in Greenock n 1926 at the age of 16 years with approximately eight pupils. The school was built up over the years, firstly with son, Lindsay then with daughter, Jeanette. It was at this point the school became the Lindsay-Wood School. It was, and probably still is, the oldest dancing school in Scotland if not the UK. It is now under the Lindsay Wood School, in the very safe and capable hands of Patti. Miss Lindsay retired in 1991 and the age of 81, but she maintained a keen interest in the school until she passed away in 2002.

Miss Lindsay was a Fellow and Examiner of the BATD and she undertook Sunday exam sessions in faraway places with the minimum of entrants in an effort to encourage teachers to become interested in the Association. Travelling to places like Wick on a snowy Sunday to examine 12 children then travel home again couldn't have been much fun, but the job was done.

Miss Lindsay organised the BATD Stage, Ballet and Highland competitions and Championships for approximately 10 years at the Kingston Halls, Glasgow with great success. It was during one of these competitions that the Scottish Lilt was danced competitively for the first time.

Miss Lindsay was a Founder member of the SOBHD and a member of the Technical Committee which planned the technique for Highland dancing. She compiled the original scripts for the lesser known dances.

Many teachers and competitors who came home from the Games in the summer regularly asked Miss Lindsay to advise them as to whether they were following Board rules to the letter.

Miss Lindsay also organised the first recognised World Highland Dancing Championship at Gourock Highland Games.

Dancing was her life and she was never happier than when she was involved in classes, examining and offering sound advice to those who asked for her assistance.

NAN KEELING

Nan Keeling was born in Springburn in 1927 and will be best remembered for the commitment and dedication she showed to the dancing world and her brilliant dancing career. Nan started dancing at the tender age of 2 and her early talent for dancing earned her the nickname the "Springburn Shirley Temple" and indeed she danced in the same show as Sir Harry Lauder when she was still a child. Nan's speciality dance was toe tap and she would regularly perform her routines tapping up and down specially made stairs on her toes, often the routines would last up to 6/7 minutes.

Nan never married and dedicated her life to dancing. Her classes were spread far and wide and she taught in Springburn, Kirkintilloch, Bishopbriggs, Glasgow, Renfrew, Beith and Ardrossan which is a feat in itself, but considering she couldn't drive it showed that she was a very determined lady.

She was a prominent choreographer for the Glasgow amateur dramatic clubs including the Minerva, the Glasgow Light Opera, the Lyric and the Pantheon clubs. She choreographed in clubs for many years and always had rave reviews.

Her professionally-staged displays raised hundreds of pounds for various charities, including the Red Cross Prisoner of War Fund, Indian Famine Relief and local disabled groups. Her pupils got the opportunity to learn most styles of dance including tap, ballet, highland, As a result of her technical knowledge and skill, she became a prominent member of the British Association of Teachers of Dancing and she sat on the Executive Council of the BATD from 1977 to 1982. She was on the Stage and Ballet Committee, the Highland Committee and was a Technical Delegate for the Highland Branch. In 1983 Nan was honoured by the Association by becoming Vice President and from 1984-1985 she was voted in as Senior Vice President.

Nan travelled the length of breadth of Britain examining for the Association and had many trips over to America and Canada and as a result Nan made many friends.

Nan not only had a wealth of knowledge and experience but as a person she was lovely to know. Her mild manner, unending patience and generosity made her a favourite teacher and examiner and people warmed to her immediately. Nan died sadly at the age of 73 in November 2000 but her memory still lives on in many teachers' and pupils' hearts.

JEAN MARINO

Jean Marino ran a very busy full-time theatre and Highland dancing school at The Studio at 10 Moray Place in Glasgow. Many BATD teachers will remember taking one or more of their professional qualifications at The Studio, examined by Jean Marino. Jean Marino's dance teaching career is believed to have emerged from her mother's refusal to let her accept an offer to join a major ballet company during the war. Instead she worked as a professional dancer in Glasgow theatres before turning her talents to teaching. Not being allowed to join the ballet was always something that she regretted. However, she threw herself into teaching and opened her first dancing school in the late 1940s in the East-end of Glasgow, successfully training students for examinations and school shows. Over the years, she taught in several areas in Glasgow gaining a keen following of Highland dancers and when she moved to The Studio in Moray Place many of them moved with her to continue their training.

As well as having very popular Highland classes and a good number of competitive dancers Jean Marino also taught all theatre branches. Teaching was of course not her only involvement in dance. She was in demand as a lecturer and also as a choreographer. Her work as a BATD examiner took her all over the UK and also North America where she met with a number of Highland teachers with competitive schools who brought their dancers to Scotland each summer to compete at Cowal and other Highland Games. This resulted in a number of overseas dancers and their teachers taking classes and workshops with Jean Marino at The Studio each summer during the competitive Highland season. Add to this, the many Highland teachers in the UK who also sought her guidance and it is clear that she was respected by her colleagues and peers.

Throughout the year Jean Marino was in demand as a Highland adjudicator and she travelled the length and breadth of the UK adjudicating hundreds of competitions and Championships. She always had great interest in the work of the SOBHD and in the 1970s she was delighted to be able to serve on the technical committee along with Jessie Stewart, Jean Ritchie and Cissie Tucker. And if this was not enough to fit into an already very busy life she also found time to organise the annual BATD Festival, held at Easter in Glasgow each year, and also the Edinburgh Stage Festival.

Jean Marino trained many dancers and teachers including her daughter Seònaid McWhirter (now Sho Botham) who followed her mother's footsteps into the dance profession. Jean Marino continued to develop her own knowledge, skills and understanding right up to the end when she died unexpectedly one evening, in her fifties. Earlier that day she had been apologising for being unable to accompany her daughter to the SOBHD Judges meeting because she felt too unwell. Typically she left behind her a number of dance books open on her bedside table.

EVELYN (LYNN) MCLAREN

Dancing was a huge part of Lynn's life since she was a very small child. Born in Edinburgh, she was the youngest of ten children. She used to go without her lunch so she could save her dinner money to pay for a weekly dance class. When her parents found out how determined she was they agreed to find the money to pay for lessons.

During the 2nd World war, Lynn found herself posted to Duns in the Scottish Borders as a member of the Land Army with her friend Ella Wynn. On arrival, she was horrified to discover there was no dancing school in the area. She placed a simple advert in a little sweet shop and over 60 youngsters turned up eager to dance. This formed the Lynella Dancing School in 1944.

For decades, she taught ballet, tap and highland dancing throughout the Scottish Borders from Eyemouth, Duns and Berwick to Coldstream, Kelso and Galashiels. When the war was over, the dancers begged her not to return to Edinburgh so she and Ella stayed to continue the dance school. She carried on teaching for over 60 years. Sharing her love of dance with her young pupils was her biggest joy - regardless of their achievements.

Her dancers performed in many shows, concerts and operas throughout the Borders incorporating ballet, tap and highland. She ran many competitions and events throughout the Borders for several years - including the South of Scotland Highland Dancing Championship.

Lynn was an Honorary Member of the SOBHD and formerly part of the Technical Committee. She became an Associate of the BATD in 1957, a Member in 1959 and a Fellow in 1981. Recognising her professional manner, knowledge and beautiful feeling for dance, Miss Sadie Simpson appointed her as an International Examiner in 1986. In 2001 she was presented with the Atholl clasp. She was always very keen to support her many pupils through their dancing exams with many becoming Associates and Members of the BATD with some also going onto become adjudicators with the SOBHD.

In 2002, Lynn was invited to Edinburgh Castle's Great Hall on the eve of International Women's Day. She was honoured as an 'unsung heroine' by the then Scottish Secretary of State Helen Liddell at a special dinner - for her lifetime's service to promoting traditional Scottish highland dancing.

In November 2004, Lynn was joined by past and former pupils at a special Ceilidh to celebrate the 60th Anniversary of the Lynella Dance School.

After a short illness, in her 90th year, Lynn passed away peacefully on 10th December 2008. She will always be remembered as a lovely lady and an inspirational member of the BATD.

EDITH DUNCAN M.B.E.

Edith started to dance at the age of three little knowing then that her first steps would lead me on to a lifetime career and a visit to Buckingham Palace.

Her first steps were in highland dancing although she had not much balance at that age so probably struggled to begin with. However Edith really loved to dance, so moved onto ballet (her favourite), tap and other subjects. Her sister made Edith practice every morning before going to school and in the evening they played at teaching dancing. Edith performed at dances at church socials, concerts, daffodil teas and in the annual dance school displays. You name it, she did it.

Edith had a course of ballet lessons in London and was due to go back there to take a ballet exam. However war broke out and shattered her dreams. As she had four brothers serving in the forces there was no way Edith could leave home. This also ended her dream of a stage career. So when other girls left, she stayed broken hearted at home. Edith's teacher told her she could teach at her school so she became a teaching assistant for many years.

At the end of the hostilities Edith headed back to the ballet teacher in London and passed her first professional exam with the R.A.D. Every summer Edith studied dance while her friends went on holiday. By then she knew this was what she wanted to do with her life. Edith then joined the highland branch of the BATD and was persuaded by examiners to qualify in other branches.

In time Edith opened her own school and has taught many hundreds of children and adults to dance, many of whom won BATD scholarships and ultimately 11 students won the Theatre Dance Council International Scholarships.

Edith's BATD membership was a good decision as she was invited to become an examiner and really loved the work. It opened up a new world as she conducted several tours to Canada and America and made many good friends there and in this country.

Many happy things have happened through the BATD. Edith was honoured to give the ballet lecture at the Centenary Conference and her pupils performed twice at the Showcase Theatre.

Edith also conducted the first Canadian Scholarship ballet class. Then she was asked to travel again to Toronto much later and teach the students and adjudicate.

Edith's greatest honour was receiving the M.B.E for services to dance in Aberdeen. This was a memorable day at the Palace meeting the Queen. This was a long way from her first steps but she still loves to dance and do a bit of teaching and coaching. She can never give it up!

To dance is to live and to live is to dance!

MAMIE DAVIDSON

Mamie began dancing at the age of four back in 1940. She was involved in a variety of dance disciplines such as ballet, highland and tap. She opened her first dancing school at the age of 16, branching out to four successful dancing schools by 1967. Mamie ran the dancing schools up until 1977 and her pupils performed in many shows donating a lot of the proceeds to charity. Mamie also ran dancing competitions where the proceeds were again given to charity.

Mamie was an examiner with the BATD (Highland, Tap & Ballet, and Majorettes) and also an adjudicator with the SOBHD where she adjudicated at many Championships and highland games around Scotland. One of her highlights was judging the World Highland Dancing Championships at Cowal. Sadly, shortly after returning from the Cowal Games Mamie passed away in 1978 at the young age of 42, but not before passing on her enthusiasm and passion for dancing to the many people she met throughout her life.

Many people will be forever grateful to Mamie for the guidance and encouragement she gave so freely, which has helped them reach their goals in highland dancing.

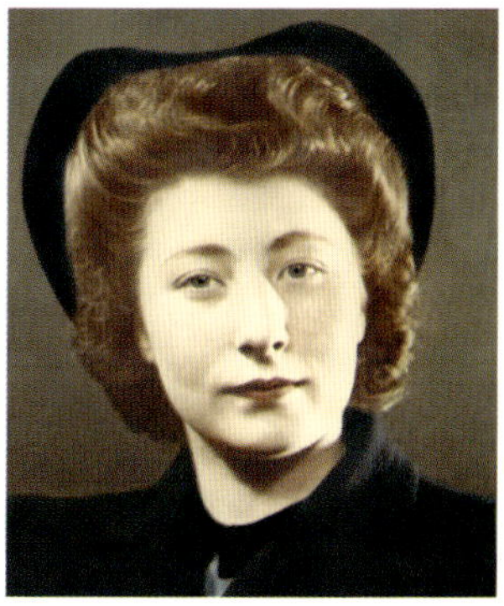

MISS CATHERINE STEWART

Catherine Stewart was the sister of Jessie and Agnes Stewart. Catherine was a strong competitive dancer during the pre-war years. In 1936 she was a Cowal winner winning the coveted MacNiven Cuthbertson Challenge trophy.

Catherine served in the WAF (Woman's Air Force) during the war and after the war married and moved to Whitley Bay where she taught all forms of dance for many years. Many pupils of hers that are well known include Harry Picken, Jessie Clark, Sally Thornton, Susan Donnachie, Arlene Carr, Ken Gooden, Helen Callow and Norman Syrat.

OUR SPECIAL LADIES AT THE BATD

Special luncheon held on 18th August 1996 at the Hilton Hotel, Glasgow
Honouring Mrs Haggarty, Miss Lindsay, Miss Simpson, Miss McLaren and Mrs Ritchie

Adult World Champions

The British Association of Teachers of Dancing Members

1948
May Falconer
Motherwell

1962
Sandra Bald
Kirkcaldy

1963 & 1964
Billy Forsyth
Bridge of Allan

1965
Wilma Tolmie
Monifieth

1967
Irene McKechnie
Grangemouth

1968, 1969 & 1972
Victor Wesley
Ayr

1969
Angus MacKenzie
British Columbia

1973
Hugh Bigney
USA

1974 & 1976
Aileen Robertson
Ayr

Adult World Champions

The British Association of Teachers of Dancing Members

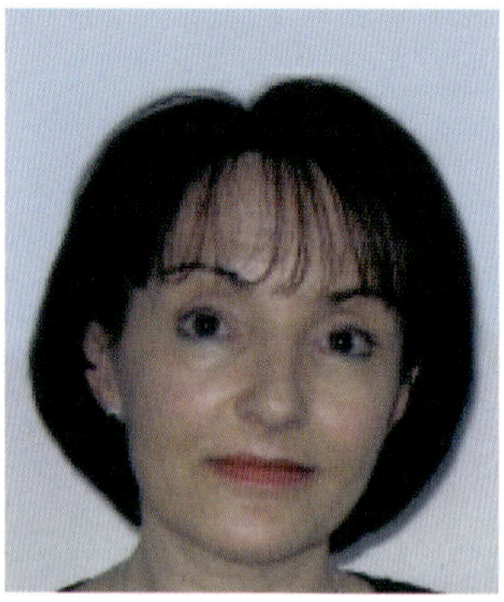

1975 & 1977
Linda Rankin
Prestwick

1979, 1980 & 1982
Christine Lacey
Alexandria

1983
Helen Fitzpatrick
Stenhousemuir

1984
Lesley Bowman
Dundee

1985, 1987, 1988 & 1989
Gareth Mitchelson
Monifieth

1986, 1990, 1992, 1997 & 1998
Gregor Bowman
Dundee

1991, 1994 & 1995
Deryck Mitchelson
Monifieth

1999, 2000, 2001, 2002, 2003 & 2005
Colleen Rintamaki
Canada

2006
Erin Rose
Canada

Junior World Champions

The British Association of Teachers of Dancing Members

1961 Betty Turkington Glasgow

1967 Lyne Erbrick USA

1973 Linda Rankin Prestwick

1977 Mary Beth Miller USA

1981 Jennifer Lindsay Canada

1983 Gregor Bowman Dundee

1986 Ann Milne Canada

1988 Deryck Mitchelson Monifieth

1991 Lorraine Brown Kilbirnie

1994 Natalie Quick Canada

1998 Colleen Rintamaki Canada

2003 Laura Cafferty Canada

2008 Alexandra Matthews Canada

1963 Irene McKechnie Grangemouth

1972 Aileen Robertson Ayr

1974 Katie Rowan Ayr

1978 Christine Lacey Alexandria

1982 Jennifer Lindsay Canada

1984 Gregor Bowman Dundee

1987 Ann Milne Canada

1990 Dawn Brennan Canada

1993 Natalie Quick Canada

1997 Colleen Rintamaki Canada

2002 Rachel McLagan Blairgowrie

2007 Fiona Lee Canada

Juvenile World Champions

The British Association of Teachers of Dancing Members

1934 Elspeth Strathern Glasgow

1956 Ann McIlroy Rothesay

1961 Irene McKechnie Grangemouth

1974 Christine Lacey Alexandria

1976 Mary Beth Miller USA

1983 Ann Milne Canada

1985 Deryck Mitchelson Monifieth

1987 Nicola Grant Kirriemuir

1991 Natalie Quick Canada

1996 Colleen Rintamaki Canada

2003 Marielle Lesperance Canada

1939 May G Falconer Motherwell

1957 Sandra Bald Kirkcaldy

1964 Cecilia Orr Forth

1975 Christine Lacey Alexandria

1981 Gregor Bowman Dundee

1984 Ann Milne Canada

1986 Deryck Mitchelson Monifieth

1990 Nadine McKenzie Polmont

1995 Colleen Rintamaki Ontario

1999 Ashley Knox USA

BATD HIGHLAND SCHOLARSHIPS

The BATD Highland Scholarships for Great Britain came about in 1991.

It was announced by the Highland Committee that any "Honours" candidate in the Highland branch, who, in the Examiners opinion has a special quality and talent, may be entered for the Highland Scholarships.

This day involves the dancers participating in a class, sitting a written paper based on questions from the grade examination syllabi and performing a solo choreography.

In 2002 the BATD paid tribute to Jessie Stewart by naming their Highland scholarships the "Jessie Stewart Haggarty MBE Highland Scholarships".

Jessie Stewart-Haggarty MBE

Sadie Simpson

The first BATD Sadie Simpson North American Highland Scholarships were held in 2002 in the Circus Circus Hotel in Las Vegas and the choice of hotel was just perfect as host for so many dancers and their parents and friends. A ceilidh followed the scholarship event and Miss Simpson's three sons Craig, Paul and Raymond entertained the audience with keyboard and song and when they sang "Mum's" favourite song "My Ain Folk" there was not a dry eye in the house and their performance almost raised the roof.

Highland Committee & Junior Forum

The British Association of Teachers of Dancing

BATD HIGHLAND COMMITTEE

The BATD Highland Committee has nine members. Seven of the members must be Association examiners.

The committee meet around five times a year. In recent years they have been responsible for updating the Highland and National exam syllabi. In 2009 they introduced a choreography examination and this year a recreational examination.

The Jessie Stewart Haggarty MBE Scholarships are one of the main events organised by the Highland Committee.

The aim of the committee is to promote the art of Highland Dancing and strive to improve technique. The committee formed a Junior Forum to encourage young members to play an active part in the Association.

Along with the SOBHD delegates, the committee discuss all SOBHD matters.

The Delegates (2010) are D.Young, C.O'Donnell, J.Shearer, S.Lees, K.O'Donnell and L.Lamont as deputy.

The BATD technical delegates (2010) are J.Shearer, S.Lees and B.Wren as deputy.

BATD JUNIOR FORUM

At the 2004 BATD Annual Conference, The Highland Committee invited some of the Junior members to establish a Junior Highland Forum, open to all BATD Highland Members under the age of 40.

The aim of the Forum is to provide a medium whereby young members can share their views, opinions and ideas about the ways in which they can promote and develop Highland Dancing, and in particular the BATD, among dancers and teachers.

They hold a meeting at The Annual Conference and elect a secretary and chairperson. They have other meetings during the year when required.

Members of the Forum "shadowed" members of the Highland Committee at the Jessie Stewart Haggarty MBE Scholarships in Paisley to help but also to learn what is involved on the day. They were involved with registering the candidates, scrutineering the class work, invigilating the written paper and controlling the music for the choreography.

Since the Forum was established, they have run a series of Highland Roadshows across Scotland, working with teachers and judges from across the country to deliver fun, exciting and informative workshops on technique, fitness, choreography and other forms of dance. The Roadshows have proved to be a highly successful venture and the Junior Forum is hoping to build on this success in the coming years.

Highland Championships

The British Association of Teachers of Dancing

VENUE	EVENT ORGANISER
Central Hall, Bath Street Glasgow	Ian Wilson
St Andrews Hall Glasgow	Ian Wilson
Kingston Halls, Paisley Road Glasgow	Mary Lindsay
Govan Town Hall Glasgow	Mamie Davidson
Palace of Arts Glasgow	Christine Aitken & Betty Turkington
Paisley Town Hall Paisley	Christine Lacey

The Wallace Trophy 1954

The British Association of Teachers of Dancing Associate Trophy

THE WALLACE TROPHY 1954

Awarded to Associate with most points in Championships

The Wallace Trophy

1954 - Sylvia Luckett

1955 - Nancy Haggarty

1956 - Sylvia Luckett

1957 - Nancy Haggarty

1959 - Sheila McMillan

1960 - Irene Dick

1961 - Sheila McMillan

1962- Sheila McMillan

1963 - Nina Hemingway

1964 - Nina Hemingway

1965 - Victor Wesley

1966 - Fay McNaughton

1967 - Sally Anne Thornton

1968 - Sally Anne Thornton
Jessie Clark

1969 - Jessie Clark

1970 - Jean Stewart

1971 - Jean Stewart

1972 - Margaret McCabe

1973 - Aileen Robertson

1974 - Aileen Robertson

1975 - Linda Rankin

1976 - Katie Rowan

1977 - Jean Crawford

1978 - Christine Lacey

1979 - Christine Lacey

1980 - Christine Lacey

1981 - Alyson Burgoine

1982 - Patricia-Ann McKay

1983 - Gregor Bowman

1984 - Gregor Bowman

1985 - Gareth Mitchelson

1986 - Deborah M. Kelly

1987 - Deryck Mitchelson

1988 - Gregor Bowman

1989 - Robyn McBoyle

1990 - Ailsa Mitchelson

1991 - Lorraine Brown

1992 - Amanda Kane

1993 - Audrey Aitken

1994 - Jeannie Buchan

1995 - Lorraine Brown

1996 - Alison Cameron

1997 - Kirstie-Anne Marsic
Leigh-Ann Plenderleith

1998 - Leigh-Ann Plenderleith

1999 - Lucia Polanski

2000 - winner unknown

2001 - Tracey Graham

2002 - Rachel McLagan

2003 - Rachel McLagan

2004 - Tanya Horne

2005 - Kelly Louise MacKinnon

2006 - Mhairi Hennigan

2007 - Nicola Brown

2008 - Fawn Russell

The Winnie Clifford Shield

The British Association of Teachers of Dancing Members Trophy

THE WINNIE CLIFFORD SHIELD

Awarded to Associate with most points in Championships

The Winnie Clifford Shield

1965 - Betty Turkington
1966 - Betty Turkington
1968 - Betty Turkington
1969 - Betty Turkington
1970 - Betty Turkington
1971 - Betty Turkington
1972 - Kenneth Gooden
1973 - Linda Nixon
1974 - Jessie Clark
1975 - Aileen Robertson
1976 - Linda Rankin
1977 - Katie Rowan
1978 - Katie Rowan
1979 – winner unknown
1980 - Christine Laing
1981 - Christine Lacey
1982 - Christine Lacey
Lesley Bowman
1983 - Christine Lacey
1984 - Christine Lacey
1985 - Christine Lacey
1986 - Gareth Mitchelson
1987 - Gareth Mitchelson
1988 - Gareth Mitchelson
1989 - Gregor Bowman
1990 - Deryck Mitchelson
1991 - Deryck Mitchelson
1992 - Gregor Bowman
1993 - Deryck Mitchelson
Gregor Bowman
1994 - Deryck Mitchelson
1995 - Deryck Mitchelson
1996 - Deryck Mitchelson
1997 - Amanda Kane
1998 - Kirstie Marsic
1999 - Leigh- Ann Plenderleith
2000 - Leigh-Ann Plenderleith
2001 - Leigh-Ann Plenderleith
2002 - Leigh-Ann Plenderleith
2003 - Gemma Baillie
2004 - Rachel McLagan
2005 - Tracey Graham
2006 - Gemma Baillie
2007 - Craig Johnston
2008 - Gemma Baillie
2009 - Gemma Baillie

John Doak

The British Association of Teachers of Dancing

Mr John Doak
President in 1930
John Doak joined the Association on the 7th June 1920

From Left: David Doak, John Doak, Jesse Doak

MARGARET ANNE BROGAN

Margaret started Highland Dancing when she was 5 years of age in the kitchen of a local lady. She then attended a local dance class run by Margaret Cassidy.

Margaret stayed with Miss Cassidy until she was 17 and had completed her Associate exam in Highland.

Miss Cassidy emigrated to Australia and Margaret took over the school.

She continued her professional exams with Jean Ritchie and finally became an examiner in 2001. Now, even although Margaret teaches many other types of dance, Highland remains her favourite.

HEATHER FRASER

Heather started dancing at the tender age of 2 1/2 years at the Sadie Simpson School of Dance in Paisley, then continued to train at the Elma Whyte School of Dance when Miss Simpson retired.

At 5 years of age, Heather commenced her first Highland class, which she loved and has continued her passion with Highland dance, dancing as part of a Scottish show case with ceilidh bands and at organised events. Heather gained her professional qualifications during her period of study with Miss Jean Ritchie.

At 19 years of age Heather opened her first dance school in Paisley, then in Renfrew a couple of years later. Heather is a Fellow and Examiner with the British Association Teachers of Dancing .

SUSAN FRASER

Susan had the honour of being appointed as an examiner of the BATD in 1990. She has travelled all over the country examining in Highland and many other branches of dancing.

Susan has also had the great honour and pleasure of conducting several examination tours in Canada. Just recently she was on the adjudicating panel of the BATD Highland Scholarships which again was an absolute delight.

Susan has met many lovely teachers through her examining career and has made lots of new friends. Susan is delighted to have had the wonderful experience of seeing some fabulous dancers through her examination work.

MAY MARTIN

May Martin started Dancing at 4 years of age, competing at 5 years and the winner of many awards and also Cowal Scottish Championships.

Unfortunately, she had to retire from dancing early owing to illness. Delighted to return into the dancing world from whence she became a BATD adjudicator and BATD Examiner. Sadie Simpson, a Trustee at the time, appointed husband Alex. as the B.A.T.D's personal Piper.

The Martin's were a dancing family, with daughter Melanie and son Clive both successful dancers.

May enjoys every connection with dancing, especially having the opportunity as an Examiner, to inform the candidates of what was pleasing and giving helpful comments for further improvement.

Having travelled many countries Examining and Adjudicating, May appreciates the lovely friends she has in dancing both at home and overseas.

May served as Vice – President of the British Association of Teachers of Dancing 2006 – 2009

DOROTHY YOUNG

Dorothy lives in Edinburgh where she has, for the past 45 years, taught Highland Dancing and her daughter, Kelly Grassick, now teaches within the school.

Dorothy is a Fellow Member of the BATD (Highland and National Branches) an Examiner of the Association, a member of the BATD Highland Committee and represents the Association at SOBHD meetings. She is also a member of the SOBHD Worldwide Judges' Panel and has been for many years. Prior to taking up teaching, Dorothy competed at Championship level and won numerous awards. She has now passed on her teaching knowledge to her students and daughter who have won many Championships over the years.

JEANETTE SHEARER

Jeanette Shearer is a Fellow and Life Member of the BATD. Her interest in Highland Dancing began over 55 years ago in Wick, Caithness as a pupil of Miss Jean Smith. Because of this far north location in The Highlands of Scotland and limited travel opportunities at this time, her dancing potential was not realised until a fortuitous meeting with Miss Jean Ritchie at the Halkirk Highland Games.

As a result of this Miss Ritchie took a great interest in Jeanette and became an enormous influence in her dancing career. Jeanette first started teaching in Wick over 43 years ago and during this time produced numerous dancers to Championship level. Jeanette has had the pleasure of lecturing, examining and judging extensively throughout the UK, Canada and the USA.

Jeanette became an Examiner in 1999 and is also a member of the Highland Committee. She is also a delegate to the SOBHD, the Technical Committee and an SOBHD adjudicator. Jeanette now lives and teaches in Crieff, Perthshire.

LESLEY E BOWMAN

Lesley began her dancing career aged four years with Miss Wilma Tolmie. She quickly moved through to the Open category and won most of the major Championships including the Commonwealth, British and Scottish Championships. When Lesley began studying for her degree in Edinburgh, Miss Frances Paterson became her teacher.

It was in 1984, as Lesley completed her B Ed. in Physical Education and Human Movement Studies that she also won the coveted Adult World Highland Dancing Championship. Lesley is a very accomplished dancing teacher and her pupils have won every major title including the Juvenile and Junior World Championships and the Adult World Championship on eight occasions.

Lesley teaches physical education and dance in a Dundee Secondary School and it is also in Dundee where she runs her dancing school. Lesley is a Fellow and Life Member of the BATD, a BATD Highland Examiner, a member of the BATD Highland Committee, Convenor of the SOBHD Judges Panel Committee and a member of the Worldwide Adjudicators Panel with the SOBHD.

CHRISTINE O'DONNELL

Christine started dancing lessons at the age of 4 being taught by well known piper, dancer and adjudicator, Iain McDonald. She competed successfully until 1975 when she passed her SOBHD adjudicators exam.

She has since adjudicated all over the UK and in Canada and America. Christine is a Fellow, Life Member and Examiner of the British Association Teachers of Dancing. She became an examiner in 1990 and has examined in the UK and Canada.

She is currently the secretary of the BATD Highland Committee and organises the Jessie Stewart Haggarty MBE Highland Scholarship weekend.

Christine runs a very successful dancing school in Paisley with 170 pupils being taught in Tap, Ballet, Modern, Majorette, Freestyle, Highland and Traditional Step Dancing.

ADELINE DUNCAN, BRITISH COLUMBIA (Deceased)

Mrs. D., as she was affectionately known, has been involved with Highland Dancing for over 75 years. She was first taught by a dance master of the "old school" in Victoria, B.C. For over fifty years she had a permanent studio in Victoria and trained many outstanding dancers including Angus MacKenzie and Jennifer Lindsay, both World Champions and BATD Members. She was a Fellow and Life Member and Examiner of the BATD. Along with countless honours she received in her outstanding career, she was most proud that she was the first person "outside of Scotland" elected an Honorary Member of the Scottish Official Board of Highland Dancing.

EVELYN LEINWEBER, ALBERTA (Deceased)

Evelyn was a symbol of Highland Dancing in Alberta and was a familiar figure at Highland Games throughout Alberta for 70 years. A highly respected teacher, she dedicated much of her life to generations of students who have had their lives enriched by her instruction and by her kind, caring ways. Evelyn held a special place in her heart for each and every one she taught and sought ways to encourage them to continue, to pursue Highland Dancing. She was an Examiner with the BATD and a member of the Scottish Official Board of Highland Dancing Adjudicators Panel. The Grand Lady of Highland Dance epitomized the strength and courage of the Scots and at the same time displayed a generosity of spirit that endeared her to all who had the good fortune of knowing her.

JANET T. MACLACHLAN, ONTARIO (Deceased)

Janet (Jenny) T. MacLachlan was an artist, historian and pillar of resource and knowledge in the Highland and Scottish Country Dance communities in Canada, the United States and in Scotland. The BATD was Jenny's Association. She served as an Examiner for many years and contributed to the Association's Bulletin with articles containing historical scripted dances that she had collected and researched over the years. Sadie Simpson was a great friend and mentor to Jenny. She inspired Jenny to establish a BATD Dance Festival in the Western Ontario Area which still continues today. Jenny also established WOHDA - Western Ontario Highland Dance Association, and was Founder of the Cambridge Highland Games along with her late husband Duncan MacLachlan. She worked hard to enrich the Scottish Dance heritage in North America, producing many exceptional highland dancers that have gone on to teaching and judging careers.

EVELYN MURRAY, ONTARIO (Deceased)

Evelyn Murray came to Canada in the early 50's and opened her dance studio shortly after that. Evelyn taught baton, jazz, ballet and tap, but her true love was teaching highland dancing. She travelled extensively, judging, examining and conducting workshops across Canada and the U.S. Along with other interested parties, she was instrumental in the formation of the Eastern Canada Highland Dancing Association. Mrs. Murray was also Secretary for the BATD Toronto District for many years. Mrs. Murray's aim in life was to enhance and encourage the art of Highland Dancing in Canada. Her dream was realized as evidenced by her many pupils who are now successful Highland dance teachers and judges. Mrs. Murray was a Fellow and Examiner of the B.A.T.D., as well as an adjudicator on the Scottish Official Board of Highland Dancing.

CURRENT CANADIAN BATD HIGHLAND EXAMINERS

Nancy Haggarty, Alberta

Nancy's first steps in dance were taken at the age of three and now like mother, Jessie, she too has dedicated her life to dancing and promoting the BAT D. Nancy taught with her mother at the world-renowned Stewart School in Alexandria, Scotland where they produced many champions throughout the years. Nancy immigrated to Fox Creek, Alberta, Canada. She continues the high standard of excellence with her students in Fox Creek as she did in Scotland. Nancy is a Fellow and Examiner of the BATD, also an adjudicator on the Scottish Official Board of Highland Dancing. Her input is always beneficial to dance and highly respected from all those that know her.

Mary Margaret Manifold, British Columbia

Mary Margaret Manifold is a Fellow and Examiner of the BATD. She started her dancing career under the guidance of Mary Isdale McNab of St. Andrews Scotland. She had a successful competitive career competing in Canada, United States and Scotland winning many titles including Pacific Coast International award, Intercontinental, US Open and Canadian Championship. She is the Secretary for BATD BC and Northwest States and continues to teach in the Coquitlam area.

Ann Milne, Ontario

In a competitive career spanning almost twenty years, Ann Milne has won every major Championship in North America, Scotland and Australia including: 4 Worlds, 12 Canadians, 13 Ontarios. Ann has trained many successful dancers. Her students' accomplishments include Ontario, Canadian, North American and Scottish Championships. Ann has extensive training in classical Ballet and Jazz. She is an award-winning Choreographer and is the Artistic Director of the performing group Celtic Accent. Ann has performed and taught workshops in Canada, USA, Australia and Japan. Ann is an Examiner for the British Association of Teachers of Dance and is on the Judges' Panel of the Scottish Official Board of Highland Dancing.

Mary Munro, British Columbia

Mary resides in Burnaby, British Columbia. She is a Fellow and Examiner of the BATD and is also on the SOBHD Adjudicators Panel. As a competitive dancer, her many awards include the Adult Canadian Championship, Adult British Overseas Championship, Braemar Most Points and Best Overseas dancer, Dancers Challenge Medal at Oban and First Runner-up in the Adult World Championship. As a judge and teacher, she has had the opportunity to travel to Australia and extensively throughout North America.

Anne Sutherland, Ontario

Anne Sutherland is a Fellow, Examiner and Life Member of the British Association of Teachers of Dancing and a SOBHD Judge. She received her dance training with the late Janet T. MacLachlan. Anne has taught and operated her own School of Dance in London, Ontario for more than 40 years. She is Chairman of the BATD Western Ontario District and the organizer of the BATD Western Ontario Highland Dance Festival. A founding member of WOHDA-Western Ontario Highland Dancing Association, she continues an active role as the Association's Professional Advisor. She is also a Past President and Honorary Life Member of ScotDance Ontario and an Independent Member and Past President of ScotDance Canada. She continues her involvement with SDC on the Examiners' Advisory Committee. Anne has produced dancers who have won championship and runner-up titles in Canada, United States, Australia and Scotland and many students who have gone on to teaching and judging careers.

Joy Allen Tolev, Ontario

Joy (Allen) Tolev started dancing at the age of 3 under the instruction of Mrs Evelyn Murray in Toronto, Ontario. During her competitive days she successfully competed in many highland dance competitions and championships throughout Canada and the United States.

She has been teaching at her own school of highland dancing in Toronto and has produced many dancers who have captured titles in various championships including the Ontario, Canadian, Scottish, Commonwealth and World Championships. There have been over 20 Canadian Championship Titles, many Scottish and Commonwealth Championship titles and runner-ups, and a World Champion who holds 10 World Titles. She is a Fellow and Examiner of the BATD, North American Coordinator of the BATD , and adjudicator on the SOBHD Judges panel.

Joseph Wallin, Nova Scotia

Joseph Wallin is a Member, Fellow, and Examiner of the BAT D and a Member of the SOBHD Judges' Panel. He is also on the Executive Council of the BATD Mr. Wallin is Chairman of the BATD Maritimes as well as Festival Organizer of the BATD Nova Scotia Dance Festival. A former Maritime Highland Dance Champion, Joseph danced with a semi-professional ballet company for three years. He has appeared in many musicals and stage shows in Nova Scotia. Mr. Wallin performed and choreographed for Canadian television for more than 20 years. Joseph has operated a very successful dance school for the past 50 years in Dartmouth, Nova Scotia. Joseph is the choreographer for the Nova Scotia International Tattoo and he is the Dance Director and Choreographer for the award winning dance troupe "Amethyst Scottish Dancers of Nova Scotia."

JEAN FORBES (Deceased)

Jean had a successful dance studio, where she taught ballet, tap and Highland in Dallas, Texas for many years. Jean retired from teaching, judging and examining for the BATD in the early 90's as she wanted to enjoy retirement with her husband, Robert in Midlothian, Texas. When Jean was younger, she used to tour with the USO entertaining the troops and that is where she met her very devoted husband of over 50 plus years. They were instrumental in getting the Highland Games started in Texas. Jean and Bob used to travel to Houston, Texas and help the teachers at St. Thomas' Episcopal School when they were trying to get their Scottish Arts Program started. We in Texas are forever grateful for their dedication. Jean was a gracious and lovely lady who will be sadly missed.

MARGUERITE REID (Deceased)

Marguerite Reid started her life-long career in the Highland Dancing world at the age of 5 when she saw a couple of Highland Dancers on a ship that her grandmother took her on for a holiday in Scotland. One look and she was hooked. Marguerite began teaching at the age of 13, with all of her cousins as her students. She accomplished much in the dancing world and taught many US Champions. Many of her dancers went on to become teachers and judges themselves. Marguerite was a Fellow Member and Examiner of the BATD and an adjudicator with the Scottish Official Board of Highland Dancing. Marguerite did it all, but her passion was to teach. She said if she couldn't teach she couldn't live. There are very few places in the dancing world where Marguerite Reid is not known and her legacy will live on through all those whose lives she touched.

MARY STEWART (Deceased)

Mrs Stewart came to Kearny, N.J. from Glasgow, Scotland in December 1951, a few months after her husband, Allan, a Major in the British military, came to the United States to start a new life for his young family. In 1953, Mrs Stewart began teaching Scottish Highland Dancing at the Masonic Temple in Kearny, New Jersey. In 2000, Mrs Stewart retired after nearly 50 years of teaching. Many people may remember Mrs Stewart as a long-time member of FUSTA and its predecessor, USHDA. She was an adjudicator with the Scottish Official Board of Highland Dancing and a BATD Examiner and Life Member.

C. STEWART SMITH (Deceased)

Born in Dundee, Scotland in 1929, Stewart was both a Scottish Highland and country dancer. He emigrated to the United States in 1950, settling in San Francisco where he was principal of the San Francisco School of Scottish Dancing. There his pupils won many Championships in the Western United States. He accepted the position of dance instructor at St. Thomas Episcopal School in Houston, Texas and moved there in the 1970's, where he inspired hundreds of young dancers in the Scottish dance arts. Stewart was a Fellow Member and Examiner for the BATD and an adjudicator with the Scottish Official Board of Highland Dancing as well as an active member of the Royal Scottish Country Dance Society. He taught and judged Scottish dance around the world at the highest levels of performance and competition.

ELIZABETH COYLE

Elizabeth Coyle was taught by her mother, Jean Ritchie and then taught with her in her School of Dance in Scotland until moving to the USA in 1982. Elizabeth has directed her own School of Dancing since then and has trained dancers from Beginner to Championship level. She is a Life Member of the BATD, a Fellow and Examiner of the Association and also an adjudicator with the Scottish Official Board of Highland Dancing.

DONNA CUSACK

Donna Cusack is a Life Member and Examiner with the BATD. She teaches Highland Dancing at St. Thomas' Episcopal School in Houston Texas, with her sister, Diane Krugh. Over the past 28 years, they have taught many United States Champions and in 1997 their student Michelle Cumagun won the Juvenile World Championship. Donna and her husband, Mike have been happily married for 24 years and have one son, Michael.

LYNNE ERBRICK

Lynne began her dancing career at the age of five. She studied Highland Dancing at the Marguerite Reid School of Highland Dancing and Ballet at the Philadelphia Dance Academy. Lynne won the Gaelic College Scholarship and spent two summers studying with J.L. MacKenzie in Nova Scotia. Lynne spent three months in Scotland where she studied with Elspeth Strathern. While in Scotland, she became the first American dancer to win the Junior World Championship. Ms. Erbirck's students have been representatives for the Eastern and Southeast Regions to the US Championships. Lynne is a Fellow, Life Member, and Examiner for the BATD. She is an adjudicator with the Scottish Official Board of Highland Dancing. In 1993, Lynne was asked to judge the World Championships at the Cowal Highland Games. She is still the only American winner of a World Championship to also be a judge. She is the director of the Pocono Highland Dancers in Stroudsburg, Pa. In addition to Highland Dancing, Lynne is a Principal in the Bangor Area School District in Pa.

DIANE MACPHEE KRUGH

Diane MacPhee Krugh has been teaching Highland for over 37 years and for the past 28 years has been teaching Highland Dancing at St. Thomas' Episcopal School in Houston, Texas where she teaches on a full time basis along with her sister Donna Cusack. Together they have produced seven different United States Champions, winning twenty-two US Championship titles. On several separate occasions their students have been in the top six overall places in the Juvenile and Junior World Championships, as well as wining many other Championships in Canada and Scotland. In 1997, one of their students Michelle Cumagun won the Juvenile World Championship. Diane travels on a regular basis conducting workshops and has adjudicated at many competitions and Championships all over the United States and in Australia, Canada, New Zealand, Ireland and Scotland. Diane is a Life Member and a Fellow and Examiner with the BATD and an adjudicator with the Scottish Official Board of Highland Dancing. Diane is happily married and has 2 children.

United States Highland Examiners
The British Association of Teachers of Dancing

BETTY LAWRENCE (RETIRED)

Born in Scotland, Betty Lawrence immigrated with her husband to the United States. After a successful competitive career, Betty followed her true love to the teaching arena and possesses the very special talent of teaching students all levels of Highland Dancing. Her belief that anyone can polish a diamond, but a real teacher will start with the rock and polish it until it becomes a diamond, is a very special skill Betty possesses from the heart. Betty was a Fellow Member and served as an Examiner of the BATD for many years. Betty was also an adjudicator with the Scottish Official Board of Highland Dancing. The number of teachers trained and examined by Betty over the many years is incalculable. Her contribution, dedication and loyalty firstly to the school of Scottish Arts and then to the Ohio Scottish Arts School has enabled our art to flourish and successfully thrive in the USA. It would be extremely difficult to find someone more dedicated and devoted to the development and teaching of Highland Dancing in the USA than Betty Lawrence.

SANDRA WEYMAN

For Sandra, Highland Dancing started with Australian champion Shirley Ayres, who instilled a strong technical foundation. When Shirley moved to Scotland, Sandra travelled to Philadelphia to study with Marguerite Reid, who continued to enhance her knowledge and saw Sandra go from winning Championships to teaching and on to becoming a judge. She considers herself fortunate to have had such wonderful teachers at home as well as being able to take classes with the expertise of several Scottish teachers, such as Jessie Stewart. A retired school teacher, Sandra now continues to work with her small dance school, many of whom have been Championship winners and USIR reps. She enjoys judging, doing workshops and now examining in the US and Canada.

New Zealand Highland Examiners
The British Association of Teachers of Dancing

JUDY CLARK

Judy has been teaching Highland and National Dancing for over 30 years. Many of her pupils are now teachers and adjudicators and many have won North & South Island, New Zealand, Australasian, British, Commonwealth and Scottish Championships. In 2005 Judy's pupil, Morgan Bamford, won the first of her five World Championships. Morgan is the only dancer who has won all Scottish Championships at Cowal from under 9 years through to 15 years. Judy is a Fellow and Examiner with the BATD. She is a founding member of ScotDance New Zealand and is the Administration Officer for ScotDance New Zealand. Judy is a member of the worldwide adjudicators' panel and has adjudicated throughout New Zealand, Australia, USA, Canada, Northern Ireland and Scotland. Judy has tutored workshops throughout New Zealand, Australia, Scotland, Canada and USA. Judy is a former deputy principal of a secondary college and is now director of Kip McGrath Education Centre in New Plymouth. In her spare time she loves to cross-stitch, read and go walking.

THE SCOTTISH DANCE TEACHERS' ALLIANCE

General History

The Scottish Dance Teachers' Alliance (SDTA) was founded in 1934 following concerns that the opinions of Scottish dance professionals were not listened to "down south". Mr Alex Warren, OBE and SDTA Past President, wrote a letter to all Scottish dance professionals inviting them to a meeting to discuss the forming of a purely Scottish society and to make a break away from the Imperial Society in London.

And so the Alliance was formed!

To be a member, you had to be a) Scottish or of Scottish descent and b) a full-time dance professional. Eventually, part-time teachers (for example, those who had another career and only taught dancing as a secondary business) were allowed to join the Alliance, but only as an Associate Member who was neither allowed to speak at meetings nor to have a vote. If they had anything they wished to be brought up, they had to ask a Full Member to bring the matter to the meeting.

Mr Warren, Mr Joe McGowan (one of the SDTA's very early members) and Mr Joe Diamond (then Secretary) travelled to London at their own expense to enable Scotland's voice to be heard. They made such a good job of it that Mr Warren (then President of the Alliance) subsequently became Chairman and President of the Official Board of Ballroom Dancing, now known as The British Dance Council.

All this began in the studio of the first secretary, Mr Joe Diamond, to be continued by Mr Jack Muir and Mr Alex Dalglish. They allowed their homes to become the SDTA Headquarters; such was their commitment to strengthening the position of the Scottish dance professionals.

As time went on, with so many Scots emigrating and promoting the SDTA in their adopted countries, the rule of being "Scottish" had to be withdrawn. The Alliance News (still in circulation today), was read avidly in the UK, United States of America, Australia, Canada, the Far East, Holland, New Zealand, South Africa and Japan. It is pleasing to note that links formed all those years ago are still in existence today – testament both to the hard work and dedication of many SDTA members and to the strength of international fraternity prevalent in the world of Highland Dancing!

Through time, bridges were built and differences between the Alliance and the Imperial Society were reconciled. At this time, Miss Jean J. C. McLellan (Past President) became a powerful force in the SDTA and all branches began to grow. It is interesting to note that during the war years, a Victory Fund was started and the Alliance raised enough money to buy two Spitfires - not bad going for a then small society.

INAUGURAL MEETING OF WHAT WAS TO BECOME THE SCOTTISH OFFICIAL BOARD OF HIGHLAND DANCING

As the SDTA continued to grow, there was unrest in the late 1940's amongst the competitors in the Highland Dancing world as there was no specific body or anyone with authority to answer queries or to correct mistakes. To address this, the STDA made a move towards establishing a representative board of control. Mr Jack Muir, then President of the Alliance, held a meeting in Stirling to which all dancers, judges, teachers and organisers (in fact, anyone with an interest in competitive Highland Dancing)were invited – and so began the Scottish Official Board of Highland Dancing which is celebrating its 60th year this year!

* Transcript of a letter written by the Honorary Secretary to George Lowe esq, at the Herald Press, Arbroath (22nd November, 1949)

Dear Mr Lowe,

The Scottish Dance Teachers' Alliance are of the opinion that "a board of control" of Highland Dancing should be formed, this body to be representative of all associations of individuals interested in the art of Highland Dancing.

The functions of this proposed "board of control" would probably be as follows:

To standardise the technique of Highland Dancing

To formulate rules governing the status of Amatuer and Professional dancers

To formulate laws governing all types of competitions

To control the granting of Championships

To ensure that only those who are competent are allowed to act as judges at any Championship or recognised competition

To deal with any important matter relevant to the art of Highland Dancing

In order to discuss the advisability of the above project, the Scottish Dance Teachers' Alliance invite you to attend, or in the case of an association, to send 4 delegates to, a meeting to be held in the Plaza Ballroom, Stirling, on Sunday 15th January, 1950 at 2pm. Since the Scottish Dance Teachers Alliance may not be cognizant of all responsible associations or individuals who should be invited to attend this inaugural meeting, each recipient of this letter is requested to get in touch with any such responsible association or individual whom they think ought to be included in this invitation, and if any such party has not received an invitation, they are requested to communicate with me at the above address.

Signed: Hon Secy.

* Transcript of a letter to James L. McKenzie (12th January, 1950) re. inaugural meeting

Dear Mr McKenzie,

Just a hast note to enclose a copy of further letter from ID Cameron. He certainly seems keen to help in any way he can. I only hope that we are able to live up to his expectations.

Lieut Col A.G.L. McLean 'phoned me today to say that as long as this attempt to form a board of control is inspired by you he is willing to attend on Sunday. He is not keen on anyone else trying to run it so that's a feather in your cap!

Tried to 'phone you tonight but your nephew informed me that you had a letter in the post for me so I am hoping there will be no delay in the post. Expect to get through to Stirling early Sunday. H.Q. probably Golden Lion.

Yrs aye,

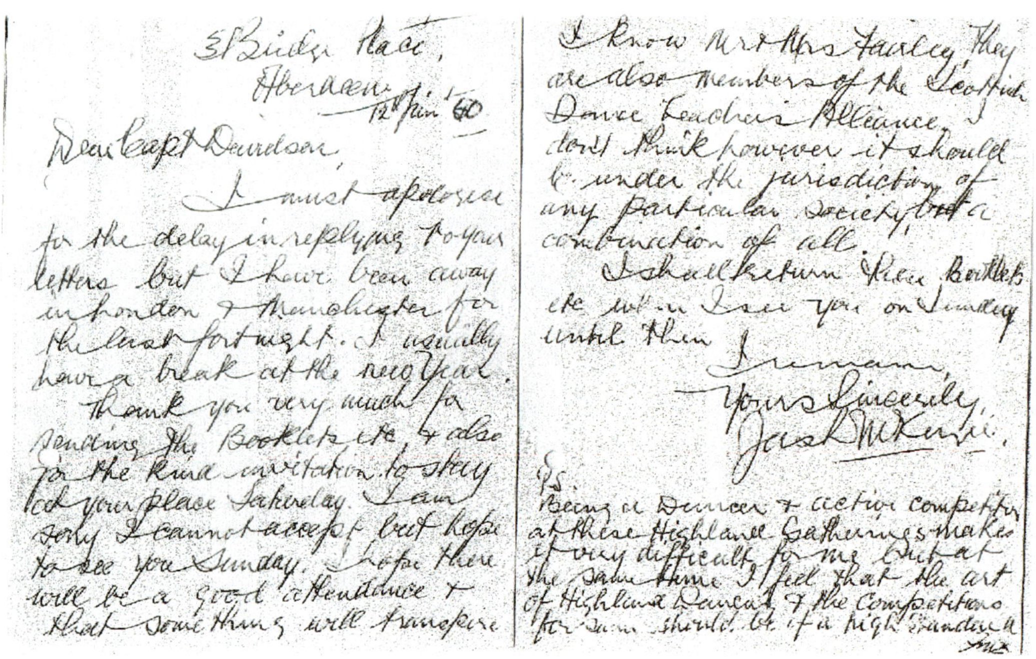
3 Bridge Place,
Aberdeen
12th Jan '50

Dear Capt Davidson,

I must apologise for the delay in replying to your letters but I have been away in London & Manchester for the last fortnight. I usually have a break at the New Year.

Thank you very much for sending the Booklets etc, & also for the kind invitation to stay at your place Saturday. I am sorry I cannot accept but hope to see you Sunday. I hope there will be a good attendance & that something will transpire

I know Mr & Mrs Fairley they are also members of the Scottish Dance Teachers Alliance. I don't think however it should be under the jurisdiction of any particular society but a combination of all.

I shall return these Booklets etc when I see you on Sunday until then I remain,

Yours Sincerely,
Jack McKenzie.

P.S. Being a Dancer & active competitor at these Highland Gatherings makes it very difficult for me but at the same time I feel that the art of Highland Dancing & the Competitions for same should be of a high standard

The Original Letter

THE HIGHLAND BRANCH

Many SDTA members have become internationally renowned in their own fields and the Highland Branch is proud to boast many world champions, both past and present.

Examiners in all branches continue to maintain the high standards set by our founder members and are proud to be able to support and serve the international dance community.

The Scottish Dance Teacher's Alliance has come a very long way from Mr Alex Warren's idea 84 years ago but hopefully we are achieving his hopes and aspirations in maintaining the standards he set in 1934.

We must never forget the debt we owe to Alex Warren, Joe McGowan, Joe Diamond, Jack Muir, Alex Dalglish, Johnny Stewart and all other members who throughout the years have helped the Alliance become what it is today.

The Highland Branch was fundamental in the establishment of the Scottish Official Board of Highland Dancing (SOBHD). Below is a transcript of the minutes of the Highland Branch held on Sunday 28th August 1949 in Miss Jean McLellan's studio. The original minute is held by Mr Billy Forsyth, past President of the SOBHD.

A meeting of the above Branch was held in Miss J. McLellan's studio on Sunday 28th August. There was a good attendance of members and a hearty welcome was extended to Miss Mary Dring from South Africa who was introduced by Mr Douglas Thomson.

Mr McKenzie, the Branch Chairman, on opening the meeting, stated that owing to the distance between the majority of members and himself, he found difficulty in keeping contact. Mr Muir then suggested that a deputy chairman be appointed, and Mr McKenzie agreed. Mr Turpie was then unanimously appointed depute chairman.

The effect of the new Highland Association was then gone into, and several statements were given by the members – some farcical and some serious although it would not serve any purpose to disclose these here.

Proposed Highland medal tests caused quite a sensation when it became known that should the parent body sanction these tests, there would be almost 200 applications without delay. It was agreed to ask the parent body to grant this at the next meeting, and the medals to be on the same line as those given for Ballroom.

Mr McKenzie agreed to go over the syllabus at the next meeting in Edinburgh. Mr Turpie then gave instruction on his dance "Scotch Broth" and members and associated members agreed to demonstrate the dance next meeting if called upon.

The proposed formation of Highland Official Board proved the most interesting part of the meeting. The chairman gave his opinion that it would make no difference to organisers of competitions who would continue to run those Championships to suit themselves. Miss Lindsay said she could not agree entirely with Mr McKenzie as she thought a little difficulty would occur at the beginning, but that the time would come when the Official Board of Highland Dancing would be looked upon as the governing body.

Mr Muir agreed entirely with Miss Lindsay, and gave a brief outline of the difficulties experienced by the Official Board of Ballroom Dancing, who had now overcome all difficulties, and are now the governing body for Ballroom Dancing. Every member present felt quite enthusiastic about an Official Board being formed, and should this come to pass the Chairman of the Board should be someone interested in Highland Dancing, but not a member of any Association. After further discussion it was agreed to place the following recommendation before the parent body: "that the Highland Branch, SDTA, get in touch with all Associations interested in Highland Dancing with a view to forming an Official Board of Highland Dancing."

Associations to be notified:

British Association Teachers of Dancing

National Association Teachers of Dancing

Imperial society Teachers of Dancing

UKAP Teachers of Dancing

Scottish Highland Association

NBRA Teachers of Dancing

Objection was taken to one of the Associations mentioned, but after a lively discussion, it was agreed to ask all associations.

The committee then met to discuss the result of the meeting, and the business to be presented at the next meeting.

The meeting closed with a vote of thanks to the chairman.

JACK MUIR (PAST PRESIDENT) 1894-1967

Jack Muir was brought up in Motherwell, the only child of parents who were dance teachers, so naturally he became a dancer. He founded the Muir School of Dancing which became known as the finest dance school in Lanarkshire.

Jack Muir and his wife, Peg, taken at Jean Hamilton's wedding

By teaching in Bellshill, Motherwell, Wishaw, Carluke, Hamilton , Strathaven and, for a short time, East Kilbride, he was renowned. The studio was in Hamilton where he and his wife "Peg" as she was familiarly known, taught mostly Ballroom Dancing. Jack taught Tap, Ballet, Highland and Ballroom six days a week and, of course, attended meetings at his beloved SDTA. He was a stalwart member, holding positions of President and Secretary.

Over the years, Jack compiled textbooks for Highland, Tap, and Ballet that told exactly how each exercise or step should be done. They were a boon to teachers and pupils alike and left them in no doubt as to what was required.

Jack was an accomplished pianist and orchestrated the music for the annual displays held in the towns in which he taught. He always had an orchestra playing at his displays.

Along with J. L. MacKenzie, Jack worked very hard in the establishment of the Scottish Official Board of Highland Dancing. Although not always in harmony, they worked with great skill and determination. Their efforts are gratefully acknowledged by the SDTA.

(Report compiled by Mrs Jean Hamilton)

James L McKenzie

JAMES L. MCKENZIE (MBE) 1905 – 1992

As a youngster, Jimmy McKenzie would hide in the corner of the barn on his father's farm and watch his sister as she was instructed by one of the dancing teachers who travelled round the rural districts teaching youngsters to dance. Jimmy would then practice secretly on his own in his bedroom.

When this was discovered by his mother, it was decided that he, too, should have Highland Dancing lessons and from then on, the shy eight-year-old boy joined the class, although sometimes against his will. The first steps he learned were taught to the tune of "Pop Goes the Weasel", played on the violin by his instructor who both played and gave instruction at the same time.

Initially Jimmy had no aspirations to become a competitive dancer but, after his family left their farm and moved to Aberdeen, he became interested in the many competitions. At the age of 12, he entered his first competition at Pittodrie in Aberdeen, now a famous football ground, and much to everyone's surprise, he placed 2nd. This was just what he needed to get him going on a long and successful competitive career.

At this time, Jimmy was fortunate to have Johnny Pirie as his instructor and although Pirie was a hard taskmaster, Jimmy's personal desire not to be beaten and the advice and encouragement from his mother, who had also been a dancer, kept him going. Willie Sutherland also gave McKenzie many valuable hints and, in spite of the rivalry between Pirie and Sutherland, their rich heritage was passed onto McKenzie who in turn passed it onto his own students. Later in his life, dancers and teachers throughout the world experienced his love of Highland Dancing as he toured extensively in Canada, the United States of America, South Africa, Ireland and other European countries giving demonstrations and lectures. For many years, James L. (or "J.L." as he became affectionately known), was the principal dance instructor at the Gaelic College in St Ann's, Cape Breton during the summer months and dancers travelled from across Canada to take advantage of his expertise.

His list of competitive success is lengthy. Some of his impressive winnings are the World Highland Dancing Championship – won three successive years at the Cowal Highland Gathering, Argyllshire in 1951, 1952 and 1953; the British Open Highland Dancing Championship, Edinburgh Festival in 1954; the Braemar Highland Games Championship, won ten times; the Aboyne Highland Games Championship, won twelve times and the Oban Highland Games Championship, won twelve times. Mr McKenzie was still competing and winning Championships when he was in his late forties. His favourite dance was the Highland Fling and, when he won the Coronation Medal at Braemar Gathering, he was thrilled to perform the Fling for the newly crowned Queen.

Mr McKenzie was the principal dancer in the instructional films of Highland Dancing produced by the Scottish Official Board of Highland Dancing and photographs of him were used to illustrate positions and movements in the original textbooks of the SOBHD. Later these photographs were changed to the now-familiar line sketches.

The rapid rise in the standard of Highland Dancing in Canada in the 1960's was largely due to Mr McKenzie's interest and encouragement and his willingness to work untiringly to educate teachers and dancers in the technique of the Scottish Official Board of Highland Dancing.

Mr McKenzie was a founder member of the Scottish Dance Teachers' Alliance and, for many years, he served as one of its favourite examiners and, certainly, one of its best ambassadors. In recognition of his dedication to the art of Highland Dancing, Mr McKenzie was granted the distinction of Member of the British Empire (MBE), which was bestowed upon him at Buckingham Palace by Queen Elizabeth II, The Queen he had danced for so many years before at Braemar. In honour at that time, Miss Elspeth Strathern, another well-known and well-loved Highland Dance teacher, choreographed the dance "A Tribute to J.L. McKenzie".

Such a man was James L. McKenzie, the lad who began dancing in a poorly lit barn loft to the scraping of a violin, the champion who danced for The Queen and the gentleman who shared his love of Highland Dancing with the world. We were deeply honoured and grateful to have had him as a member of the Scottish Dance Teachers Alliance.

Bibliography

Hutchison, Bert Who's Who in Highland Dancing, Winnipeg, Manitoba, 1970

Webster, David Scottish Highland Games. Edinburgh, Scotland: Reprographia, 1973

ELSPETH G. STRATHERN 1922 – 1995

Another renowned member of the Scottish Dance Teachers' Alliance was the previously mentioned Miss Elspeth Strathern. Born in Glasgow, she was a foremost authority in the world of Highland Dancing. In addition to Highland Dance she was trained in classical ballet, stage, modern and tap. Elspeth won the World Highland Dancing Championship at the age of 12. Following this accomplishment, she gave her first dancing display at the Cooper Institute in Cathcart, Glasgow, where so many people turned up that somebody called the Fire Brigade and the show was stopped until all those standing had left the hall.

Miss E Strathern

Miss Strathern began her teaching career with Lillian MacNeil and eventually opened her own school at the Rutherglen Town Hall where she taught a number of dance disciplines for many years. At all times she displayed fair and undivided loyalty to each and every one of her pupils regardless of ability or potential. In return, she earned their loyal, devoted and life-long respect. To her, each and every child was special and her approach was always one of encouragement. Linda Rankin, one of Miss Strathern's World Champion students, remembers her fondly as "having the ability to create a positive teaching and learning environment that was technically, professionally and psychologically complete. She was more than just a teacher and to many of us became as important and well-loved as any family member." During her teaching career, Miss Strathern produced more World Champion Highland Dancers than any other teacher of Highland Dancing. Many of her former students are now well-known teachers and judges of Highland Dancing.

When Royal Doulton produced their series of "Dancers of the World", Miss Strathern was called upon for her technical advice and supplied photographs of Sandra Kennedy, another of her World Champion students, from which the creator made the original mould for the dancer in this series.

Elspeth married John (known as Jack) McLean and they had two daughters - Avril and Meryl - who both enjoyed their dancing lessons but were not competitive dancers. Upon retirement, circa 1980, Elspeth and Jack moved to Vancouver BC, Canada where they lived for twelve years.

Miss Strathern taught and adjudicated throughout Great Britain, North America and Australia. She was an adjudicator for the Scottish Official Board of Highland Dancing, an Examiner and Fellow of the Scottish Dance Teachers' Alliance, a Fellow of the British Association of Teachers of Dancing and an Honorary Member of the SOBHD.

As mentioned, Miss Strathern choreographed 'A Tribute to JL McKenzie' in honour of the man himself. This dance gained much popularity, particularly in North America where Miss Strathern and Mr McKenzie were popular workshop and summer-school instructors. It is interesting to note that both Miss Strathern and Mr McKenzie were judges at the first-ever Canadian Inter-Provincial Championships which were held in Ottawa, Ontario in 1974. In 1995, the Scottish Dance Teachers' Alliance donated a trophy in memory of Elspeth Strathern to ScotDance Canada and the trophy is now competed for annually and presented to the winner of the 12 & 13 year-old Canadian Inter-Provincial Championship.

A most gracious and professionally generous lady, Miss Strathern will long be remembered for her willingness to share her vast experience and knowledge, not only with her pupils, but also with her fellow professionals.

(Biography compiled in 2007 by Donna-Jean Ostrander. Contributors: Linda Rankin and Meryl Campbell)

MAY FALCONER

May Falconer won the World Highland Dancing Championship in 1939 as a juvenlille and in 1948 was the World Adult Champion. She went on to coach 6 world champions and 23 Scottish Champions. She was an Honorary member of the SOBHD, member of UKA & BATD, Fellow and Examiner of the SDTA & Member of the SOBHD judges panel. May was also Convener of the Judges Meetings for a time.

May Falconer

May originally lived in Millburn Street, Motherwell with her Mum and Dad. It was her Dad Jimmy (who was originally from Elgin) who got May into Highland Dancing. However she became seriously ill at the age of twelve after a ruptured appendix and spent nearly a year confined to a wheelchair. That didn't stop May.

She got back into her dancing and was also a pupil of The Sunshine School of Dancing in Glasgow where she studied Tap, Ballet & Ballroom. May married Jimmy Ballantyne who was an excellent Ballroom dancer and the two of them loved to demonstrate their talent regularly in the Empire Theatre in Motherwell. Jimmy also made May's Highland shoes in colours such as red, green, yellow and gold.

May was a laboratory technician in Dalziel until later on when she moved to Stanmore House in Lanark to work with handicapped children. It gave her far more satisfaction and she loved the challenge.

May always put her love for Highland Dancing first. She travelled all over the country competing in Highland Games and competitions with her Dad close by for support. When she danced her heart was always in the dances.

She taught in the Orange Hall in Motherwell and also organised competitions in many places. She attended every meeting she could and anyone who knew May would tell you she loved to voice her opinion, and she certainly did on many occasions. May could make you laugh and cry at the same time. She was great fun to be with and loved to travel. She drove hundreds of miles to judge and every new car she bought would be given a name. If you got wet or dirty at a competition, you could go into the boot of May's car and could be kitted out in full, including the shoes as she kept a suitcase in her car filled with spare clothes and shoes. Nearly every place she visited, she bought at least one pair of shoes.

A most interesting character but sadly she died at the age of 76 from Cancer.

CURRENT HIGHLAND BRANCH EXAMINERS

GREGOR BOWMAN

Gregor started dancing at aged 8 in Dundee where he was born and grew up. He had a successful competitive dancing career over 25 years in the UK and overseas with some of his achievements being:

The World Championship 8 times

The Commonwealth Championship 7 times

The British Open Championship 16 times

The SOBHD Oscar Award 14 times

The Champion of Champions Championship of Australia

North American Championship

Northern Canadian Championship

Atlantic International Championship

Ontario Open Championship

He has also danced in the impressive Ajax football stadium in Amsterdam in front of 60,000 people. On two occasions he was also a guest performer with the Scottish Dance Company of Canada in their production of Immrama and performed as a soloist at the Edinburgh Tattoo on 2 occasions.

Gregor is a Fellow, Examiner and member of the Executive Council of the Scottish Dance Teachers' Alliance and currently the Highland Branch Convener. He is also a member of the SOBHD worldwide panel of adjudicators.

Gregor continues to teach workshops and adjudicate throughout the World and has the opportunity to visit many countries through Highland Dancing such as France, Hungary, Holland, Turkey, Japan, Dubai, South Africa, Canada, USA and Australia.

Outwith Highland Dancing, Gregor works for the Royal Bank of Scotland specialising in Lean methodology.

GAIL DANYSK

Gail Danysk is a Fellow and Life Member of the SDTA, a member of the SOBHD Adjudicators' Panel and Chair of both the ScotDance Canada Judges' Committee and the ScotDance Canada Advisory Committee. As a dancer, she was examined by James L McKenzie on his first examining tour to Western Canada.

She was also examined a number of times by SDTA's wonderful ambassador, Ms. Elspeth Strathern. Highland Dancing has filled Gail's life as a dancer, teacher, judge, and more recently as an SDTA examiner.

She was the original director of the Gillie Callum Highland Dancers in Calgary, and has chaired the ScotDance Canada Championship Series the three times it was held in Calgary. Gail is a school teacher currently in the position of Kindergarten Specialist for the Calgary Board of Education.

LYNNE HAMILTON

Lynne Hamilton started tap and ballet with Jack Muir when she was 3 years old. On reaching 7 she started Tap and Highland with Mrs Margaret Todd and was trained in Ballet by her mum, Jean Hamilton. Mrs Todd trained Lynne for all her Highland exams and competitions and for this Lynne will always be truly grateful.

Lynne was a highly successful competitor in Highland up until she was 21 and has been choreographer for numerous musicals and pantomimes over the years.

She taught with Mrs Todd for 30 years and also opened her own school in Forth in 2000 teaching Highland, Tap, Ballet, Jazz, Disco and Cheerdance.

Lynne is a Fellow and Examiner with the Scottish Dance Teachers' Alliance and an Adjudicator for the Scottish Official Board of Highland Dancing. She has adjudicated, examined and conducted workshops in Scotland, England, Ireland, Holland, America and Canada.

NINA HEMINGWAY

Nina has been teaching Highland Dancing for more than 50 years. Her dancing career began at the age of three in Maryhill, Glasgow with Bessie Findlay for Highland and Evelyn Murray for Tap and Ballet. Evelyn later immigrated to Canada and continued teaching there.

Bessie Findlay retired from teaching when Nina was sixteen years old. Consequently Nina continued her dance education under the expert tuition of Elspeth Strathern. Elspeth trained her for all of her professional exams and Judges test. Being taught by Elspeth was by far the most educational and enjoyable classes of her dancing life.

Nina's daughters Fiona and Catriona Campbell are both SDTA members and SOBHD Adjudicators. Many of Nina's pupils have enjoyed success in competitive dancing, also performances for BBC Television and trips to many places including Japan, Canada, USA, Italy, Switzerland and France.

TREVOR HICKS

Trevor was born in Port Elizabeth, South Africa. He began his career in Highland Dancing at the age of 12, qualifying as a teacher at 18 when he opened his own dancing studio. Following a move to Johannesburg, he studied Highland with Jean Voss under whose guidance he won all the Championships of the time throughout South Africa, including the South African title in 1974.

His competitive career saw him compete not only in South Africa but also in Scotland in 1976 where he was third overall in the British Championship in Edinburgh and fourth overall at the World Championships at Cowal.

Trevor is Fellow, Examiner and Life Member of the SDTA as well as an SOBHD adjudicator.

His experience in the field of dance extends to Ballet, Theatre, Classical Mime & Dance Drama as well as Irish dancing. In all these fields he has accumulated many awards and accolades. Apart from heading his own studios, he has also examined, adjudicated, taught workshops and conducted lectures in England, Canada, the USA, throughout South Africa and Rhodesia. A past Chairman of the Official Board of Highland Dancing (SA), Trevor now lives in London.

SANDRA BALD-JONES

Sandra was a student of Miss Betty Haggart, one of the original members of the SOBHD Technical committee. When the SOBHD was first formed, Sandra along with Marjory Rowan, and Betty Jessieman, presented the "new" technique at a Press Conference in Ayr. Besides Highland Dancing, Sandra studied many forms of dance including: Ballet, Tap, Modern Stage (Jazz), Old Time, Ballroom, and Latin American. She was featured on many TV shows, and before settling down to teach in Canada, toured North America with Scottish Variety Shows.

Sandra was successful in winning every major Championship in Scotland, including the World Juvenile and the World Adult Championships. In fact, the year she won the Adult Worlds, her young student Helen Thomson was the 8 years and under Scottish Champion.

Sandra has taught in Hamilton, ON for over 45 years, during which time she has had many students who have been very successful in competitions. Her students have won all major Championships, including Canadian, Scottish and Worlds. There are a number of great Highland Dance teachers who were at one time students of Sandra's; many of whom have also produced Champions and many have been successful in passing their Judges' exam. She has also taught workshops all over N.A./S.A./Australia/N.Z. and Scotland

Sandra's first major professional project was "Feux Follets", the Canadian Folk Ensemble, which toured all of Canada, Europe and Japan.

Sandra has created hundreds of choreographies and been involved with numerous dance projects, but perhaps the most memorable was the 1981 and 1986 Edinburgh Tattoo, when Sandra's Schiehallion Dancers joined forces with Donna's Annabarrach Dancers of Ottawa, to perform in the Edinburgh Military Tattoo. This honour was again extended to Canadian Dancers in 2002 when Sandra directed an amazing Canadian Team and in 2003 when her own Schiehallion Dancers again took part.

Sandra was nominated for the Dora Mavor Moore Award for her original Choreography in "The Needfire" and this work was also chosen for the prestigious Governor General's Award Show and was nationally broadcast on television.

In 1996, another goal was accomplished with the forming of The Scottish Dance Company of Canada. It was a dream of Sandra's to promote Highland Dancing at the highest possible level and along with Gladys Forrester, Wenda Crawford and Joyce Kite, this dream was realised. The Scottish Dance Company received rave reviews for their original production of "Immrama" which showcased outstanding choreographies and dance performances with an original script and music score composed by Neil Dickie.

With Cathy Hynd, Sandra started the World Of Highland Dancing Conference in Las Vegas 1980 and has been involved in the running of it when it was held every 3 or 4 years until 2006....There have been 9 Conferences!.

Along with Loree Vellner contributed Highland Dance words and terminology to The Dictionary of Dance 1996.

Qualifications and Credentials:

Fellow and Examiner SDTA

Fellow and Life Member BATD

Life Member ScotDance Ontario

SOBHD Judges Panel

Honorary Member ScotDance Canada

Founder Scottish Dance Company of Canada

Director Schiehallion Dancers

Past Executive member ScotDance Canada and ScotDance Ontario.

MARGARET LIVINGSTONE

Margaret has been a successful competitor and loyal Member of the SDTA since passing her Associate exam in 1977 under the expert tuition of Miss Elspeth Strathern. When Miss Strathern retired, she was privileged to be taught by Sheena McDonald.

Her own students were fortunate to have danced in Italy, Spain, France, Russia and the "Great wall" in China! Margaret is an SDTA delegate for the SOBHD and since becoming an Adjudicator in 1989 has been honored to adjudicate both in Scotland and abroad. Margaret has also conducted workshops both in the UK and abroad.

Gaelyn McGregor

Gaelyn McGregor is a Fellow and Examiner with the Scottish Dance Teachers' Alliance and an adjudicator with the Scottish Official Board of Highland Dance. She travels internationally examining, adjudicating and instructing workshops and has developed many champion dancers over the years which include her daughter Colleen McGregor. She has been the principal teacher since 1977 of the McGregor Studio of Dance in Winnipeg, Canada holding classes in her studio as well as at Balmoral Hall School for girls.

As a dancer, Gaelyn's highlights were winning the British Overseas Adult Championship in Musselburgh, 5th Runner-up in the Adult World Championship and Best Overseas Dancer at the Royal Braemar Gathering as well as countless Manitoba and Mid-Canada Championships, 1st Runner-Up in the Intercontinental Championship, the pre-cursor to the Canadian Championships and the Northern Canadian Championship.

Gaelyn was the first recipient of the "Lord Strathcona Award" sponsored by the St. Andrew's Society for her tireless contributions of keeping the Scottish Heritage and Culture alive in Manitoba.

Margaret is an active Highland Branch Committee Member and was Highland Branch Entries Secretary for nine years. As a Fellow of the SDTA since 1991 it is the ultimate achievement to serve as an SDTA Examiner to which she was appointed in 2009.

JANICE MCQUARRIE

Janice Macquarrie, a former champion Highland dancer began her dancing career in Antigonish, Nova Scotia at age nine. She competed for fourteen years then went on to train many dancers in her area. Many of her students have won major awards including Nova Scotia, Canadian and North American titles as well as first and second runner-up positions in World Championships. She is also an award-winning choreographer and has choreographed many pieces for Nova Scotia tourism as well as different events throughout her province.

Janice holds her Fellow certificate with the Scottish Dance Teachers' Alliance and is a full panel adjudicator with the Scottish Official Board of Highland Dancing. She has enjoyed judging and giving workshops throughout Canada as well as Scotland, Australia, New Zealand and the United States.

Besides running her dance school, Janice is also a Grade two teacher with the Strait Regional School Board in Antigonish.

SHEENA MCDONALD

Sheena started dancing at a very early age and trained in ballet/tap at the Glasgow Ballet School which she now teaches, along with Highland and wheelchair dancing.

Her Highland training was given by her sister Anne and with this training she won many Championships including the Juvenile World's and three times winner of the Adult's (no junior in the good old days). Both Anne and Sheena studied together to become examiners with the SDTA and Judges with the SOBHD. Sheena's granddaughter, Sheena junior, has joined the family tradition.

Sheena has toured Australia, Belgium, Canada, Holland, Japan and the USA. As an Independent member of the SOBHD she is at present on the current technical and judges committee.

Sheena's career was crowned when she was the recipient of the Atholl clasp for her dedication to Highland Dancing.

PATRICIA MCMASTER

Pat is formerly from Scotland and has been in Canada since 1974. She was a full time student at the Lillian McNeil School of Dance in Glasgow, where she received her Highland training from Elspeth Strathern.

In addition to being an examiner, Life member and Fellow of the SDTA and SOBHD Judges Panel, Pat has qualifications with BATD, ISTD in Tap and Modern and also advanced RAD Ballet.

She successfully runs her own studio in Niagara-on-the-lake, Ontario. Her students have won many Championships in Canada, USA, Australia and Scotland including the Junior and Juvenile World titles. Pat has also judged the World and Commonwealth Championships.

IRENE MILLER

Irene Miller is an Examiner and Life member of the SDTA and started dancing at the age of 3. Ms Miller became qualified in all branches and became an examiner in the Highland branch. Ms Miller is an adjudicator with the SOBHD and was a delegate for the Alliance for a number of years. She has examined and judged overseas and is a member of the Highland Branch Committee.

Irene began her teaching career at the age of 15 and enjoys teaching choreography in all branches. She has been a member of the SDTA for over 40 years.

MYRA MILLER

Myra started dancing at the Lillian McNeil School of Dance, Glasgow. Her teachers being Elspeth Strathern - Highland, Nancy Moore - Stage and Lillian McNeil - Ballet.

After taking qualifications with the SDTA and BATD Myra taught at the Lillian McNeil School for four years before opening her own classes in East Kilbride.

For the past thirty years her pupils have competed successfully in the UK, Canada and the USA.

Myra represents the Alliance on the SOBHD Technical Committee and was recently elected to the Judges Committee. She is also the SOBHD Delegate for the Caledonian Club of San Francisco's

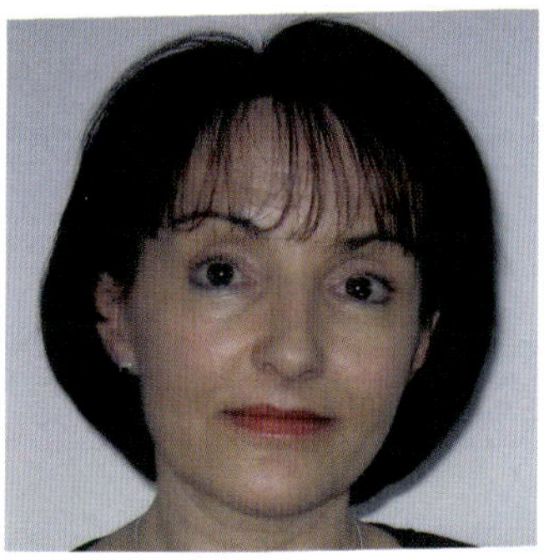

LINDA RANKIN

Linda started dancing at the age of six and had the honour of training under the expert eye of Miss Elspeth Strathern for the whole of her competitive and professional training. During her competitive career she won all major British Championship titles. Her ultimate success was achieved when she won the World Championship title three times, Junior in 1973 and Senior in 1975 and 1977.

In the interests of Highland Dancing, Linda has travelled extensively worldwide, competing, lecturing and judging. She is a Member of the BATD, a Fellow of the UKA and a Fellow and Examiner with the SDTA. She also has a teaching qualification from the Royal Country Dance Society. Linda is currently ScotDance Canada's Head delegate to the Scottish Official Board of Highland Dancing in Edinburgh and serves on the Board's Registration, Disciplinary and Quality Assurance Committees.

Linda has been involved in Highland Dancing now for over thirty years and ran her own dancing school in both Glasgow and Beith. She is currently Principal Teacher of Pupil Support at Garnock Academy, one of the largest high schools in the west of Scotland.

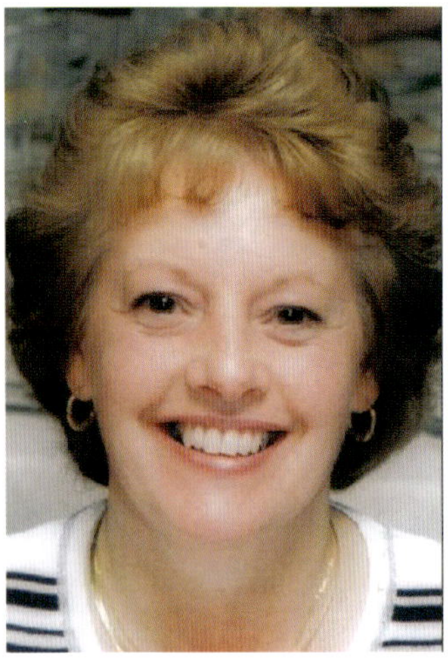

AILEEN ROBERTSON

Aileen Robertson has judged many Canadian, United States and Australian Championships and teaches workshops throughout the world. She has recently returned from her first trip to New Zealand.

Aileen started dancing at the age of seven from which she continued her career by winning every major Championship title in Scotland including the British Open, United Kingdom and Commonwealth. She also won the mid Canada Championship in Winnipeg. The highlight of her career was winning the World Championship three times, the junior title in 1972 & the adult in 1974 & 1976. Aileen also won the Oscar Award for Champion of Champions.

Aileen is a fellow and examiner of the Scottish Dance Teachers Alliance & was taught by Elspeth Strathern. She is a life member of the BATD & a member of the UKA.

Aileen is Head delegate to the SOBHD representing Fusta & is on the Registration Committee of the SOBHD. She is depute delegate for the SDTA on the SOBHD technical committee.

Aileen has a successful dancing school based in Ayr, having had many successes in choreography as well as training pupils to world-class level.

MARGARET TODD (RETIRED EXAMINER)

Mrs Todd is a life member of the SDTA and before retiring was on the Highland branch examining panel. As a teacher of dance and piano she has guided many pupils to a very high standard in competitive field. Among her pupils is Lynne Hamilton, another examiner with the SDTA.

As an independent member of the SOBHD she served for many years on their technical and judges committee and on the judge's panel.

With her resignation as an independent member Mrs Todd was made an honorary member of the SOBHD and was also a recipient of the Atholl clasp for her life long dedication to Highland Dancing.

BILL TROOCK

Born and raised in Edmonton Alberta, Bill has been an active teacher, adjudicator and choreographer for over 30 years. His students have won many Championship titles throughout North America and Scotland, including three Canadian Inter-Provincial titles. In addition, his students have successfully finished in the top six in the Juvenile, Junior and Adult World Championships.

Bill began dancing at the age of 6 with Pat Horlor. Over the years, his teachers have included Angus MacKenzie, Heather McGregor and Evelyn Jones.

He is a Member of the World Wide Judges' Panel of the Scottish Official Board of Highland Dancing (S.O.B.H.D.); a Fellow and Examiner with the Scottish Dance Teachers' Alliance (S.D.T.A.); a Member with the British Association of Teachers of Dancing (B.A.T.D.); Independent Member of ScotDance Canada; Life Member of the Alberta Highland Dancing Association.

In 1986 & 2000, he chaired the ScotDance Canada Championship Series held in Edmonton. Bill continues to play an active role with ScotDance Canada as the National Chair for the Competition Organizers Committee and a member of the Advisory Committee. He also serves on the Executive of the Edmonton Highland Dancing Association and Highland Dance Teachers & Judges of Alberta.

Bill has travelled extensively throughout Canada, United States, Australia, South Africa and Scotland adjudicating, examining and conducting workshops. In 2006, Bill travelled to New Zealand to conduct workshops and had the honour of judging their first SOBHD Championship and then again in 2007 judged the first New Zealand National Championship.

In 1995 along with his teaching partners Kelly Abrahart and Jacques Bourgouin, they opened the Strathcona School of Dancing where they continue to teach together. In addition to his dancing, Bill is currently employed by Sabre Inc. as the Senior National Sales Manager.

The Scottish Dance Teachers Alliance
Current Highland Branch Examiners

The following list contains current Highland Branch examiners who did not supply a biography:

Miss Deborah Ward

Miss Jean Hislop

Miss Donna Cram

Mrs Irene Baird

Mrs Caroline MacNicol

Highland Branch Examiners Dinner

The SDTA is proud to recognise their members who have won the adult world Championship.

May Falconer

J.L.Mackenzie

Sheena Mcdonald

Sandra Bald

Irene Mackecknie

Victor Wellsley

Angus Mackenzie

Aileen Robertson

Linda Rankin

Helen Fitzpatrick

Lesley Bowman

Gregor Bowman

Jacqueline Smith

Tony Cargill

Central Scotland Championships

The Cental Scotland Championship was started in 1974 and the organiser was Miss Elspeth Strathern

The first venue was the Woodside Halls in Glasgow and the age groups were under 12 years, under 16 years and adults.

Due to increase in the number of entries bigger premises had to be found and the next few venues included Hamilton Town Hall, Palace of Arts, Jordanhill College and St. Andrews College.

The present venue is The Kelvin Hall in Glasgow and this has two large arenas to accommodate the vast increase in number of today's competitors so much so that we now have pre-Championships and Championships in single ages.

The motto in the Glasgow coat of arms is "let Glasgow flourish". Ours should be "Highland Dancing is flourishing".

Past Presidents

2004 - 2007	Warren Brown
2001 - 2004	Betty Sutherland
1997 - 2001	Sheena McDonald
1982 - 1996	Johnny Stewart
1973 - 1981	Nancy Moore
1971 - 1972	Jean J McLellan
1970 - 1971	John McKinnie
1969 - 1970	Alex S. Warren
1961 - 1968	Joe McGowan
1957 - 1960	Paul H. Collins
1953 - 1956	Jean H. Lindsay
1952	Alice McEwan
1949-1951	Jack Muir
1948	John G. Warren
1946-1947	Roger McEwan
1944-1945	Nellie Warren
1942-1943	Douglas Thomson
1935-1941	Alex S. Warren
1934	Joseph A. Warren

THE PRESIDENT'S BALL — Andrew McCowan

Composed to commemorate the Diamond Jubilee of the Scottish Dance Teachers' Alliance and presented to SDTA President Johnny Stewart at the President's Ball on 5 March 1994.

The President's Ball

Composed to commemorate the Diamond Jubilee of the SDTA

From right: Loree Vellner, Elspeth Strathern, James L. McKenzie, Sheila McGillivray, Christine Robertson, Margaret Todd.

The SDTA held a workshop from which Margaret Todd left to conduct her first examining tour.

The United Kingdom Alliance of Professional Teachers of Dancing

THE HISTORY OF THE UKA

By David Roberts

At the turn of the century, "Ballroom Dancing" was very different from today. With the Charleston still to emerge in 1907, the Foxtrot in 1914 and the 'Modern' Waltz in 1920, the scene was one of "Sequence Dancing". These were the Lancers, Quadrilles, Waltz and Polka etc., plus some of the Old Time dances which still survive to this day.

Although the BATD had been formed in 1892, there were no Examinations or Syllabus. In 1902, at Finnegan's Ballroom, Manchester, several dance teachers in the North met together and decided to form an Alliance. They were all "Dancing Masters & Madames" and all full time professionals. An account was opened in the name of "The United Kingdom Alliance of Professional Teachers of Dancing and Kindred Arts" and each paid the handsome sum of a □ guinea (10/6 or 52 □ p) as subscription. It was agreed that the 'brains' behind the idea Mr. James Finnegan, would be the acting President. By the beginning of 1903, twenty one members were enrolled. To promote the new Alliance, a Conference was held in Seven Sisters Road, Holloway, London in June 1903 and the first President elected was Mr W. H. Roe of London. Mr Alf Brown became Secretary and Mr J. B. McEwan of Glasgow, the Treasurer. Among the register of those who attended at that first Conference were people whose names may not be too familiar but their dances survive to this day: Mr Tom Almond (The Fylde Waltz and Barn Dance): Mr A. Morris (Veleta); Tom Hayton (Carina Waltz) and one of the motivators of the formation of the Alliance, James Finnigan (Military Two Step). It was interesting that under Kindred Arts and the Alliance Constitution covered opera and sword fencing.

1905 Saw the first overseas members and Mr S. F. Conley, Mr W. F. Brown and Mr Tom Walton (Boston Two Step) all joined the Alliance from the USA. 1907 saw the doubling of the subscription fee to 1 guinea (£1.05) and all members were issued with a certificate and badge. At this stage, examinations did not exist. Only members who were full time Professionals were accepted on the recommendation of the existing membership.

1908 Mr J. Wilkinson of Australia, joined the membership list and the total membership for the year was 56. Although an Annual General Meeting and Election were held each year, it was 1911 before a large scale event was planned. This was held at Derby Castle in the Isle of Man. It lasted for a full week with lectures, discussions and competitions. At this event, it was decided that this style of conference would be an Annual event and Blackpool was decided upon as the next venue.

At the outbreak of World War 1 in 1914, the membership stood at 75. This same year saw the founding of the Scottish Branch (as it was called then). The Alliance continued through the war and in 1916, Conference left Blackpool and was held in Morecambe Tower Ballroom. At this event, it was decided to form Areas in Lancashire and Yorkshire. In 1923, the famous 'Hibbert' family joined the Alliance (You will all remember Madame Lily Fishwick (Hibbert) who served the U.K.A. with great gusto for many years, being Secretary of the Ballroom Branch.

1924 The U.K.A., along with seven other Society delegates, met in Blackpool and 5 guineas subscription was paid to form The Central Council. This developed into The Official Board of Ballroom Dancing and later The British Council of Dance (BDC). By 1926, the membership (still restricted to full time Professionals only) stood at 100. Madame Hibbert attended a meeting in 1928 during which rules were discussed for all Societies.

1930's Saw great headway in the World of Dance and of course in the Alliance and examinations and medal tests in Ballroom, Theatre and Operatics were in full swing. When 1939 saw the outbreak of War, with much of our membership involved with the war effort, the Alliance went through the quietest years of its existence. With our dear Louie Wilkinson at the helm as President, she guided the U.K.A. through the war years and examinations and meetings still continued.

1946 Another Finnigan, Joan and her husband Frank Gibson, joined us together with Cecil Raw, Jack Bradley and Miss Jean Rowbotham. By 1949, the Alliance was bigger and stronger than 10 years earlier and the Annual Conference was held in Edinburgh.

1949 Also saw the Alliance playing an innovative role in Highland Dancing. An incident at the Cowel Highland Gathering in that year, saw a dispute which proved difficult to resolve. In consultation with Miss Peggy McDonald (the Chairperson of our Highland Examiners), Marjory Fairley (our President) and her husband Harry, called a meeting between all the Presidents of Associations. This was held at Mr Mowet's studio in Stirling in January, 1950. The S.O.B.H.D. was formed as a direct result of this action.

1950 Conference was held in July, in the Blackpool Winter Gardens, organised by Madame Illet (also organiser of The British for many years) with Louie Wilkinson in the Chair, Madame Fishwick Vice President and Harry Boyle as General Secretary. At this event, the Scottish Country Dance Branch was formed, being the first of its kind in this dance form and also, the London Area was formed. The Theatre Branch held its own Conference in Manchester the following week. Lecturers at Blackpool included Eric Hancox, Frank Gibson and Harry Boyle. This Conference also saw another first for the UKA the first ever Official Board of Ballroom Dancing Scrutineers' Examinations were held. Fifteen candidates took the examination and this was the start of the system that now exists throughout the world. The famous 'Gainsborough Glide' won both the Inventive at this event and also The Official Board Trophy, compiled by our own Marjorie Fairley. Frank Gibson was elected the new President and Miss Jean Rowbotham became Treasurer. Motions passed included one that the General Secretary is automatically an OB delegate.

1951 The Irish Area was formed and the U.K.A. promoted the All England Championships at Hammersmith Palais. We were proud that our Technical Advisor, Mr Eric Hancox had been appointed Chairman of the newly formed Official Board Latin American Technical Committee with the portfolio to standardise the technique. The OB Sequence Advisory Committee was formed. Conference took place at the Savoy Hotel, Blackpool from 18-20th July, with Frank Gibson, President.

Another immortal dance, the 'Lilac Waltz' devised by Alf Halford won both our Inventive and OB Trophy. It is interesting from the Conference Report, that Eric Hancox conducted the 'Fun & Games' at the annual dinner. (A scene that I have tried to picture but have great difficulty). The Highland Branch was flourishing with Ada Calder as Secretary (remember Branch Secretaries processed all the medals and certificates then) and they welcomed new members from as far afield as Australia and Argentina.

1952 Conference was held at the Savoy Hotel, Blackpool 6-8th July. Frank Gibson President. The EC then consisted of just 4 members, plus the President, Vice Presidents and General Secretary. This was the 50th Jubilee year and Alf Halford again won the Inventive with the 'Jubilee Tango'. Lecturers included, Connie Grant, Eric Stonehouse, Dougie Hall and Sylvester Burrows (who was a member of our EC for many years). The Highland Branch reported a large increase in medal tests and Miss Moira Ronald took over as Branch Secretary, a lady who was to take the Branch on a big upward curve. The Northern Area started a fund for a new chain of office with a donation. It was reported that less than 10% of the membership were attending Area Meetings. Eric Hancox as Chairman of the New OB Latin Committee expressed disappointment that more were not taking the new professional Latin exam.

1953 A General Meeting was held in the Grand Hotel, Manchester in February. The purpose of the meeting was to adopt the accounts for the previous year. It was resolved at this meeting to hold Conference in June because of accommodation in Blackpool being fully booked for the Royal Show. At this Conference, the posts of General Secretary and Treasurer were combined. Mjr Eric Hancox was elected President. Alf Halford again won the Inventive with the 'Westminster Waltz'.

1954 General Meeting was again held in the Grand Hotel in January. Conference was held in The Savoy Hotel 11-13th July with Eric Hancox President. Harry Boyle resigned as General Secretary and Mr Wilf Ashworth took over the post. Mdme Fishwick became President with Frank Gibson, Jean Rowbotham and Ernest Derby as Vice Presidents. The EC were Sylvester Burrows, Arthur Hall, Edith Taylor and Mr A. Smith. John Evans from North Wales won the Inventive with the 'Louetta Tango'.

1955 The General Meeting again held in Manchester in January. An apology was given for Mr Wilfred Orange who had been caught in a snow drift on his journey from London. Conference was held in the Savoy Hotel, Blackpool 3-5th July. Phyllis Haylor lectured on training methods and Eric Hancox taught mambo. Joyce Simmonds of Rhyl won the Inventive with 'Melody Two Step'. Marjorie Fairley was elected President.

1956 The Bi-Annual Meeting was held in the Grand Hotel, Manchester during January, with Conference again at Blackpool's Savoy Hotel. Marjorie Fairley was President with Mdme Fishwick, Harry Boyle and Eric Hancox Vice Presidents. Inventive winners Sylvester Burrows 'Candlelight Waltz' and John Evans 'Riversdale Waltz' (OT).

1957 Bi-Annual Meeting in Manchester. The General Secretary, Mr Ashworth submitted his resignation. Mr Sam Ferguson was appointed to take his place from the Conference onwards. Part-time teachers were to be allowed to take Fellowship exams, previously restricted to full-timers. A study into the possibility of becoming a Limited Company was started. Mjr Eric Hancox partnered by Ann Green taught the Blues Jive. Conference was again in the Savoy Hotel and for the first time in the Alliance's history, the President did not attend. Marjorie Fairley was overseas at this time. Mr Harry Boyle was elected President.

1958 After just a few months in the office, Mr Sam Ferguson resigned as General Secretary in January at the Bi-Annual Meeting. The President, Mr Boyle, agreed to take over the position in a caretaker capacity until a successor was found. It was also passed that 'Persons qualified by examination with a recognised body', may join the Alliance without further examination. Sam Clegg was elected Chairman of the Ballroom Branch. Conference was held at the Alma Lodge Hotel, Stockport on 20/21st July and at this Conference, Miss Louie Wilkinson took over as General Secretary, a position she held until 1990.

1959 The Bi-Annual Meeting was conducted during February and Conference was held for the first time since 1903, in London. The venue was the Cora Hotel and Harry Boyle was returned as President unopposed with Miss Rowbotham, Mr Gibson and Miss Taylor as Vice President. Mr Gibson took over upon his arrival. Conference went back to the Savoy in Blackpool when Mr Sam Clegg was elected President with Jean Rowbotham, Frank Gibson and Edith Taylor as Vice Presidents.

Meeting in Edinburgh in 1960's

1961 The Bi-Annual Meeting was held in April in Manchester with conference in Blackpool on 10/11th June at the Savoy. It was at this Conference that Eric Rowland was welcomed as a new member, together with Bobby Short and Marjorie Rowan. Sam Clegg was returned as President.

1962 This year saw Conference move to the Pump Rooms in Bath and in the absence of the President, Miss

Rowbotham took the chair. Sir Billy Butlin, Mr P.J.S. Richardson and Dame Anna Neagle were all granted Honorary Membership. Miss Edith Taylor was elected President with Doreen Beahan, Louie Wilkinson and Bob Dale as Vice Presidents.

1963 The last Bi-Annual Meeting held, after which it was voted that they be discontinued. Scotland was to be the venue for Conference and the Carlton Hotel, Edinburgh the chosen venue and Edith Taylor was again elected President with Bob Dale Senior Vice President.

1964 Conference held at the Imperial Hotel, Blackpool 18/19th July. Edith Taylor in the Chair. Miss Taylor was again elected and Mr Dale Senior Vice President.

1966 Back to London for Conference at the Bedford Corner Hotel on 18/19th June when U.S.A. Area was formed. Edith Taylor again President.

1967 The Midland Hotel, Manchester hosted Conference. Our U.S.A. Area came under scrutiny of the International Council of Ballroom Dancing and we were prohibited from conducting tests in the U.S.A. It was passed that President could only hold office for three consecutive years.

1968 The Majestic Hotel, St. Annes was the chosen venue for Conference with Edith again retaining the Chair.

1969 Scotland again at the North British Hotel Edinburgh. Much discussion on 'The Morley Scheme' for amateurs to teach. As there was not a quorum, the meeting was changed to an Extraordinary General Meeting but after a while enough members arrived to form the desired quorum. It was voted that a committee be elected to make a general review of the Alliance and report to the 1970 Conference. The end of 1969 saw my entry into the Alliance and together with John and Arlene Leach, I was examined at Bob Dale's Studio in Albert Square, Manchester by Miss Janet Ball.

1970's Was probably the greatest era of the Alliance when Bob Dale, Tom Walker and Jimmy Benwell all brought their magic touches to the UKA as Presidents. 1971 was my Conference debut when I spoke to support the motion that Associates be given voting power needless to say it got through and for the first time in the Alliance history. Associates voted for the President and Council.

Right from its founding in Manchester in 1902 and first Conference in London 1903, the UKA was set to be a leader in the Dance World. Always being the leader over the years we were innovators setting the trends for others to follow. The Alliance continued uninterrupted even through the war years. The 50's and 60's saw some internal strife but by the end of the 60's a forward thinking leadership was to change the direction and prospects of the Alliance.

The 70's & 80's saw what will always be regarded as crucial years for the UKA. A period of great turmoil from which the Alliance developed from its parochial roots into a truly International Organisation. Conference was held in 1970 again in the Winter Gardens. Demonstrators at the dinner were Michael Houseman & Valerie Waite and Phil Cockram took both Inventive prizes. The membership at this time stood at 800 with more than 40% being from the Old Time Branch, 30% Highland, 25% Ballroom & Latin and a mere 5% Theatre. At this Conference, a motion was carried that the position of President could only be held for a maximum of three consecutive years. Mr Bob Dale was returned as President with Mr Walker, Mr Sage and Mr Basketter as Vice Presidents.

1971 June saw a change of venue to the Cliffs Hotel, Blackpool for the Annual Conference with Bob Dale in the Chair. Rita Pover taught the 'Balmoral Blues', a prize winner at Slough. The first Latin Inventive competition was won by Doris Latham of Burnley with the Samba Menorca. Phil and Janet Jackson demonstrated in the evening. During the previous 12 months, more than 200 new members entered the Alliance. A motion was carried that Associates could now have voting powers. Previously only those with Membership degrees had voting powers. This was proposed by Mr Walker and seconded by yours truly.

1972 The Imperial Hotel, Blackpool hosted the Conference with Bob Dale again in the Chair. A change in construction had already become evident by 1972 with Old Time 30%, Ballroom and Latin 30%, Highland 32%, and Theatre 8%. Mr Tom Walker became President with Edith Taylor, Phil Cockram and Jane Ball as Vice Presidents. Bob Dale proposed that the U.K.A. became a Limited Company and on September 3rd, 1972 at an Extraordinary Meeting at the Midland Hotel, Manchester a Limited Company was formed.

1973 And Conference was back at the Winter Gardens. During this year, Miss Edith Taylor was appointed Examination Secretary thus taking over the work previously done on an individual branch basis. Tom Walker was again returned as President with Mr Benwell, Miss Taylor and Mr Dale as Vice Presidents.

1974 Again at the Winter Gardens, the name of Ted Burroughs appeared in the Winning Frame for his 'Barbara Swing'. During this Conference Mr Walker gave reasons why the U.K.A. should support the Amateurs' Coaching Scheme as it was the way the Dance World would eventually go. He was heckled and told he was completely wrong.......? More than 700 members had joined since Conference 1973.

1975 Still at the Winter Gardens with Tom Walker in the Chair. Ted Burroughs, Ken & Vi Agar and Bob & Wyn Oliver heading the winning list for the Inventives. Tom Walker finished his three year term of office and in his speech he said, "I leave a Society very different from the one I joined 16 years ago and what I have started, I intend, with your help, to continue". Once again, more than 600 new members were welcomed since the last Conference. Mr Jimmy Benwell was elected President with Tom Walker, Bob Dale and Edith Taylor as Vice Presidents.

1976 Saw a record number of members attending Conference with Jimmy Benwell again returned as President.

1977 Was the year that the Blackpool Office was opened. Conference was again at the Winter Gardens and membership passed the 3,000 mark. This was the year that I was first elected a Councillor of the U.K.A.

1978 Saw the Disco Medal Tests introduced. Bob Dale was again elected as President with Mr Beeton, Miss Taylor and Mr Dawson as Vice Presidents. It was this year that John Leach and Bryan Allen joined the Council and the new office in Manchester was opened.

1979 Again at the Winter Gardens with Bob Dale in the Chair. For the first time ever, there was a dead heat for President between Edith Taylor and Paul Beeton. After a re-vote, Edith was elected.

1980 Saw the Conference move to the Norbreck and Edith Taylor again took the position of President. The death of Mr Fred Dawson was sadly recorded at this Conference.

1981 The introduction of the first Professional Disco Examinations. Still at the Norbreck and the year that Ted Burroughs was elected to the Council and my first year as an Official Board Delegate.

1982 Had a very hard winter and burst water pipes at the Blackpool Office damaged £1000's of stock. Luckily we were insured. Conference was once again at the Norbreck. Donnie Burns & Gaynor Fairweather were the demonstrators at the Dinner. The start of the AGM was delayed whilst the General Secretary, Louie Wilkinson, returned to the Manchester Office for some vital documents!!! Bob Dale was elected to serve another term as President.

1983 Conference at the Norbreck Castle again and Bob Dale was re-elected as President.

1984 Saw the introduction of a Rock 'n' Roll Syllabus for Amateurs and Professionals. It is interesting to note that another prominent Society within the last few months (of 1996) is advertising in the Dance Press that they have "the only Rock 'n' Roll Medal Test and Professional Syllabus in the UK". Bob Dale was re-elected as President and at the top of the Hat Parade yes, that's right not Hit Parade but Hat Parade, was Miss Judy Clegg who won the "Glamorous Hat Competition".

1985 Miss Jean Rowbotham was elected President at Conference at the Norbreck with Eric Rowland, Bob Dale and Derek Young taking the Vice President's positions.

1986 Norbreck again. Miss Taylor was elected President with Ted Burroughs, Eric Rowland and myself as Vice Presidents. The exercise and Movement Faculty was introduced. A motion opposing the imposition of Juvenile Dress Rule was given to the OB delegates as the membership felt it would lead to a decline in entries for these events. A proposal by Mr Dale and myself to drop the word Professional from our title was defeated. We do battle with the VAT and win so we de-register! A very costly legal battle.

1987 Once again at the Norbreck and Miss Taylor was returned unopposed with Vice Presidents Ted Burroughs, Bob Dale and myself. It was asked that OB delegates submit that Inventive Competitions should be controlled so that the dances for selection should be named in advance so that a good cross section of rhythms could be introduced. (This still sounds like a good idea). The UKA's suggested rule change that 'Adjudicators should not be allowed to adjudicate participants that they have trained' was also defeated at the rule change meeting.

1988 Back at the Norbreck and this year we were graced by the presence of Frances Shand Kydd (Mother of Diana, Princess of Wales) who had contributed to our Hebridean Dances Syllabus which had been compiled by Sheila McKay. Edith was re-elected as President with Ted Burroughs, Bob Dale and myself as Vice Presidents. It was during 1988 that everything was brought under one roof at Blackpool and later that year, I was appointed Deputy General Secretary to assist Miss Wilkinson at the Blackpool Office.

Frances Shand Kydd & David Roberts

1989 Ted Burroughs was elected President at Conference again at the Norbreck with Janet Ball, Eric Rowland and Bob Dale elected as Vice Presidents. This year saw the pilot scheme for a written exam for Professionals introduced on a voluntary basis and this year, we were pleased to welcome many more overseas visitors than in the previous years.

The U.K.A. was beginning to settle down into a new era as we saw the retirement from the General Offices of both Louie Wilkinson and Edith Taylor.

The 90's also presented new challenges with the appointment of an entirely new Head Office Staff, the purchase of new premises (and subsequently, the further purchase of the adjoining building) and eventually to the palatial 12,000 sq ft of Centenary House. We truly went into the 90's prepared for the future. We have seen a change of the Company name to the United Kingdom Alliance (although the original title rights remain) a postal vote for President, together with the new post of President Elect, the creation of our Annual Mini Conferences at Weston, Aberdeen, Kirkcaldy and London, and the general development of the UKA into a truly International Alliance which is a major player in the Worldwide Family of Dance. All of this has been achieved by being totally independent and by facing the future and embracing the changing face of dance head on.

2002 The UKA celebrated its Centenary as a totally individual, independent body, which was well equipped to launch into its second Century. President of the Society was David Roberts; Senior Vice President was Anna Bain; Vice Presidents were Eric Rowlands and Sue Burroughs. At the Annual Conference, one of the dance displays was conducted by Billy Forsyth, President of the Scottish Official Board of Highland Dancing, who presented the 'Edinburgh Tatoo Dancers' who displayed very colourful, up to date work in addition to the traditional sword dance. Billy then presented David Roberts with an 18th Century picture of Edinburgh Castle in recognition of the support which David had provided to Highland Dancing. At the Aberdeen Mini Conference the guests in attendance included Irene Baird and Heather Jolly who were both from Canada.

2003 This year saw Malcolm McLean, Fellow and Examiner of the UKA and an SOBHD Adjudicator awarded an MBE for services to the community which included teaching of Highland, National and Hebridean Dances to the Western Isles of Scotland. Billy Forsyth received an honorary membership of the society. Anna Bain and Rhona Lawrence presented sponsorship towards the first ever Scottish National Highland Dancing Championships which were held at Cowal Highland Gathering. The Adult Winner was Ross Croll from Dundee. Janet Gardner received her Life Membership of the UKA.

2004 President : Jackie Sanderson; President Elect : Ann Green; Senior Vice President : Anna Bain; Vice Presidents : Eric Rowland and Sue Burroughs. This year at the Annual Conference in Blackpool lecturers included Gregor Bowman, Former World Highland Dance Champion.

Rohna Lawrence & Ann Green

2005 President : Ann Green; President Elect : Jackie Sanderson; Senior Vice President : Graham Crookes; Vice Presidents : Sue Burroughs and Rhona Lawrence. Rhona was presented with an award by Ann Green in recognition of her services to the Annual Highland Gathering event held in Aberdeen.

2006 President : Ann Green; President Elect : Jackie Sanderson; Senior Vice President : Graham Crookes; Vice Presidents : Sue Burroughs and Rhona Lawrence. A Major face-lift was carried out at Centenary House with an expanded Examination Service Department taking over another floor and the creation of a new multi purpose studio and meeting room.

2007 President : Jackie Sanderson; President Elect : Ann Green; Vice President : Rhona Lawrence. Billy Forsyth was awarded an MBE for his outstanding contribution to Highland Dancing. The Annual Conference in Blackpool was dedicated to the memory of Bob Dale who had been president 16 years earlier. One of the demonstrations at the Annual Conference was provided by the Highland Oscar Winners.

Oscar Winners 2007
Eilidh McMillan, David Wilton, Heather Adams, Charlene McMahon

2008 President : Jackie Sanderson; President Elect : Ann Green; Vice President : Rhona Lawrence. Mina Mckay received a Lifetime Achievement Award at the Aberdeen Highland Gathering from Jackie Sanderson and Betty Jessiman was welcomed as the 'Queen of Highland' for her services to dance.

2009 President : Ann Green; Vice President : Paul Beeton. Highland Gathering Championship held at Holyrood Park, Edinburgh. Rhona Lawrence and Christine Lacey, Chairman of SOBHD introduced to Prince of Wales. Dancing demonstration given at the Annual Blackpool Conference by Nicola Bowie, Victoria Buchan, Jan Louise Doherty and Lynne Lawrence. President Elect Paul Beeton passed away in June 2009.

2010 UKA gains CDET Validation. Annual Blackpool Conference is dedicated to Paul Beeton

Rhona Lawrence and Christine Lacey meet Prince Charles.

SHEILA MCKAY

"Our Sheila"

Sheila McKay, as she was known nationally and internationally, was born on 26th March, 1920. She was the youngest in a family of four, having two brothers and a sister. Born in Leslie, where she spent all her childhood and most of her teens, those early years she remembered as being a very happy period in her life.

Sheila's mother, Mary, being a talented dancing teacher, taught all her own children to dance. She actually had Sheila dancing at the age of two. Little did Sheila know then, just how much those first few steps were going to influence the rest of her life. By the age of six she was competing in dancing events all over Scotland. Four years later she was off to London with her elder brother John.

In London she danced for Queen Mary and went to Buckingham Gate where she competed against adult dancers (being the first child to do so). The newspapers got hold of the story about the "young girl from Scotland" travelling all over London and they nicknamed her "Sheila the Hustler."

In 1934, she went on to win the World Highland Dancing Championships and this was followed by her holding for five years the Scottish Tap and Russian Dancing Championships. At the age of twelve she started to teach dancing but continued to compete and entertain. For four years she entertained on the liner S.S. Paris the liner was sunk during the Second World War whilst serving as a troop carrier.

Sheila left school at fifteen and worked fulltime for one year teaching dancing. She then left Leslie to stay in Edinburgh where she worked in the Waverly Market Circus. She did Russian, ballet, highland and tap dancing and as well as dancing she was trained to work as a bareback rider on the horses. Sometimes she would help out with the elephants. Her most daring exploit was practising on the tightrope. On one occasion, the tightrope-walker, whose assistant had fallen ill, asked Sheila to assist him. Part of his act included walking the rope through a ring of flames 95 feet up in the air with Sheila on his shoulders. Mary, Sheila's mother had been listening to coverage of the event on the radio. When the broadcaster mentioned "Sheila, the little lady from Leslie," Mary realised it was her daughter he was talking about and she promptly fainted.

Not long after the circus event Mary Bain died and Sheila, at the age of nineteen, returned to Leslie to stay with her father. During the war Sheila went to work in munitions and was employed by a company in Leslie named De-la-Rue. Before war broke out they had manufactured pens but then they went into the production of tracer bullets and moulded parts for aeroplanes. Even during this period the dancing prevailed. Sheila taught the girls in the factory to dance and they formed a dancing troup naming themselves "the Blue Bird Girls", they entertained at concerts and factories in the area.

Sheila and her husband Bruno had two children, a son Andrew, born in 1947, and a daughter Anna, born in 1953. It should be mentioned that Anna, true to the Bain tradition, follows in her mother's footsteps and is 'dancing mad'. As well as teaching dancing full-time, Anna judges competitions and is a fully qualified examiner.

During the first year of the war, Sheila met King Peter of Yugoslavia and Queen Wilhelmina of Denmark, who had both come to Britain as refugees.

After the war, Sheila continued with her dance tuition and built up a dancing school with over two hundred pupils. Some of her former students are scattered all over the world and many of her pupils have become champions. Sheila communicated with people from the U.S.A., Canada, South Africa, New Zealand, Australia, Tasmania, Finland and Japan. They wrote to her as friends and for information on the various dancing events taking place within the United Kingdom.

Although Sheila wouldn't say so herself, she was probably the best known figure in the Highland Dancing World. Her name certainly became synonymous with dancing. She was also at the heart of the Scottish Highland Games Association as the organiser of many of the dancing events. Through her work with the games she had friends from all backgrounds including Frances Shand-Kydd, mother of Princess Diana. She also admitted to often 'putting her foot in it'. Once when sitting in the middle of the games field at Tobermory, Isle of Mull, she did just that. Helping Sheila with the dance entries was a middle-aged lady who Sheila jokingly called her "gaffer for the day". Her helper didn't appreciate the word 'Gaffer'. During the day a helicopter had been passing back and forth. Sheila, thinking that it was for pleasure trips remarked, "That boy's making plenty siller the day". Sheila's gaffer then replied with , "Oh no my dear. That's my husband. Our daughter's getting married tomorrow and that's him bringing over some of the guests from the other islands".

Right up until a few months before her death, Sheila taught five nights a week and travelled to various events nearly every weekend. A born organiser she ran numerous competitions and took a very active part in the Highland Games. One of her indoor competitions, The Kingdom o' Fife Championships attracts over 600 dancers to Glenwood School, Glenrothes each October, whilst the United Kingdom Championships held in Musselburgh cater for about 800 dancers. The activities were endless and she amazed us all with her boundless enthusiasm and energy.

Even when she was getting on in years she never lost her dancing talent. Once a mother expressed surprise at how well Sheila could dance. Rather than being flattered by the comment she curtly rebuked the mother by saying, "I would never ask a bairn tae dae what I couldna dae masel". The magic has been transmitted as evidenced by the abilities of her numerous dancers.

Not only was Sheila an outstanding teacher she was also very much a family person who worked closely with her daughter Anna and adored her son Andrew and his family. Those who were close to her agree that she was one of the best, noted for her consideration and generosity. We all have a lot to be thankful for to that wonderful lady Sheila McKay.

MOYRA RONALD MEMORIAL TROPHY

UKA Championship Trophy for most points over Highland and National

Moyra Ronald Chaired the UKA Highland Branch Meetings which were held in the Madame Ada Studio in Regent Terrace, Edinburgh. Ms Ronald organised the Highland Examination Centres. Examiners at that time were Janet Ferguson, Cissie Tucker, Esther Clarke, Betty Jessiman, Adeline Calder, Peggy MacDonald and Rachel McFadzean.

Every Year the Trophy is awarded to the dancer receiving the most points over Highland and National.

Jan Louise Doherty
with the Moyra Ronald Trophy
2003

MOYRA RONALD MEMORIAL TROPHY RECIPIENTS

1977	T Potthast	Clydebank
1978	A Simpson	Barrhead
1979	Christine Lacey	Alexandria
1980	Christine Lacey	Alexandria
1982	Jacqueline Smith	Wishaw
1983	Christine Lacey	Alexandria
1984	Shirley Fraser	Alford
1985	Shirley Fraser	Alford
1986	Deryk Mitchelson	Monifieth
1987	Deryk Mitchelson	Monifieth
1988	Deryk Mitchelson	Monifieth
1989	Lorraine Brown	Kilbirnie
1990	Kathryn Walker	Peterhead
1991	Susan Urquhart	Ellon
1992	Lindsay Reid	Stirling
1993	Lindsay Reid	Stirling
1994	Louise Elliot	Carrutherstown
1995	Lindsay Reid	Stirling
1996	Deryk Mitchelson	Monifieth
1997	Eilidh McMillan	Ayr
1998	Eilidh McMillan	Ayr
1999	Joanna Buchan	Peterhead
2000	Rachel McLagan	Blairgowrie
2001	Joanna Buchan	Peterhead
	Eilidh McMillan	Ayr
2002	Joanna Buchan	Peterhead
	David Wilton	Forfar
2003	Jan Louise Doherty	Newburgh
2004	Joanna Buchan	Peterhead
2005	Ayleigh Jeffrey	Wishaw
2006	Anthea Bundy	Grangemouth
2007	Gemma Baillie	Aberdeen
2008	Sophie Brown	Letham
2009	Irene McAvoy	Carron
2010	Heather Cameron	Stirling

EXTRACT FROM 'THE HIGHLAND DANCER'
July 1950

Betty Fraser Jessiman, Huntly, Aberdeenshire

It gives us a great deal of pleasure to present Miss Betty Jessiman of Huntly, Aberdeenshire, Scotland as our first outstanding lady dancer. Miss Jessiman is certainly one of the best known Highland Dancers in the world today and without fear of contradiction we say one of the very best. To quote from the Oban Times – 'Her dancing is meticulous and polished, but with a lightness and feeling'. The essence of a champion Highland Dancer!

Having danced since the age of four, it would likely be impossible to name all the Championships and prizes this amazing person has collected, but to name a few – The Open British Championship (1959 and 1960), the North of the Forth (Open – 1961), North of Scotland (Open); the Edith Kirkham Trophy for the best female dancer at Aboyne (1960) and top placings at London, Cowal, Aberlour, Dornoch, Turriff, Arisaig, Abernethy – the list is endless.

Last year at the Cowal Gathering in Dunoon an upset occurred which truthfully shocked those interested in Highland Dancing all over the world. As many of the readers know, Cowal runs a qualifying competition, that is, the top six dancers in the Open may compete for the World Championship. In the first round Miss Jessiman received first place in both the Fling and Seann Triubhas and third in the Sword dance. The others qualifying gained just one prize each. Victory was virtually assured for the Huntly dancer who had been second or third in this competition five times previously. However, the unexpected happened – the Championship was won by another finalist and Miss Jessiman was again second.

To whom does the credit go for training and perfecting this talented dancer? Undoubtedly a large amount of it is due to the dancer herself, but her mother, Helen Fraser Jessiman, Miss M Guthrie and Mr J Allardyce of Aberdeen all contributed immeasurably towards developing the champion as she is today.

Miss Jessiman is a teacher of Highland, Ballet and Tap, is an examiner and fellow member of the United Kingdom Alliance of Professional Teachers of Dancing and a member of the British Ballet Organization. Among her promising girl pupils are her nieces, Patricia and Ann Peters (Patricia has won the Under 18 Aberdeenshire Trophy at the Edinburgh Festival for the past three years) and also young Frances Gordon. She seems to be upholding the Aberdeenshire tradition of producing outstanding male competitors in Alex Scott, Michael Esson, Cameron Gordon and Joe Simpson – the latter having won the Scottish Boys Championship for the past two years.

As you will see from the picture, Betty Jessiman wears the dress recommended by the Scottish Official Board of Highland Dancing (SOBHD) which she feels, and the writer certainly agrees, is a much smarter garb than the old outfit. In fact she says she would never wish to dance in anything else.

Naturally as benefits a dancer of her standard she is interested in improving and furthering Highland dancing and therefore feels that since the formation of the SOBHD there has been a decided improvement in the general standard. Her words are 'they have done a tremendous amount of work – and continue to do so'.

Last January the children of South Uist were treated to a unique and beneficial experience in that Miss Jessiman was their teacher for two weeks. Her own impressions of the trip were that it was perhaps the happiest two weeks of teaching she has ever done due to the great enthusiasm of the children.

For the benefit of our readers she was kind enough to give her opinion on what constitutes a good highland dancer (excluding the fact that they must be technically good) and so as not to misinterpret any of her ideas we quote 'A dancer who can perform with ease and grace and with feeling – be able to interpret the spirit of the dance – and above all, enjoy doing it. They should be beyond the stage of visibly counting. A dancer could be technically perfect, be able to count 1 and a 2, 3, 4 – measure perfectly an eighth quarter or half turn but still look like a mechanical toy wound up! This has all to be mastered – but once attained the dancer must learn to execute it with ease and enjoyment.'

She feels the dancers today could improve by having more confidence in the judges' decisions and competitors must be taught to take the bad with the good.

Apart from her accomplishments in the competition and teaching fields she has had many interesting experiences. In 1958 she was one of eight who performed before Queen Elizabeth and Prince Philip – the first highland dancers ever to appear at Holyrood Palace. She has toured France as the solo Highland dancer with a Scottish Country Dancing group, taken part in an International Dancing Festival in Ireland and danced in a Military Tattoo in Dublin. When the Scottish National Ballet was formed Miss Jessiman was asked to appear with the company on television.

As previously mentioned Miss Jessiman's mother was a dancer, likewise her three sisters. Quite a dancing family! The 'Jessiman Sisters' arranged their own dancers and made their own costumes – a great time must have been had by all concerned.

Among her ambitions is the hope of a tour abroad, either alone or with a group. We cannot express how pleased we would be if this trip materialised and at this time would like to hint that the possibility might not be too far removed – all going well.

The writer is and has been extremely impressed with the humbleness of the champion Scottish dancers she has had the pleasure to meet. Could it be that they have really learned the true definition of a sportsman – 'a person who can take loss or defeat without complaint, or victory without gloating and who treats his opponents with fairness, generosity, courtesy etc.'

'The Highland Dancer' wishes to thank Miss Betty Jessiman most warmly for her contribution to this issue. We feel sure that everyone will enjoy reading about such an outstanding member of our 'clan.' May we again say how delighted we would be if she would visit us and wish her the very best in the forthcoming summer.

Miss Jessiman attained her dream at the Cowal Highland Gathering by winning the Adult World Championship in 1961.

Betty Fraser Jessiman

VICTOR W. WESLEY

Victor W. Wesley, is a long standing distinguished member and examiner of the United Kingdom Alliance

He is the only Highland Dancing Champion to win the Adult World Championship held at the Cowal Highland Gathering in Dunoon and win it under three variations of judge's panels:

(A) Freestyle judges panel

(B) Transition of half freestyle and SOBHD panel.

(C) And completely under he SOBHD panel and jurisdiction. Which completed a historical hat trick.

At 21 years of age he emigrated to the United States to study classical Russian Imperial Ballet under the tutelage of some of the greatest names in the history of classical ballet, James Jamieson, Helene Antonova, Sonja Woijcikowska, George Ballanchine, Alexandra Danilova, Anthony Tudor Sir Frederick Franklin, Agnes DeMille, many of whom with links directly to the Ballet Ruses, and the Serge Diagaliev Company and who themselves danced with Vaslav Nijinsky, Anna Pavlova, and Leonide Massine in this company.

Through hard work and dedication to succeed he quickly rose through the ranks of the Corp, Soloist, and Principal dancer making his name within the professional ballet world.

Through the elevation and fame he was invited to appear all over the world, dancing and partnering some of the worlds most famous and recognised ballerinas.

During his career he danced and earned the prestigious title of Premier Danseur, has danced the leading principal male roles in the classical repertoire of many of the worlds foremost professional ballet companies, and has also taught and restaged works for these companies.

His talents in dancing are far-reaching and very accomplished, as he has not only received notoriety as a choreographer of outstanding merit. He has received accolades from Royalty, Presidents, Senators and leading dignitaries from throughout the world for his outstanding career. Victor has taught former world champion highland dancers and has had a most distinguished career as a teacher of classical ballet and character dance, culminating with becoming the Artistic Director and Choreographer of a Professional Ballet School and Company.

In 2004 Victor passed the Scottish Official Board of Dancing Judges exam under the guidance and tutelage of Mr Ritchie Gibson a senior Board member and also a long standing member and examiner of the United Kingdom Alliance.

Victor is now a recognised member of the SOBHD international judges panel, whereby he has gained great respect by his peers as an adjudicator of the Board, and is further in demand as a lecturer at Board affiliated organisations conventions and events.

It is with the greatest humility and pride that I have arrived at being a member of the SOBHD World Wide Judges Panel and serve as a represented member and delegate of the Board, with this in mind I look forward to many years, and a long career as a recognised member of such a distinguished organisation.

With a long and illustrious career in dancing and a host of accomplishments behind me it is with the utmost respect and sincerity and too the greatest honour that I convey my well wishes to the members of the Board and the SOBHD itself on the 60th Anniversary Celebration of it's founding.

Congratulations Happy Birthday BRAVO.

BOBBY WATSON

Bobby Watson was a born dancer and performer – he loved an audience. His enthusiasm and energy for dance were infectious. He stimulated people's interest in Highland and Scottish Country Dance worldwide.

Bobby followed in the dancing footsteps of his mother and from an early age he toured the dance circuits, becoming the World Junior Dance Champion in 1926 at Cowal Highland Games. Because of his stature and particularly small feet he was known as 'Nipper Watson'. Bobby went on dancing and winning.

He trained as a motor mechanic, and although interested in cars, it was dancing that was in his blood, and in 1936 he became a full time professional dancer following a successful audition with The Brighton Follies. Along the way, elocution lessons were given to soften his broad 'Aberdeen' accent, and acting, singing and comedy were added to his repertoire. During this period he met his wife Mavis, a particularly accomplished and experienced professional dancer who greatly influenced Bobby's life and career.

BOBBY AND MAVIS WATSON

At the end of World War II, Bobby found himself being 'called up' again......this time it was a request from his mother to take over her dancing school! And so he returned to kindle the northeast with his energy and enthusiasm. Mavis played an active part in Bobby's dance and performance career. They were perfectionists and so their dancers had to be likewise.

Bobby's teaching, performance and judging career to him, to Highland Games, festivals and shows from Aberdeen to America, Fraserburgh to France, Aboyne to Africa, Turriff to Tokyo and so on. He continued to compete until he was in his 40's, he last performed at the age of 70, and he taught until he was 82. Throughout his life he was an influential figure in the Highland Dancing World being a co-founder of the Scottish Official Board of Highland Dancing in 1950.

His performances were not confined to village and stately halls, or theatre stages; he was a pioneer of Scottish dance on television, where he danced in and choreographed shows such as The Kilt is my Delight and The White Heather Club. Bobby's Highland Dance Performers – The Deeside Dancers – and his Scottish Country Dance performers – The Clan Hay Dancers appeared with him at home and abroad and on television. Bobby Watson's contribution to Scottish Country Dance was recognised in 1986 by the Royal Scottish Country Dance Society when they awarded him their highest accolade, the Society Scroll.

Known for his infectious enthusiasm and boundless energy, Bobby was delighted too, when the Lord Provost of his home city presented him with life-time use of his own special car registration number, NRG 1. Bobby Watson played a part in the life of hundreds and thousands of people, his pupils, his fellow dancers and judges, non dancers and so many others who all remember him for his high standards, but most of all for his 'energy and enthusiasm' and good sense of fun.

Bobby Watson, Aberdeen's own 'Lord of the Dance' died in October 1997.

DAVID WILTON

Through a love of the sport from the age of five, David Wilton has forged himself a place in the pantheon of Highland Dancing greats and written his name into the history books as one of the most successful male dancers of all time. A six-times World Champion, in 2007 David became the first male (and only the second dancer ever) to win consecutive Juvenile, Junior and Adult titles at Cowal.

His achievements throughout the world include 12 UKA Championships, 12 British crowns and eight Scottish triumphs in the blue riband Dunoon arena. Taught by his mother, UKA Examiner Delma, David has also enjoyed multiple successes in the North American Championship, Australia's Champion of Champions event and the SOBHD Champion of Champions Oscars. In summer 2010, he was poised to emulate his mother in becoming a Fellow of the UKA.

Future aspirations include becoming a UKA examiner and SOBHD judge. David's desire to contribute to the continuing development of Highland Dancing extends beyond the ability to share his talent and expertise with future generations of dancers and into his life's other great passion, bagpiping. Countless competitors have appreciated his musical skills, either at events where David has played or through his first CD, Diversity, which rings out in dance classes across the globe.

He skillfully juggles his competitive dance career with that of being a member of the Scottish Power Grade One band and a successful solo piper who secured a place in the prestigious Gold Medal Piobaireachd competition in 2010, his final Honours degree year at Glasgow's prestigious Royal Scottish Academy of Music and Drama.

JEAN REYNOLDS 12/3/1924 TO 25/10/2000

Jean Reynolds started her teaching career at the age of twenty in the Poole's Synod Hall Edinburgh and later extended her classes to East and Midlothian. Her classes were very popular mainly because of Jeans' lively personality and true passion for dance which she conveyed to her students. She produced exciting and colourful annual school displays in the Usher Hall which was always filled to capacity.

Jean provided her pupils with a variety of opportunities from competing at the Highland Games where she would encourage them to "Dance to the hills," to dancing professionally with the White Heather Club or with amateur groups such as the Southern Light Opera Company in the Kings Theatre or to entertaining the patients in the Edinburgh Royal Infirmary on Christmas Day. "Practise makes perfect" was another of Jeans' favourite words of advice to her pupils.

Jean as a child was taught Ballet by Madam Ada and Highland by Sydney Black, she competed at the Highland Games where no doubt she would have been a striking figure with her yellow McLeod Tartan kilt and plaid, her vivid red hair and her lovely smile which expressed her love of dance.

Jeans ethos was "It's not just enough to teach the steps, I try to reach dancers' hearts as well as their feet." She did just that for many of her students. A unique and fun loving character to whom many dancers owe their gratitude for passing on her love of dancing.

Australian Board of Highland Dancing Inc

Letter from the President - Judith Monteith

LETTER FROM THE PRESIDENT OF THE AUSTRALIAN BOARD OF HIGHLAND DANCING

Miss Christine Lacey
Chairman Scottish Official Board of Highland Dancing
Heritage House
32 Grange Loan
Edinburgh, Scotland EH9 2NR

Dear Miss Lacey,

It is with great pleasure that I take this opportunity on behalf of the Australian Board of Highland Dancing Incorporated executive, our State and Regional Committee executives and delegates, and Affiliated Association members to extend hearty congratulations to the Scottish Official Board of Highland Dancing as it commemorates 60 years as the governing body for Highland Dancing world-wide. A wonderful achievement with numerous accomplishments attained due to the dedication of many persons affiliated with the Board throughout the 60 years.

This year 2010, is also a very special and memorable year for the Australian Board of Highland Dancing Incorporated as it celebrates its 50th Golden Jubilee under the auspices of the Scottish Official Board.

Our sincere appreciation is extended to the many persons associated with the SOBHD, whom over our affiliated years have given of their time, expertise and advice to assist in achieving the many goals set over this long period of time. Many of these persons are not with us today, but it is the legacy of their foresight, inspiration and devotion to Highland Dancing which remains with us all as we continue to work towards further strengthening and promoting of the dance now and in the future.

A special thank you to all our SOBHD delegates who assisted the ABHDI in its prior years, to Mr. Billy Forsyth who came to Australia to attend an ABHDI Board meeting and from whom we gained considerable knowledge and advice, to Miss Marjorie Rowan who answered all our many queries over a long period of time, to former delegate Gareth Mitchelson who met with the ABHDI Executive whilst visiting Australia and to our current SOBHD delegates, Marion Clow, Gillin Anderson, Christine Crowe, Janette Jamieson, Mary Neill and Betty Wren and your good self who gave of your time recently for discussion whilst in Australia. We have enjoyed the pleasure of the company of many overseas Judges and Teachers who have imparted their knowledge and expertise generously at our ABHDI Technical and Board meetings and workshops over the years.

Best wishes to the present SOBHD executive and all our fellow colleagues world-wide as we celebrate the past 60 years and work towards the future to uphold the present high standards.

Best wishes,

Judith Monteith.

President ABHDI

HIGHLAND DANCING IN THE AUSTRALIAN COLONY IN THE 19TH CENTURY

(Some information gleaned from notes formulated by the late Mr. D. Scotland O.A.M. B.E.M.)

In the mid 1830s the first Scottish immigrants arrived in Australia and during the next two decades many more Highlanders and Lowlanders followed. Prior to this period there were only a small number of Scots in comparison including about 100 convicts transported from Scotland to the Port Arthur Penal Colony, Tasmania.

During the 1850s many emigrated as a result of the clearances in Scotland. Although some of these immigrants were to settle in both country and city areas within the vast States and Territories of Australia, Victoria became the most popular colony in which to settle during this period. Unfortunately, there are few records available as to who were the Highland Dancing teachers at this time.

It is obvious that amongst the early arrivals from the United Kingdom, be they convict or free settlers there must have been Scots who had learnt Highland Dancing in the land of their birth. Early Highland dancers in Australia were mostly males and there is mentioned in correspondence of that period, that at functions, be it a wedding in Sydney or one of the growing cities, a Station or a Settlers Homestead that an exhibition of Highland Dancing covering Fling, Reel or Swords performed over sticks or brooms was given.

The earliest evidence of Scottish societies holding dancing competitions was recorded in The Melbourne Herald in 1860. This was a report of the 'Grand Caledonian Gathering' - a two day festival from 30th November to the 1st December 1860. Another early Highland Dancing competition organised within Australia was held on New Year's Day 1869 at the Albert Ground, Redfern, Sydney, as part of the Highland Gathering organised by the Duke of Edinburgh's Highland Rifle Brigade. There were four competitors who performed the Highland Fling, Sword Dance and Highland Reel. The judge was a Mr. John Clark. The results show that the winners were a Mr. J. H. Campbell (Highland Fling), Mr. Culbert (Gillie Callum) and Mr. Donaldson (Highland Reel). No mention was made of the fourth competitor.

Over the following years the number of competitors gradually increased and in 1874 the winner of each adult event received a prize of two pounds. Another new venture at that time, was the holding of a Highland Dancing competition for boys. Mr. John Clark is again recorded as being the Judge but what his experience or qualifications were, is unknown. In 1879 the Gathering saw two new events added to the Dancing Competition namely the Sailors Hornpipe which was open only to bona fide sailors from ships in port and a Highland Fling for young ladies. On January 2nd each year, the names of the winners appeared in the Sydney Morning Herald, the leading paper of the day in New South Wales. By 1878, The Highland Society of New South Wales had come into existence and became the organisers of this event.

Because of the interest shown, Agricultural Shows in many State country towns began to add a Highland Dancing competition to their program. These events were attracting greater numbers of spectators and, with cash prizes being given in the dance sections, it was creating greater competition. There are not many of these outside Highland dancing events held today.

HIGHLAND DANCING IN THE 20TH CENTURY

(Information gleaned from M. S. Allen, SOBHD Judge)

Early in the century the number of teachers conducting schools of Highland Dancing grew in all States and Territories of Australia. This was due not only to the migration policy of Australia at the time, but also to the genuine love of this discipline by those who had previously participated in this country as competitors.

Due to the vastness of the country and difficulty in regard to transport and costs involved, it was rarely possible for dancers to compete outwith their area of domiciliation. Teachers and judges held no particular Highland Dance qualification only a love of the dance. There were many differing steps, styles and costuming during this era. Each State and Territory of Australia had its own particular style and each State and Territory believed that it was correct.

Interest in Highland Dancing had increased and the teaching was widespread in the cities as well as the country areas. Competitions were held by the Highland Games Organisers, Scottish Societies, within the dance section of Eisteddfods, and at Agricultural Shows particularly in country areas.

Information regarding Highland Dancing technique was mainly by "word of mouth" in Australia before the formation of the Australian Board of Highland Dancing. As a result, the experienced dancer became aware of the style wanted by a particular judge and tried to adjust the style and steps to accommodate the "point of view" of that particular judge. Original dances began to be lost with the embellishments that were added to give effect. Even the bows to introduce dances were exaggerated and overdone.

With the end of World War 11 there was a great resurgence of interest in Highland Dancing, not only by Australians themselves but also by the Scots migrating to Australia. It became obvious that unrest in technique and judging was prevalent in most States and Territories of Australia with a strong desire for uniformity. We were indeed most fortunate that the same desire for uniformity was also evident about the same time in Scotland itself which resulted in the formation of the Scottish Official Board of Highland Dancing in 1950.

JOHN COUSINS

Mr. Cousins was born in Scotland in the mid 1880's. He was a successful Highland Dancer in Scotland following the various Highland Games in his days as a young man. Having migrated with his parents and brothers to Australia prior to the First World War he resided firstly in Victoria and later in Sydney. His love of Highland Dancing was always with him. He was a well known and respected Judge of Highland Dancing in New South Wales.

CHANGES AFOOT IN HIGHLAND DANCING WITHIN AUSTRALIA

By the 1940's, John Cousins came to believe that he must take steps to try and bring Highland dancers back to the work that he had danced in Scotland.

In 1945, Mr. Cousins decided to open a Highland Dancing School and asked Maree Fairfield (Allen), a young successful competitive dancer, to be his assistant. This became a very difficult time for his pupils as the teachers of the time, while having respected him as a Judge, could not understand his desire to change the styles.

However, he persevered (as did his pupils) and decided in the late forties and the early fifties along with Mrs. Doris Stokes (a teacher and a Judge who resided in Newcastle, NSW) and Maree Fairfield to try and bring teachers and interested persons of the day together with hope of standardising Highland dancing in New South Wales.

Mr. Cousins was one of the recognised Teachers who attended the first meeting called to bring about what was to become the Australian Board of Highland Dancing in 1960. His interest in Highland Dancing never waivered. His pupils will remember the tapping foot and his whistling of the dance tune throughout class.

Mr. Cousins died in July 1966 and was sadly missed by the Highland Dancing community.

VERA LACEY

It was due to the tenacity and perseverance of a few persons in Australia who were desirous of securing a standardisation of Highland Dancing within Australia and thereto affiliation with the newly formed SOBHD. Vera Lacey was one such person. Besides studying law she was a performer for the very well known theatre company within Australia for many long years, J. C. Williamson.

Mrs. Lacey, as British Ballet Organisation's Australasian representative, and keen upon Highland dancing examinations being incorporated into an affiliated Highland branch, knew it would be extremely difficult to achieve a standardisation of Highland Dancing within Australia and for the many teachers to make the necessary changes to what they had been teaching for years on somebody else's say-so.

Hence she realized how necessary it was to accept an arbitrator such as the newly formed Scottish Official Board and set off on what was, at that time, a long and costly trip to Britain to attend SOBHD meetings, observe and take films of Highland Dancing in Scotland and seek as much technical information and advice as was possible to bring back to Australia.

Vera Lacey was instrumental in the setting up of the initial meetings of what is now the ABHDI and offered the British Ballet Organisation's premises in Sydney free for meetings and later ABHD Judges' examinations. She remained in her original position as the BBO Australasian representative and as an examiner for the BBO and NDAA until her passing in 1978.

INITIAL STEPS WHICH LEAD TO THE FORMATION OF THE ABHDI

In the early 1950's two Highland Dancing Associations were formed with the common object of introducing uniform technique into Highland Dancing, judging and dress similar to that of the newly formed Scottish Official Board of Highland Dancing in Scotland. These associations were The Scottish Dancing Association of Australia (SDAA) and the National Dancing Association of Australasia (NDAA) both of which remain relevant examining bodies in various states of Australia to this day.

Highland Dancing was flourishing in other states of Australia, especially Victoria. However, due to infrequent public transport and the high costs involved with travel across the vast areas of Australia at that time one could have been on another planet. The Victorian Scottish Dancing Association (VSDA) was formed on the 3rd August, 1954 and was striving to follow SOBHD technique also. The VSDA is still functioning strongly to this day in Victoria and has been an examining body for a long period of time.

With distance, cost and time re travel between Scotland and Australia being prohibitive and communication with the SOBHD in early years most difficult due to the slowness of all overseas mail systems at that time, trying to achieve conformity within Highland Dancing was almost impossible.

SCOTTISH DANCING ASSOCIATION OF AUSTRALIA. (SDAA)

It was Mr. John Cousins and Mrs. Doris Stokes (both respected teachers and judges of the time) and Miss Maree Fairfield (Allen) a dancer and competitor and assistant teacher with Mr. Cousins, who initiated the first meeting of the SDAA in the early 1950's which resulted in the formation of the Scottish Dancing Association of New South Wales on the 5th August 1953 which later became the Scottish Dancing Association of Australia. Medal tests in Highland Dancing were introduced shortly thereafter. Miss Fairfield (Allen), now a respected Judge and long serving member of various Highland Dancing committees, was the first Secretary of the association and is a Foundation and Life Member of the SDAA

NATIONAL DANCING ASSOCIATION OF AUSTRALASIA. (NDAA)

The inaugural meeting of the NDAA was held in 1951 in Sydney with Mrs. Vera Lacey as Director and Mrs. Dorothy Kerr BEM, the Honorary Secretary at that time. The first Highland Dancing examinations held within Australia were conducted by the NDAA and were demonstrated initially to approximately fifty local teachers in May 1952. In setting up the syllabi it was decided that technique must be as per the technique set down by the SOBHD and contain theory questions for all grades. Mrs. Kerr retained the Secretarial office of the NDAA up until her retirement in 1999.

It was due to the foresight of persons connected to these two associations that the initital meetings were instigated which led to the formation of the Australian Board of Highland Dancing Incorporated as it is known today.

DOROTHY KERR B.E.M. D.Ua.

Dorothy Kerr's contribution to Highland Dancing within Australia is considerable and with her drive and vision to lift the art of Highland Dancing within Australia she did achieve much success. Following the SOBHD steps from the initial 16mm film produced in Scotland she passed such knowledge on to teachers in NSW cities and towns and in other States.

For her services to Highland Dancing she was honoured with the British Empire Medal and also recognised as Duine Uasal with post-nominal rights of use of D.Ua for service to the Celts by the Celtic Council of Australia. Her encouragement, advice and assistance to the younger teacher will be remembered by many across Australia.

As the ABHD's first Hon. Secretary she was instrumental in gaining support and approval for the ABHDI to conduct Judges' examinations within Australia. In collaboration with Vera Lacey and Mabel MacInnes she introduced the first Highland examinations into Australia in 1952 and registered the first Championship under the auspices of the SOBHD. She was a Registered Judge, examiner and great teacher culminating in two of her pupils winning the World Championship. Being honoured along with four other distinguished world Highland teachers in Las Vegas in 2004 meant a great deal to Mrs. Kerr. She was a mentor to many teachers.

Mrs. Kerr indeed left us with a great legacy on her passing in 2008.

MAREE ALLEN

Born in Arncliffe, Sydney, NSW, Maree Allen (nee Fairfield) has been involved in Highland Dancing since age of five and remains very active in judging and administration in NSW and Australia. She is one of the longest serving SOBHD Judges in Australia having passed the SOBHD Judges Test in Scotland in 1962.

It was in 1945 that Mr. John Cousins invited Maree, at the time a very successful competitive dancer, to become his assistant and later in partnership, to teach what he knew from experience was the authentic Highland Dancing he had learnt in Scotland as a young man. Both became foundation members of the Scottish Dancing Association of Australia whose beginnings commenced in the early 1950's and instrumental in the formation of the ABHD. The studio produced many successful competitive pupils.

When as former President of the ABHDI, Maree worked diligently for recognition of ABHDI qualified Judges by the SOBHD. Maree serves to this day on Highland Dancing committees with much dedication, commitment and integrity.

FORMATION OF THE AUSTRALIAN BOARD OF HIGHLAND DANCING

It was, in April 1960, that a reply was received from Ms. Elspeth Strathern, then Secretary of the Scottish Official Board of Highland Dancing, to a request from various persons within Australia wishing to be affiliated as a combined body with the Scottish Official Board of Highland Dancing, Edinburgh, Scotland.

A circular emanating from the Scottish Official Board of Highland Dancing, Edinburgh, was circulated to all interested parties within Australia. Here below verbatim is correspondence received from Miss Strathern dated April 1960.

PROPOSED GOVERNING BODY OF AUSTRALIA

Dear Sirs,

Further to our recent circular letter regarding the formation of a Governing Body of Australia, we have now received quite a number of replies in favour of setting up such a body, under the auspices of the Scottish Official Board of Highland Dancing. As previously stated, we feel that such matters as the granting of Championships, titles, formation of a Judges' Panel, etc. could best be accomplished by representatives in the area.

It has been suggested by one of the Australian Associations that a meeting in each State could be held in the first instance to which all Associations and organisations in highland dancing should be invited to attend. At this, delegates to the inaugural meeting of the Governing Body could be chosen (the Official Board have two delegates from each represented member and each affiliated Association can each send one representative). Suggestions could also be forwarded from these meetings which would form the nucleous of the Agenda for the Inaugural meeting.

In order to make progress as quickly as possible, we suggest that the State meeting should be held before the end of June with a view to having the Inaugural Meeting of the Governing Body prior to the end of September.

We fully appreciate the difficulties of travel, etc. in your Country but feel sure that the setting up of Governing Body to control your domestic affairs would greatly benefit Highland Dancing generally.

Mrs. V. Lacey, 22 Tyron Road, Lindfield, NSW, has kindly offered the use of her studio for the Inaugural Meeting and we put forward the suggestion for your consideration.

Yours sincerely,

Elspeth Strathern

INITIAL MEETING OF INTERESTED HIGHLAND DANCING ASSOCIATIONS IN AUSTRALIA AND NEW ZEALAND

Following the receipt of Miss Strathern's letter, Mrs. Dorothy Kerr, Honorary Secretary at that time of the National Dancing Association of Australasia (NDAA) and the British Ballet Organisation (BBO) invited, by correspondence dated 5th May, 1960, all interested persons to attend a general meeting to be held on 19th May, 1960, at the premises of the NDAA/BBO, 505 Pitt Street, Sydney, New South Wales.

The meeting had been called in view of the fact that there would be in Sydney on that date, representatives from New Zealand, Tasmania, The Victorian Scottish Dancing Association, and the Ballarat and District Guild and various country centres, all of whom had expressed an interest in the forming of an Australasian Governing Body.

Recorded within minutes of such meeting chaired by Mrs. Vera Lacey with Mrs. Dorothy Kerr as Honorary Secretary were the following persons:

- The Honorable Richard Thompson, Member of the Legislative Council and Chairman of the City of Sydney Eisteddfod.
- Mesdames Green, O'Hara, Burnett, Barker, Burdett and Mr. J. Waddell of the Victorian Scottish Dancing Association.
- Messrs. Stanton, O'Sullivan, Cousins, Hughes, Temple, Walker, Cashin, Clubb, Powell and Mesdames Wathin, MacInnes, Lane, Henning and Stokes of the Scottish Dancing Association of Australia.
- Mrs. D. Graham, Miss P. Peters and Mr. J. McKenzie of The National Dancing Association of Australasia.
- Mrs. G. Zillies, of the Ballarat and District National Dancing Guild, Victoria.
- Mesdames Perfect and Williams of Christchurch, New Zealand.
- Mrs. Ellis of Dunedin, New Zealand.
- Mrs. Joan O'Neill, of The Tasmanian Caledonian Society, Launceston, Tasmania.
- Mr. John Miller of the Highland Society of New South Wales.

The Chairman invited all those present to give their view on the proposed formation of an Australian Governing Board and it appears from minutes that all were most favourable to this suggestion.

Mrs. Lacey in thanking those present for coming long distances to attend, requested that a combined effort be made to solidify the work of the SOBHD in Scotland.

ST LAURENCE CHRIST CHURCH BUILDING

505 Pitt Street, Sydney, New South Wales

A large part of the building was the home of the National Dancing Association of Australasia and British Ballet Organisation for many years and where the preliminary meetings to consider the formation of an Australian Governing Body for Highland Dancing took place from 1960, and meetings were also held there in the initial years of the Australian Board of Highland Dancing following its formation. The New South Wales State Committee of Highland Dancing also held meetings at this venue in earlier days.

The first ABHD Judges' examination to be conducted in Sydney, and for sometime after, were held on the top floor. These examinations were usually conducted on a Sunday commencing early morning as were the initial Australian Board Meetings and one would certainly not lose concentration at either activity as the church bells would chime for a minute or two just prior to the commencement of each church service throughout the day.

The Grand Australasian Highland Dancing Championships for many years were held on the top floor until a fire gutted the interior completely in the late 1980s. The top floor was a theatre style venue with stage and off-side dressing rooms. The Scottish Theatre Shop managed by Mrs. D. Kerr, initially located on the second floor and later the lower floor, sold all things Scottish. The ground floor on one side was used as a ballet studio and the opposite side housed a kitchen which catered for those souls in need of food and care. The building was owned by the Saint Laurence Church which was located next door, part of which can be seen to the left in the picture.

No doubt many Australian and overseas Highland judges, teachers and dancers well remember this venue.

INTERIM MEETINGS

Due primarily to the vast distance between States and Territories, and also the cost of travel, it was not possible for all interested organisations Australia wide to be able to attend the meetings deemed necessary if the goal of forming an Australian Governing Body for Highland Dancing was to be achieved.Distance and high cost of travel to Australia was also a difficulty for the interested New Zealand teachers. Hence, it was the New South Wales domiciled delegates from various associations who met on a further two occasions to initiate organisational procedures necessary if the primary goal was to be achieved.

Further correspondence, dated 7th June, 1960, was received from Miss Elspeth Strathern who advised the following:

"At the meeting of the Official Board held on Sunday, 22nd May, a proposition was put forward by members to the effect that:

'each State should have its own committee, representative of all appropriate Associations in that State - for example - Western Australian Scottish Dancing Union for Western Australia - and from each of these committees, one or two delegates be appointed to form a controlling body for Australia.'

Joan O'Neill

The proposition is put to you for consideration, as we thought it would help to bridge the tremendous distances separating the various Associations from each other."

A draft constitution was compiled based, as far as possible, on the SOBHD constitution of that time and was circulated to Associations Australia wide. A bank account was opened from donations received from within Australia and from New Zealand persons in the name of "The Australasian Board of Highland Dancing" with the amount of £10.0.0 banked and the balance of £1.7.3 in funds to be held by the Secretary as petty cash. It was suggested that the inaugural meeting of the Australasian governing body be convened and interstate associations notified and asked to nominate two delegates to attend this inaugural meeting.

Honorary ABHDI Judge, Piper and NDAA Teacher and Examiner for many years, Joan represented Tasmania at the initial meetings held in Sydney during 1960 to discuss formation of a Governing Body within our country under the auspices of the SOBHD. Now retired but still teaching piping, Joan gave many years to Highland Dancing especially in the State of Tasmania where she was the inaugural President of the Tasmanian Regional Committee of Highland Dancing.

Marna Rooney (Tredrea)

Marna came to Australia from Scotland in 1958. She commenced teaching in South Australia and joined The Athol Highland Dancing Association of South Australia. Marna represented her association at the inaugural meeting of the Australian Board of Highland Dancing on September 22nd, 1960 and remains very involved with the Australian Board to this day as a Judge and often as a delegate for her State Committee. She has served on such committee from time to time in various Executive positions.

THE INAUGURAL MEETING

ORIGINALLY KNOWN AS 'THE AUSTRALASIAN OFFICIAL BOARD OF HIGHLAND DANCING'

SYDNEY, NEW SOUTH WALES 22ND SEPTEMBER, 1960

The inaugural meeting of what is now the Australian Board of Highland Dancing Incorporated took place on September 22nd, 1960, and was held at The Highland Society of New South Wales, 145a George Street, Sydney.

The Chairman, Mr. J. Miller, (The Highland Society of New South Wales opened the meeting. Honorary Secretary, Mrs. D. Kerr (National Dancing Association of Australasia) was present as were delegates from The Highland Society of New South Wales, The Scottish Dancing Association of Australia and The National Dancing Association of Australasia.

Those present included many names of past judges, teachers and other interested persons—Messrs. Long, McKenzie, Crawford, Temple, Stier, Cashin, Walker, O'Sullivan and Cribbin and Mesdames Lacey, Rooney, McInnes, Henning, Cribbin and Walker.

Apologies and best wishes for every success were received by telegram and correspondence from the individual persons and interstate associations including the Victorian Scottish Dancing Association, The

Dandenong Highland Dancing Association, The Western Australian Scottish Union, and The Highland and National Dancing Teachers Association of South Australia who were all unable to attend the meeting.

Cost of travel and the time restraints associated with travel across the vast distance of Australia had once again limited the number of interested associations however the Chairman, Mr. J. Miller, opened the meeting welcoming Mrs. Marna Rooney and Mr. Ken Crawford, delegates who had travelled the long distance from The Athol Highland Dancing Association of South Australia to attend the meeting.

The Chairman gave a brief outline on what progress had taken place since the receipt of Scottish Official Board circular of April 1960 had been received. Discussion emanated upon the proposed constitution which the Secretary had forwarded to all interstate associations with a list of suggested alterations which had been received from the Athol Highland Dancing Association of South Australia. Following discussion the constitution was finally accepted.

Following an election of Office Bearers namely Mr. J. Miller (President), Mrs. D. Kerr (Hon. Secretary) and Mrs. R. Henning (Assistant Secretary) the President closed the meeting at 11.25p.m.

ATTENDEES AT INTERIM, INAUGURAL AND EARLY MEETINGS OF THE ABHDI

TASSIE GREEN

Tassie Green introduced SOBHD technique into Victoria in 1954 and was actively involved in the formation of the Victorian Scottish Dancing Association. Tassie Green was a well known respected and accomplished teacher and adjudicator who continued to take a keen interest in all aspects of Highland Dancing and also the Victorian State Committee well after her retirement. She was one of the Victorian representatives at the inaugural meeting of the Australian Governing Body in 1960.

Whilst Mrs. Green sadly passed away in April 2008, the commitment she gave to Highland Dancing, particularly in Victoria, will be remembered in the "Tassie Green Award", this award being presented to members of the Victorian State Committee of Highland Dancing Inc. in recognition of their outstanding contribution to SOBHD in Victoria.

ROSE McLELLAND B.E.M. (Nee MacColl)

Rose MacColl was born in Edinburgh, Scotland in 1907. Her family came to Australia in 1913 for her father, Archie, to tutor the Mackay Pipe Band. Archie McColl was a gold medalist at Oban and a winner of the Macrimmon Shield in Scotland in about 1912. Rosie, as she was known to many, was a dancer for many years competing and winning Championships in and around Queensland in the 1920's

As a member of the Caledonian Society & Burns Club she promoted Highland Dancing in South East Queensland and Northern New South Wales and was one of the representatives for Mackay/Brisbane at early ABHD meetings and also organized the ABHDI Judges examinations in Brisbane in the sixties.

In 1978 she received the British Empire Medal for her services to Highland Dancing. Rosie was 98 when she died in 2005.

NORMA BURNETT

Norma Burnett, as a representative of the Victorian Scottish Dancing Association, attended the first interim meeting in Sydney on the 19th May, 1960, to discuss the formation of an Australian Governing Body under the auspices of the Scottish Official Board of Highland Dancing.

Mrs. Burnett attended ABHDI meetings as a delegate for the Victorian State Committee for a number of years and was the ABHDI Junior Vice President for a period in the seventies as well as Secretary of the Victorian Scottish Dancing Members Association for many long years until her passing.

Norma's passion for Highland Dancing is carried on by her two daughters, Gaye and Gillian who are both Judges as well as her granddaughter and three great grandchildren who are all Highland dancers.

ABHDI AND STATE AND REGIONAL COMMITTEES

State and Regional Committees function in all State and Territories of Australia with the exception of the Northern Territory. The earliest committees were formed in the early sixties with other State and Regions following shortly thereafter. All State/Regional Committees are affiliated members of the ABHDI which in turn is an affiliated member of the SOBHD. Because of the immense distances between pockets of Highland Dancing teachers in some States it has been necessary to establish Regional Committees in the one State e.g. Queensland and Western Australia. As numbers of teachers and dancers grew or diminished within some State and Regions, there has been a necessity to change status from time to time.

JUDGES AND TEACHERS

Judges and Teachers are represented through the various dance Associations or through the examining bodies with headquarters in their particular area of domiciliation. In one exceptional case where a dance school is situated near central Australia and on the border of another State, the teacher and dancers have been permitted by the ABHDI to affiliate outwith their State due to convenience of travel.

EXAMINING BODIES

The examining bodies are namely the National Dancing Association of Australasia, The Queensland Scottish Dancing Association, The Scottish Dancing Association of Australia, The Victorian Scottish Dancing Association and the Yarra Valley Highland Dancing Association. These examining bodies were the backbone of the acceptance and spread of SOBHD technique into Australia due initially to the foresight of a few persons in NSW and Victoria in the very early fifties and well prior to affiliation with the SOBHD. All remain strong to this day promoting SOBHD technique and support many of our Highland Dancing events.

STATE AND REGIONAL COMMITTEES

State and Regional Committees Australia wide hold General meetings four to seven times per year as well as an Annual General Meeting and each committee is responsible for conducting of Judges and Technical meetings as well as the Championship Step Lectures, Organisers and Scrutineering sessions throughout each year within their State/Region. All minutes of such meetings are forwarded to the Australian Board of Highland Dancing Inc. State and Regional Committees usually organise at least one Championship within their area. Each State and Regional Committee has a Registrar who registers the dancers domiciled within their area only and such details are forwarded to the ABHDI bi-annually. State and Regional Committees register competitions held within their domain and continually fund raise for the Champion of Champions event and other worthy causes with the holding of annual recitals, debutante balls, sausage sizzles, camps, Scottish evenings and a variety of other events.

STATE AND REGIONAL COMMITTEE REPRESENTATIVES

Each State and Regional Committee is represented upon the ABHDI with State Committees permitted 3 delegates and Regional Committees 1 delegate with exception of South Queensland Regional Committee which has 2 delegates due to the large number of dancers registered within their area. It is the dedication and work ethic of persons affiliated with the ABHDI, State/Regional committees and especially teachers that Highland Dancing continues within Australia as migration of persons from Britain has greatly diminished over recent years.

DELEGATES

Delegates from State and Regional Committees come together twice per year at the Australian Board for a two day meeting on each occasion and sometimes for a special meeting on the evening prior to aforementioned meetings when required. The ABHDI also conducts Judges, Technical and Championship Step Lecture sessions, conducts the Champion of Champions Championship of Australia and administers the rules and regulations as laid down by the SOBHD/ABHDI. The Board executive usually rotates each three year period between some states within Australia.

THE CHAMPION OF CHAMPIONS CHAMPIONSHIP OF AUSTRALIA

This Championship was first mooted at the Australian Board of Highland Dancing in 1974 and the conditions set down were that the Championship was to be held at a different State venue every two years and whenever possible in conjunction with the Australian Pipe Band Championships. Competitors entering must produce evidence showing they have won either a 1st, 2nd or 3rd overall placing in a previous registered Championship. The Champion of Champions Championship of Australia is always held on the Saturday and Sunday at Easter.

The first Champion of Champions Championship was held in 1976 in Adelaide, South Australia with the South Australian State Committee of Highland Dancing being the organisers on behalf of the Australian Board of Highland Dancing.

This is Australia's most prestigious Championship events and there are only three age groups namely 7-12 years, 13-15 years and 16 years and over.

Championship prizes covering specific values are awarded to each place winner from 1st to 6th along with a Championship sash. The host State is responsible for these awards. Each State holding the Championship strikes its own medals to be presented to individual place winners in each of the four individual dances. The Australian Board also provide a small cash amount to the winner and the winner's teacher of each Championship.

A special Australian Champion of Champions medal award is awarded to the highest placed Australian dancer in each of the three Championship age groups. These medals are presented by the Australian Board of Highland Dancing. Each of the three recipients also receive "The Frank Cleves Perpetual Trophy Award" donated by Mrs. M. Reichelt in memory of her father who worked extremely hard to further Highland Dancing in Mount Gambier, South Australia.

Ten to twelve judges are usually engaged to judge this event and, along with our own Australian judges, many of the judges have been invited from overseas countries such as Scotland, Canada, United States of America and South Africa.

We have also had the pleasure of dancers from those countries, as well as New Zealand, competing and being successful at this event. Generally, the State or Regional Committee organising the event will also include one of their particular regional Championships along with accompanying events on one of the two days of competition.

Australian judges, teachers and dancers together with their families, travel from all States and Territories of Australia to attend this event and there is always an excited "buzz" at the venue. Do come join us "downunder".

CHAMPION OF CHAMPIONS CHAMPIONSHIP OF AUSTRALIA WINNERS 1976 - 1986

1976 Adelaide, South Australia

	7—12 years	*13, 14, 15 years*	*16 years & over*
1st	**Kerry Venables, Qld**	**Sharon McPherson, Qld**	**Debra Stuckey, SA**
2nd	A Brown, Qld	Janene Simpson, Qld	Ellen Sommerville, Qld
3rd	Amanda Venables, Qld	Debbie Madsen, Qld	Christine Brogan, NSW

1978 Sydney, New South Wales

	7—12 years	*13, 14, 15 years*	*16 years & over*
1st	**Kylie Sommerville, Qld**	**Tracey Daly, Qld**	**Sharine Nicholson,NSW**
2nd	Sharryn Key, Qld	Kym Swanson, NSW	Sharon McPherson, Qld
3rd	Wendy Neilsen, NSW	Linda McNeill, NSW	Donna Brooks, NSW

1980 Brisbane, Queensland

	7—12 years	*13, 14, 15 years*	*16 years & over*
1st	**Lesley Clough, Qld**	**Tracey Daly, Qld**	**Catherine Herzig, Qld**
2nd	Kathryn Welburn, Qld	Kylie Sommerville, Qld	Janene Simpson, Qld
3rd	Anthea Fulton, NSW	Cindy King, Qld	Donna Brooks, NSW

1982 Ringwood, Victoria

	7—12 years	*13, 14, 15 years*	*16 years & over*
1st	**Allyson Evans, Qld**	**Lesley Clough, Qld**	**Dianne Carrick, NSW**
2nd	Margaret Pallaras, Vic	Kathryn Welburn, Qld	Catherine Herzig, Qld
3rd	Rachel Spoehr, SA	Anthea Fulton, NSW	Tracey Daly, Qld

1984 Glenorchy, Tasmania

	7—12 years	*13, 14, 15 years*	*16 years & over*
1st	**Melissa Ho, Qld**	**Christine Larson, Qld**	**Donna Chalmers, ACT**
2nd	Heather Clough, Qld	Sharon Roberts, NSW	Dianne Carrick, NSW
3rd	Bronwyn Ho, Qld	Fiona Wood, NSW	Tracey Daly, Qld

1986 Adelaide, South Australia

	7—12 years	*13, 14, 15 years*	*16 years & over*
1st	**Bronwyn Ho, Qld**	**Lesley Burns, SA**	**Janene Simpson, Qld**
2nd	Leonie Meincke, Vic	Melissa Ho, Qld	Agnes Steele, SA
3rd	Heather McIlwain, NSW	Allyson Evans, Qld	Tracey Daly, Qld

CHAMPION OF CHAMPIONS CHAMPIONSHIP OF AUSTRALIA WINNERS 1988 — 1998

	7—12 years	*13, 14, 15 years*	*16 years & over*
1988	**Sydney, New South Wales**		
1st	**Carleen Ho, Qld**	**Kendall Cordes, ACT**	**Anne Milne, Canada**
2nd	Renee MacGregor, Qld	Jodie Orr, Qld	Tracey Daly, Qld
3rd	Simone Cowley, ACT	Bronwyn Ho, Qld	Justine Daly, NSW

	7—12 years	*13, 14, 15 years*	*16 years & over*
1990	**Brisbane, Queensland**		
1st	**Renee MacGregor, Qld**	**Sharon McGhee, Qld**	**Christine Larson, Qld**
2nd	Carleen Ho, Qld	Lisa Phelan, Qld	Tracey Daly, Qld
3rd	Jane Tapfield, NSW	Katrina Pope, Qld	Jodie Orr, Qld

	7—12 years	*13, 14, 15 years*	*16 years & over*
1992	**Launceston, Tasmania**		
1st	**Lisa Barker, SA**	**Carleen Ho, Qld**	**Grace Watson, Vic**
2nd	Sarah Johnston, Qld	Renee MacGregor, Qld	Justine Daly, NSW
3rd	Andrea Ho, Qld	Katie Bell, SA	Kylie Sommerville, Qld

	7—12 years	*13, 14, 15 years*	*16 years & over*
1994	**Geelong, Victoria**		
1st	**Natasha Millwood, Tas**	**Lindsay Reid, Scotland**	**Justine Daly, NSW**
2nd	Jeaness Muir, Qld	Lisa Barker, SA	Jacqueline Aird, Scotland
3rd	Melody Lutwyche, Tas	Natalie Powell, Qld	Bronwyn Ho, Qld

	7—12 years	*13, 14, 15 years*	*16 years & over*
1996	**Adelaide, South Australia**		
1st	**Natasha Millwood, Tas**	**Jane McArthur, Tas**	**Jackie Smith, Canada**
2nd	Karina Mosley, NSW	C. Lanthier, Canada	Justine Daly, NSW
3rd	Craig Johnston, Qld	Nicole Cook, Qld	Sarah Johnston, Qld

	7—12 years	*13, 14, 15 years*	*16 years & over*
1998	**Newcastle, NSW**		
1st	**R. McLagen, Scotland**	**Natasha Millwood, Tas**	**Gregor Bowman, Scotland**
2nd	Cobie Williams, Vic	Alana Maybury, Qld	Amy Martin, NSW
3rd	Karen Cameron, Scotland	Karina Mosley, NSW	Grace Watson, Vic

Australian Board of Highland Dancing Inc

Champion of Champions Championship of Australia

CHAMPION OF CHAMPIONS CHAMPIONSHIP OF AUSTRALIA WINNERS 2000 — 2010

	7—12 years	*13, 14, 15 years*	*16 years & over*
2000	**Brisbane, Queensland**		
1st	**Chantelle Burke, NSW**	**Karina Mosley, NSW**	**Amy Roach, NSW**
2nd	Carissa Wiblin, NSW	Craig Johnston, Qld	Tony Cargill, Scotland
3rd	Zara Lim, Tas	Katie Trydal, Canada	Natasha Millwood, Tas
2002	**Launceston, Tasmania**		
1st	**L. Zalewski, New Zealand**	**Rebecca Fleming, NSW**	**Sarah Johnston, Qld**
2nd	Meaghan McPhee, Qld	Chantelle Burke, NSW	Craig Johnston, Qld
3rd	Emily Brown, Vic	Tiffany Elvin, Vic	Katie Trydal, Canada
2004	**Melbourne, Victoria**		
1st	**M. Bamford, New Zealand**	**David Wilton, Scotland**	**Craig Johnston, Qld**
2nd	Laura Andrews, Qld	Chantelle Burke, NSW	Natasha Millwood, NSW
3rd	Emily Brown, Vic	L. Salewski, New Zealand	R. McLagan, Scotland
2006	**Adelaide, South Australia**		
1st	**Erin Hopkins, Scotland**	**Emily Brown, Vic**	**Craig Johnston, Qld**
2nd	Jemma McCarthy, Qld	Laura Andrews, Qld	David Wilton, Scotland
3rd	A-M. Feierabend, WA	Emily Ingram, Tas	M. Lesperance, Canada
2008	**Newcastle, NSW**		
1st	**Anthea Bundy, Scotland**	**Jamie Conrick, Canada**	**David Wilton, Scotland**
2nd	Abby-Jane Taylor, NZ	Shayliesh Emmett, Vic	Katie Trydal, Canada
3rd	Sarah Hanel, SA	Emily Brown, Vic	Kyle Marston, NSW
2010	**Caloundra, Queensland**		
1st	**Abby-Jane Taylor, NZ.**	**Rebecca Smith, NSW**	**Kyle Marston, NSW**
2nd	Holly Keir, New Zealand	Fern Doyle, Qld	Emily Brown, Vic
3rd	Sarah Bourke, Tasmania	Chanel Aitkin, WA	Katie Trydal, Canada

OZSCOT AUSTRALIA

OzScot Australia, under the direction of Cheryl Roach OAM, is based in Bathurst NSW, and was established in 2000 by Amy and Cheryl Roach. OzScot showcases highland dancers from all the states and regions in Australia.

OzScot Australia has performed at the Edinburgh Military Tattoo in Scotland in 2002, 2004, 2007 and 2009. A team of 150 dancers was provided for the Salute to Australia by the Edinburgh Military Tattoo in Sydney in 2005, and again in 2010 provided a team of 100 dancers from all states and regions of Australia.

With a colourful and unique blend of traditional and contemporary highland dance, OzScot was proud to be the only international guest performer at the Oman Military Tattoo in November 2005. This was the first time females have been invited to perform, and the first time dancers were included in the Tattoo, which commemorated the 35th reign of the Sultan.

In 2008 OzScot Australia performed at both the Virginia International Tattoo and the Royal Nova Scotia International Tattoo. At the Nova Scotia Tattoo, OzScot performed very successfully its own special style of choreography.

OzScot Australia was delighted to accept an invitation to perform at the Basel Tattoo in 2009. This was OzScot's first performance in Europe. The Australians were very well received and the choreography.

The choreography provides a fresh approach to entertain the modern audience of today. The team has several dancers who have held or are currently holding Regional, State and Australian Championship Titles. It consists of dancers who are either at college, university or are professional women.

The OzScot Australia dancers have received excellent reviews and very high praise for their achievements. Because the team is selected from various parts of Australia, the first time the team works together is on arrival at the international event at which they are to perform.

This means intensive rehearsal to provide the splendid performances that the dancers are able to achieve.

The choreography provides a fresh approach to entertain the modern audience of today. The team has several dancers who have held or are currently holding Regional, State and Australian Championship Titles. It consists of dancers who are either at college, university or are professional women.

Some of the dancers in the team are no longer competitive dancers but are dancing and performing for entertainment only.

The OzScot Australia dancers have received excellent reviews and very high praise for their achievements.

Because the team is selected from various parts of Australia, the first time the team works together is on arrival at the international event at which they are to perform.

This means intensive rehearsal to provide the splendid performances that the dancers are able to achieve.

The dancers represent the Celtic community of Australia promoting Australia, Highland dancing and enjoy lasting friendships through dance.

Australian Board of Highland Dancing Inc
Past & Present Presidents

CURRENT ABHDI EXECUTIVE AND IMMEDIATE PAST PRESIDENTS

Judith Monteith
President

Elizabeth McLauchlan
Secretary

Julie Thomas
Senior Vice President

Carolyn Woollett
Junior Vice President

Dianne Harrison
Assistant Secretary

50th Golden Jubilee
of the
Australian Board of
Highland Dancing Inc

1960 2010

Donna Atkinson
Treasurer

CONGRATULATIONS

K. Roe & M. Paterson O.A.M. D.Urr

60th Diamond Jubilee
of the
Scottish Official Board
of Highland Dancing

N. Kennedy & M. Allen

Federation of United States
Highland Dancing Teachers and Adjudicators

Miss Christine Lacey, Chairman

Scottish Official Board of Highland Dancing

Heritage House

32 Grange Loan

Edinburgh, Scotland EH9 2NR

Dear Miss Lacey,

On behalf of FUSTA, its members, and the Board of Directors I would like to extend our congratulations and best wishes to the Scottish Official Board of Highland Dancing (SOBHD) on the occasion of its 60th Anniversary. It is fitting that a 60th Anniversary is symbolised by the diamond, which comes from the Greek root word adamas and means unconquerable and enduring. The organisation's anniversary is a time to celebrate the longevity of the Board, reflect on numerous accomplishments, and ponder upon its goals and hopes for the future.

It is commendable that the SOBHD has long been able to deal with contemporary issues, plan for the future, and also preserve the past. This successful record of achievement and progress provides its own commentary on the leadership, judgment and foresight of the remarkable people who have served on the Board throughout the past 60 years. It is an exciting time to be a member of the worldwide Highland dancing community. There is a feeling of optimism, co-operation, respect and admiration for the views and ideas each organisation has to offer. All Affiliated Members have the opportunity be a part of changes that will be made in the SOBHD, now and in the future.

I would further like to express our appreciation to our trusted advisor and Head Scottish Delegate, Aileen Robertson. Our other delegates, Katie Rowan, Gillian Lawrence, Nicola Grant and Dawn Fraser must also be thanked for their dedication and the time they devote to representing FUSTA. It is a pleasure to collaborate with these talented ladies whose knowledge and guidance are invaluable.

Congratulations on reaching this milestone! Best wishes to all as we continue to work together to promote Highland Dancing excellence throughout the world.

Best Regards,

AnneDonlan
FUSTA President

FUSTA...Twenty Five Years and Going Strong!

Written by Christie Freestone on the Occasion of FUSTA's 25th Anniversary.

Few Highland Dancers today remember a time when there was not a FUSTA organization in the United States. However, those of us who remember when Primary dancers were called "Babies," Premier dancers were called "Open" and "Best Dressed" referred to how well you wore your kilt (not to Hollywood's Top Ten) remember all too well! In those "Pre-FUSTA" days, Highland Dance flourished in many segregated areas of the country. Dancers often spent their entire competitive dancing career venturing no farther than a tank of gas would take them. An eastern area champion could reign and retire without ever dancing a propelled pivot turn with their western counterpart. North, South, East, West... and never the twain shall meet! Little did we know that Highland Dancing in the United States was about to change....

The vision for a national organisation came in the spring of 1979, when the idea of a national Highland Dance Championship was introduced to the Detroit area dance teachers. The United States was the only country in the Highland Dance world which did not host a national Championship competition. While the idea appealed to the local area teachers, it was imperative that all areas of the country embrace the concept for a U.S. Championship to become a reality. The idea was taken to the Grandfather Mountain Highland Games that summer, where it was introduced to a select group of judges and teachers from around the country. The response was overwhelming! The next step of the journey was to secure national support.

At the Professional Highland Dance Conference in Las Vegas, Nevada in 1980, Jeanne Roberts and Janis Burkhardt facilitated the first organisational meeting of U.S. teachers and judges attending the conference. Finally, East met West and North met South! Consolidated in their desire to sponsor a United States Highland Dance Championship, officers were elected and commissioned to initiate a national organisation representing all regions of the country. The Federation of United States Teachers and Adjudicators of Highland Dance (FUSTA) was established!

The founding officers, armed only with their enthusiasm, began the complex task of creating a national organisation from the ground up.

The first officers were: Christie Freestone, President; Jeanne Roberts, Vice-President; Janis Burkhardt, Secretary and Diane Krugh, Treasurer. They were responsible for naming the organisation, designing the logo, writing the by-laws, raising funds, instituting traditions, as well as generating the framework upon which the organisation would continually build.

Fusta's First Officers: Diane Krugh, Jeannie Roberts, Christie Freestone, Janis Burkhardt

FUSTA PRESIDENTS

Jumping the Hurdles and Leading the Way

Over the past 25 years, eleven dedicated individuals have held the office of FUSTA President. They have imparted the essence of Highland Dancing in the United States immeasurably.

Each entered their term of office with unique goals and are remembered for their varied accomplishments.

CHRISTIE FREESTONE

The first FUSTA President (1980-1982), never imagined that her original dream of having a national Championship would evolve into the prestigious organisation FUSTA is today. "The time was right, the enthusiasm was high, and the need had come for the United States to take its rightful place in the world of Highland Dance. I was inspired by the great American Highland Dancers and teachers of my day, and it was important to me to ensure that the American dancers, teachers and judges of the future would be respected around the world always!"

JANIS BURKHARDT

The second President of FUSTA (1982-1983), dedicated her term to escalating the prestige and recognition of the regional finalists. As President, she solicited funding through a letter writing campaign, contacting over two thousand Scottish organisations throughout the United States. As a result of her efforts, many U.S. Governors wrote personal letters of congratulations to their state Highland Dance finalists. "I am proud I was able to continue to carry the torch in developing FUSTA into a professional organisation."

ANN JOHNSON

Ann Johnson is the only individual who has served as President twice. She recalled the most difficult moment in her first Presidency (1983-1985) as her most significant contribution. "I am probably most remembered for correcting a scrutineering error. This particular error resulted in the wrong dancer being awarded a U.S. Championship title. Not correcting the error would have been a contradiction in the standard that FUSTA had worked so diligently to establish."

MARGUERITE REID

Marguerite Reid, fourth President of FUSTA (1985-1987), was the instigator of the first meeting between FUSTA and the Scottish Official Board of Highland Dancing (SOBHD). Establishing communication between these two organisations was a priority during her term. She was remembered as saying, "The standard of dance has definitely improved since the establishment of FUSTA.

SHARON FARRAR

Sharon Farrar, fifth President of FUSTA (1987-1989), is best remembered for her efforts and accomplishments in securing tax exempt and incorporation status for FUSTA. She had the foresight to recognise the changing needs of a growing organisation. In response to these changing needs and to our desire to be an SOBHD Affiliated Member, Sharon initiated the revision of the original by-laws to make FUSTA's organisational structure acceptable to the SOBHD. In 1988, during Sharon's term, the Board approved FUSTA's application to be an Affiliated Member. "My most enjoyable and memorable duty as President was to give a toast of honor to our USIR finalists as they prepared to compete at Alexandria, Virginia in 1988 and Monterey, California in 1989. The excellence of our United States dancers is a tribute to FUSTA's success."

SANDRA WEYMAN

Sandra Weyman entered her term as President (1989-1991) during a rather difficult time in FUSTA's history. "I spent many hours in phone calls and personal contacts, facilitating open communication between the regions. It was important to me to promote and encourage harmony among the regions. I wanted all members to appreciate the contributions of each other to Highland Dancing." The results of a survey she created led to the shifting of FUSTA's focus from simply hosting the United States Inter-Regional Championship to that of a more nationally incorporated organisation.

JEANNIE BRAUN

Jeannie Braun's accomplishments as FUSTA's seventh President (1991-1993) include sponsoring the first national workshop tour open to FUSTA members and delegates in all regions in the U.S. She must also be remembered for her efforts in the first co-sponsored FUSTA/ScotDance Professional Conference in Las Vegas in 1992, as well as the institution of the first national registration scheme of U.S. Highland Dancers. "I fondly acknowledge all the many willing workers.... for nothing happens without their co-operation and hard work."

ELIZABETH COYLE

Elizabeth Coyle, eighth President of FUSTA (1993-1995) saw the initiation of the World Wide Registration scheme during her term of office. Elizabeth maintained a passionate desire to achieve national identity for the FUSTA organisation during her presidency. Like other past Presidents, she credits FUSTA with, "raising the standards of Highland Dancing in the United States."

CATHERINE HYND

Catherine Hynd, the ninth President of FUSTA (1995-1997) achieved a stronger voice for FUSTA on the SOBHD by attending the first Liaison Meeting in Glasgow, initiated the revision of the FUSTA bylaws, published a competition list, printed the FUSTA brochure, provided duplicate judge's sheets for U.S. Championships, established a Judges' Committee and produced the FUSTA tape/CD of music for dancing. Emphasis was decidedly on service to the members of the organisation. "This is not about what I have done, but about what we have done: three sharp, efficient officers, bright, objective regional delegates, willing committee chairmen and the general membership have made it possible to provide greater service to our members and to move FUSTA toward strong national leadership and independence."

NANCY STROLLE

Nancy Strolle (1997-1999) focused her term of office on motivating and encouraging the membership to become involved in "their organisation." Under her leadership, the bylaws were completed. Nancy was the first President to take part in actual SOBHD Board Meetings and the SOBHD AGM. This was one of many turning points in the history of FUSTA that have served to make the organization the dynamic force in the United States that it is today. "How wonderful it was to have had the opportunity to attend the various SOBHD meetings and help to bring a "face" of FUSTA to Scotland and bring a better understanding of the SOBHD back to FUSTA.

Our attendance at those meetings helped to open the door to better relationships. After all, we were all working towards the same goals…that of furthering Highland Dancing even if we weren't always on the same page."

BILL WEAVER

Bill Weaver, FUSTA's first and only male president (1999-2003) helped to increase communication by establishing the FUSTA website. During his two terms as President, he worked to foster global change by pushing for a true worldwide board that included an organisation which represents Scotland as an entity separate from the SOBHD which continues to be developed. Bill's hard work was responsible for the fact that overseas organisations such as FUSTA are now being treated as peers by the SOBHD as evidenced by the fact that FUSTA and other organisations have been given more autonomy to act on many domestic issues as well as being asked for input on various global issues and problems that come up for discussion. "Although people may not agree with every decision the President makes, I feel that I had the strength to act on my convictions always in the best interests of FUSTA and Highland Dancing."

ANN JOHNSON

Ann Johnson, in her second term as President of FUSTA (2003-2009), believed that FUSTA's focus had not really changed since the organisation was founded in 1980, but it had expanded. In the early years the focus was building the organisation. As FUSTA grew and became more established, it successfully balanced meeting the needs of its diverse membership with assuming a larger role in the worldwide community of Highland Dance. She believed that the challenge for the future would be to maintain that balance to ensure FUSTA's longevity. "One of the things I find most appealing about FUSTA members is their collective willingness to make significant changes without compromising the integrity or ideals of the organisation. Each change has become a part of FUSTA's story, defined its history and shaped its future."

ANNE DONLAN

Anne Donlan, the current FUSTA President, came to office in 2009 after 15 years of service on the Board of Directors. As Vice President, Anne succeeded in persuading all the competitions in the United States to register with FUSTA. She compiled a Competition Organisers' Manual that is issued to Organisers when they register and is updated on a regular basis. This manual is invaluable when new people assume the role of Organiser. Anne also wrote a USIR Manual that records the details of running a USIR. "It is a privilege for me to serve as FUSTA President, after serving in the positions as Eastern Region Delegate, Secretary, and Vice President over the course of the past 15 years. As FUSTA celebrates its 30th Anniversary this year, we reflect on how far we have come and look forward to the future and expanding on our achievements, meeting the needs of our membership, and continuing to work with the SOBHD and member organisations to promote Highland Dancing throughout the world."

USIR – PAST AND PRESENT

The first 29 years as written by Diane MacPhee Krugh

The first USIR (United States Inter Regional Championship) was in 1981 and 12 miles from the center of freedom, our Nation's capital, Washington, D.C. The host hotel was located in the heart of Alexandria, Virginia, just a few miles away from the USIR venue. The day was hot and sunny when all those dreams became a reality and history was being made for Highland Dancing in the United States. Since that time we have had 28 USIR Championships in 20 different cities all around the country.

Over the years FUSTA has had to alter the original format of the Championship to accommodate the ever-increasing number of competitors. For the first twelve years, dancers competed in four age groups: 12 Years and Under, 15 Years and Under, 17 Years and Under and 18 Years and Over. Then the top three dancers in each age group received recognition. By 1993, participation had grown to the point that FUSTA decided to add an 11 Years and Under group and changed the 12 Years and Under to 13 Years and Under. In 2004, the number of dancers recognised in each age group grew from three to six. Additionally, each U.S. Champion earns a bye for the following year's regional contest and automatically receives a spot at the USIR.

The USIRs not only have raised the standard of Highland Dancing in the United States but they have also built camaraderie amongst the country's Highland Dancing community. Before the USIR, Highland Dancing competitions were primarily regional, making opportunities to meet other dancers from around the country very limited. Now dancers look forward to travelling each summer to new cities and states, to see old friends and make new ones during a long weekend that includes sightseeing, banquets and dances (not the Scottish kind!). It is unanimous that everyone enjoys the social gatherings. Parents mingle with other parents at breakfasts, afternoon teas, or evening wine and cheese, while teachers and judges have their own time to socialise.

One of the highlights of the USIR weekend is a special lunch or dinner that honors that year's USIR representatives. This event also includes the announcement of a new Hall of Fame member and the winners of the FUSTA Academic Scholarships.

Traditions associated with the USIR have evolved over its twenty-nine years. For example, at the first Championship, the dancers were given punch cups and the very first USIR toast was made to the dancers around the swimming pool of the host hotel. Now, those punch cups are presented to the teachers who have dancers attending the USIR for the first time and all the teachers who have had a representative at the USIR get recognised the day of the Championship.

At the second USIR in Portland, Oregon, Lynne Dickson Abbott from Australia thought we should recognise the dancer/teacher partnership that had gained the most aggregate points in the USIR. Ms. Abbott donated the Australian Achievement Award - a lovely wooden boomerang for the dancer, plus an opal ring for the dancer and his/her teacher. After nine years, in 1994, the award was changed to the perpetual FUSTA Achievement Award – a crystal bowl presented to the dancer who gained the most aggregate points. In 1998, that award was retired.

The FUSTA Officers And The New SOBHD Banner
USIR 2007 Irvine

Until 1997, a Dancer of the Day Trophy was presented to the winner of a dance off. Now, all the US Champions dance a four-step Victory Fling. Since 1999, all the teachers of the U.S. Champions are presented gold charms signifying the year their dancers won. In addition, each U.S. Champion in the 11 and Under, 13 and Under, and 18 and Over age groups receives a monetary scholarship in honor of three special ladies, Mrs Marguerite Reid, Mrs Betty Lawrence and Mrs Jessie Haggerty, MBE.

The Parade of Regions is one of the traditions that has remained the same over all these years. Dancers from each region line up behind their banners and are presented to the audience in a display of regional pride. Each dancer is then presented a certificate of accomplishment.

We have come a long way from those early years. We as teachers have grown from strength to strength in our knowledge and appreciation of Highland Dancing. We consider it an honour and a privilege to have our students be part of Highland Dancing history. A special note of thanks and gratitude to those great talents, past and present, from Scotland who educated us and fostered the growth of Highland Dancing in the days before FUSTA. From each of us in the United States to all in Scotland, thank you for sharing your love, appreciation, technique and dedication. We are truly grateful!

The First USIR ***Alexandria, Virginia 1981***

UNITED STATES INTER-REGIONAL Championship WINNERS

	LOCATION	*7 & U13*	*13 & U16*
1981	Alexandria, VA	Susan McKee	Cheryl Fisher
1982	Portland, OR	Penny Bruce	Michelle Powell
1983	Oberlin, OH	Kim Demsey	Susan McKee
1984	San Diego, CA	Laura Carruthers	Mary Hokeness
1985	Grandfather Mtn.	Laura Carruthers	Susan McKee
1986	Chicago, IL	Laura Carruthers	Alison Mittig
1987	Portland, OR	Jennifer Miller	Alison Mittig
1988	Alexandria, VA	Jennifer Miller	Laura Carruthers
1989	Monterey, CA	Kimberly Capitani	Laura Carruthers
1990	Denver, CO	Kimberly Capitani	Laura Yosowitz
1991	Nashville, TN	Nancy Fredrickson	Jody Vandenbossche
1992	Minneapolis, MN	Ashley Knox	Kimberly Capitani

	LOCATION	**16 & U18**	**18 & Over**
1981	Alexandria, VA	Shirlee Finch	Kathleen Campbell
1982	Portland, OR	CherylFisher	Harry Farrar
1983	Oberlin, OH	Cheryl Fisher	Kay Hamilton
1984	San Diego, CA	Michelle Powell	Harry Farrar
1985	Grandfather Mtn.	Valerie Langston	Cheryl Fisher
1986	Chicago, IL	Karen Campbell	Cheryl Fisher
1987	Portland, OR	Audrey Chang	Cheryl Fisher
1988	Alexandria, VA	Alison Mittig	Cheryl Fisher
1989	Monterey, CA	Alison Mittig	Kathleen Drummond
1990	Denver, CO	Rebecca McConnell	Harry Farrar
1991	Nashville, TN	Laura Yosowitz	Lynda Maxwell
1992	Minneapolis, MN	Laura Yosowitz	Laura Carruthers

USIR: 1981 Champions

USIR: 1983 Champions

UNITED STATES INTER-REGIONAL CHAMPIONS

	LOCATION	7 & U12	12 & U14	14 & U16
1993	Seattle, WA	Ashley Knox	Melissa Webster	Kimberly Capitani
1994	Altamont, NY	Ashley Knox	Michelle Cumagan	Melissa Webster
1995	San Diego, CA	Ashley Knox	Bree Brownlee	Melissa Webster
1996	Houston, TX	Megan Kimsey	Ashley Knox	Michelle Cumagan
1997	Chesapeake, VA	Megan Kimsey	Ashley Knox	Michelle Cumagan
1998	Detroit, MI	Mary Susan Sinclair	Kate DeGood	Ashley Knox
1999	Portland, OR	Courtney Sutcliffe	Jocelyn Case	Ashley Knox
2000	Philadelphia, PA	Holly Dorger	Courtney Sutcliffe	Kate DeGood
2001	Long Beach, CA	Cosette Aguirre	Courtney Sutcliffe	Mary Susan Sinclair
2002	Denver, CO	Eleanor Carrick	Carla Gardner	Mary Susan Sinclair
2003	Grandfather Mtn, NC	Shannon Anfindsen	Carla Gardner	Courtney Sutcliffe
2004	Minneapolis, MN	Hillary Lewis	Kelsey Crane	Carla Gardner
2005	Mt. Vernon, WA	Meghan Palmer	Shannon Anfindsen	Kelsey Crane
2006	Saratoga Springs, NY	Kathleen Black	Lauren Cooper	Kelsey Crane
2007	Irvine, CA	Georgianna Schwartz	Alison Ashworth	Lauren Cooper
2008	Denver, CO	Meghan Palmer	Jean Stein	Lauren Cooper
2009	Nashville	Kaylee Finnegan	Jean Stein	Mikhaila Markham

	LOCATION	16 & U18	18 & Over
1993	Seattle, WA	Jennifer Hastings	Karen Fisher
1994	Altamont, VA	Kimberly Capitani	Laura Yosowitz
1995	San Diego, CA	Kimberly Capitani	Lynda Conner
1996	Houston, TX	Melissa Webster	Chrissy Taft
1997	Chesapeake, VA	Melissa Webster	Lynda Conner
1998	Detroit, MI	Michelle Cumagan	Melissa Webster
1999	Portland, OR	Michelle Cumagan	Chrissy Taft
2000	Philadelphia, PA	Erin Hannigan	Michelle Cumagan
2001	Long Beach, CA	Kate DeGood	Kira Cogswell
2002	Denver, CO	Kate DeGood	Kira Cogswell
2003	Grandfather Mtn NC	Jocelyn Case	Kira Cogswell
2004	Minneapolis, MN	Kari MacNaughton	Kate DeGood
2005	Mt. Vernon, WA	Kari MacNaughton	Kira Cogswell
2006	Saratoga Springs, NY	Carla Gardner	Kate DeGood
2007	Irvine, CA	Carla Gardner	Kari MacNaughton
2008	Denver, CA	Kelsey Crane	Kari MacNaughton
2009	Nashville, TN	Lauren Cooper	Kari MacNaughton

USIR: 2000 Champions

Parade of Regions, Grandfather Mountain, 2003

Champion Courtney Sutcliffe and Eilidh MacMillan (Scotland) dance Choreography at ***USIR 2001*** with the Queen Mary ship in background

USIR: 2007 Champions

USIR: 2008 Champions

FUSTA MILESTONES

1980 The first FUSTA meeting is held at the Professional Highland Dance Conference in Las Vegas, Nevada.

1981 The first USIR is held in Alexandria, Virginia.

1982 The FUSTA Newsletter is published for the first time with Sharon Farrar as editor.

1983 FUSTA is incorporated as a non-profit tax exempt corporation.

1988 FUSTA becomes an Affiliated Member of the SOBHD.

1992 FUSTA establishes a national dancer registration scheme and soon becomes part of the SOBHD Worldwide Registration Scheme.

1995 FUSTA President Cathy Hynd attends the first SOBHD Liaison Meeting on August 21, 1995 in Glasgow. A FUSTA representative has attended this meeting every year since its inception.

1996 FUSTA holds its first Midwinter Meeting in Chicago, IL.

1996 Bill Weaver creates FUSTA's first website.

1998 FUSTA establishes the policy of sending its President to the SOBHD AGM and November Meeting every year. Nancy Strolle becomes the first FUSTA President to attend.

2004 FUSTA establishes an academic scholarship for our college-bound dancers.

2005 FUSTA invites our Head Delegate to the SOBHD, Miss Aileen Robertson, to attend the FUSTA Midwinter Meeting annually.

2005 FUSTA celebrates the 25th USIR at Mt. Vernon, Washington.

2006 FUSTA establishes the FUSTA Hall of Fame.

2007 FUSTA National Scrutineering Certification Course is introduced.

2008 FUSTA Competition Organizers' Manual is written and distributed by Vice President, Anne Donlan.

2008 FUSTA honors Jessie Stewart Haggarty, MBE for her contribution in developing Highland Dancing worldwide and especially in the United States by establishing a scholarship in her name to be presented to the Adult Champion at the USIR.

FUSTA...

the ***legacy*** and ***future*** of
Highland Dance in America!

MID-WINTER MEETING

Way back in 1996, FUSTA's Board of Directors had advanced from "Snail Mail" to scheduled conference calls, however, this innovation proved to be expensive and difficult due to everyone's schedule and a three hour time difference within the U.S.

It was a cold, snowy weekend in February 1996 when we met at the Drake Hotel in Chicago, a somewhat centralized location for everyone. This was the first "Mid-Winter Meeting" that has become an important part of FUSTA's workings today. By the way, every officer and delegate paid for their own transportation, accommodations and food for this initial meeting.

That weekend we set up an annual scholarship for the winner of the 11 & Under USIR Championship group in the name of Marguerite Reid. (Later the Betty Lawrence scholarship was established for the winner of the 13 & under USIR Championship.)

Additionally we established a U.S. Judges Committee which was chaired by Lynne Erbrick, provided duplicate judges sheets free of charge to all US Organizers, and put together a list of annual competitions and Championships in the U.S. which were granted by the SOBHD. As a result of this meeting, Vice President Nancy Strolle produced a P.R brochure as an aid to Scottish Dancing for parents and other interested people. Lastly, we were able to brainstorm ideas for a potential CD of Highland Dancing music. With the generosity of several well known pipers, technical support from Andrew Hart, and the musical ears of dance teachers Sheila Mittig and Marguerite Reid, we were able to produce a CD album of Highland Dancing Music... "Dance to the Piper" which turned out to be a musical and financial success, and remains a favorite among Highland Dancing CD's throughout the world.

Many FUSTA committees and activities were enhanced at this first meeting held out with the USIR event.

Present were:	CathyHynd, President	
	Nancy Strolle, Vice President	
	Linda Armstrong, Secretary	
	Mary Recknagel, Treasurer	
Regional Delegates:	Anne Donlan, East	Pat Johnston, Southeast
	Bill Weaver, Midwest	Andy Aitken, Southwest
	Ann Johnson, Northwest	Kay Hamilton, West

It should be noted that all of the above FUSTA Board members are still very active in FUSTA today, and have continued to make significant contributions to our organization.

Submitted by: Cathy Hynd, President, 1995-1997

FUSTA SCHOLARSHIP

Early in 2004, FUSTA established a scholarship program. The fundamental idea behind the program was to support and encourage through financial aide, our next generation of professionals. High school seniors, entering their first year of college are encouraged to apply.

The scholarship application is a three part process. Students need to complete the application, send three letters of recommendation and write an essay (based on one question out of 3 given in the application). While this scholarship is not a need based award, the committee, comprised of a chairperson and 2 members, read and evaluate each application.

The program to date has been very successful. Our scholarship has increased from $500.00 to $1,000.00 and the number of applicants has risen each year. In 2008 our program was named the FUSTA Scholarship in memory of Harry Farrar IV. Through the generous sponsorship of the Farrar family, FUSTA will be able to provide scholarship money to its dancers for many years.

This year a scholarship for college students has been added to the FUSTA Scholarship program. The Eunice Baird Whittlesey Memorial Scholarship ($500) for students in college or graduate school is donated by the Donlan Family in memory of Anne's Mother.

Winners to date:
2004 – Megan Kimsey
2005 – Elizabeth Fishback
2006 – Hannah Faustman
2007 – Susan Tapp
2008 – Cosette Aguirre
2009 – Sarah Clark

COMPETITION ORGANIZERS MANUAL

In 2007, Anne Donlan assembled the Competition Organizers' Manual, devising a new numbering system for competition stamps, and contacting each organizer in the U.S. inviting them to participate. A Regional Competition Organizer Liaison was appointed for each of the six regions in the U.S.

It became clear that it was time for US competition organizers to come together, provide mutual support, act as resources for one another, and insure that there was a baseline of consistency for all dance competitions. The idea was to assist Organizers who need help, provide current information to all organizers and encourage building a network for US competition organizers.

SCRUTINEERING CERTIFICATION PROGRAM

The first course and first certification test was given to invited members and non-members of FUSTA at Irvine in July 2007. Twenty-six passed the test and became FUSTA Certified Scrutineers (FCS), thirteen of whom qualified to be FUSTA Certified Scrutineer/Instructors. The goal was to train trainers from each region who would in turn teach the course, give the test, and certify more scrutineers. FUSTA would eventually have a deep pool of people certified to scrutineer at the regional selection competitions and the USIR. A Scrutineering Manual was written by Jim Kalat and edited by Mary Recknagel and Nancy Strolle. Mary also developed the first test and course. Betty Lawrence, FUSTA's Head Scrutineer for many years, led the work of refining the certification test and assisted in proofing and updating the manual. The manual is available on the FUSTA website www.fusta.us along with a list of FUSTA Certified Scrutineers.

FUSTA NATIONAL JUDGES COMMITTEE

The FUSTA Judges' Committee was formed by Cathy Hynd during her term as FUSTA President in 1996. She appointed Lynne Erbrick as the chairperson and there was a judge representative from each of the FUSTA regions that formed a judges' committee. Lynne served in the position from 1996 through 2001 and proved to be very successful in the formation and functions of the newly formed committee. John Hynd was elected to succeed Lynne in 2001 and has continued in that role until the present time. The Judges Committee is an important part of FUSTA. It liaisons with the SOBHD and keeps our judges informed and up to date with all matters relating to judges. Over the years, we have worked to establish credibility with the Judges and Technical Committees of the SOBHD and now feel very satisfied with our accomplishments...for the benefit of all. The chairman is on the Board of Directors of FUSTA, maintains accurate records and attendance of all U.S. judges, provides prescribed reports to the SOBHD, communicates regularly with National Regional Judges' Committee members and performs duties as requested by the SOBHD and the FUSTA Board of Directors. Current regional members of the FUSTA Judges' Committee are: Sandra Weyman, East; Holly Hodgkin, Midwest; Gail Bacon, Northwest; Margaret Howard, Southeast; Andrea Tronnes, Southwest; and Cathy Hynd, West.

FUSTA NATIONAL REGISTRAR

The primary duty of the National Registrar is to make sure that the SOBHD World Wide Registration Scheme runs smoothly and efficiently in the United States. Each of the six regions have their own area registrar and the National Registrar works closely with those registrars in handling the problems that are encountered along the way. One of the additional responsibilities of this position is being a member of FUSTA's Executive Board. Diane Krugh has held this position since 2000.

FLASH FROM THE PAST... INTO THE FUTURE

Edinburgh, July 1958 - John Hynd, center, is the first U.S. winner of the British Overseas Championship at the International Festival of Dance. He is currently the Judges' Chair and a member of the FUSTA Board of Directors. Others in the photo are from left, Marjory Greig, Kirkcaldy; unknown; Shonah (Jamieson) Robinson (co-winner, British Overseas), SOBHD judge in South Africa; Betty Jessiman, Huntly, winner of the British Open Championship; Sylvia Henderson, Crossgates; Elizabeth (Farmer) McLaughlin, SOBHD judge and current President of the Australian Board of Highland Dancing; Sandra (Bald) Jones, SOBHD judge and a member of ScotDance Canada's executive committee; Paul Collins, President, Scottish Dance Teachers' Alliance.

FUSTA ...THE FUTURE

The future of FUSTA looks bright! It is rewarding to see that many of our former dancers have become teachers and judges, as well as competition organizers, scrutineers and are willing to help out in many ways at both competitions and Championships held in the United States. A current example is that the co-chairs and key committee chairs of the 2010 USIR event are all former USIR champions. All of FUSTA's regions are full of enthusiastic, experienced and interested young people to carry on our traditions. Many young teachers have taken an active role in regional activities and are taking membership exams from the examining bodies. A dozen or more have indicated an interest in taking the Judges Test, and are studying for the upcoming exam later this year in Anaheim, California. Many of these future leaders are the products of our founding members, Past Presidents and national and regional leaders who are providing guidance and encouragement to our younger members. We are proud of these young people, and know that Highland Dancing in the United States has a strong future.

FUSTA HALL OF FAME

JEANNIE BRAUNS

Jeannie Brauns was born in 1928 in Trenton, NJ. She graduated from Rider College and then worked for the state of NY. Besides her family, her passion in life was Scottish Highland Dancing. Throughout her life, she had formed many lifelong friendships within the Scottish community around the world. Jeannie founded the Albany Area Capital District Braemar Highland Dancers in 1962, later opening another school in Rome, NY. Many of her dancers went on to compete at numerous Championships including the U.S.I.R. She was the founder of the Scotia Highland Dancing Competition and dance organizer for the Capital District Scottish Games. In 1981, she opened the Braemar Summer School of Highland Dancing and Kiltmaking. She was a member of several organizations, past president of FUSTA and Daughters of Scotia. Jeannie was also a life member of the SDTA. (d. 2005)

MARGARET CALLANDER

Margaret Callander was born in Cleveland, Ohio. She began dancing at the age of 5. She is a Life Member of the BATD and has been a Member of the SOBHD Judges' Panel for many years. In 1955 she won at the Edinburgh Festival. She began teaching in 1950. Her students have won many awards in the United States, Canada and Scotland. She was secretary of USHDA before FUSTA was created. USHDA was comprised of members from the present Midwest Region and Eastern Region. From members of this association, FUSTA was born. Margaret was one of the founders of the Ohio Scottish Games, which led to the organization of the Ohio Scottish Arts School. For the past 28 years the School has promoted Highland Dancing to students from the United States and Canada. The School promotes teacher training and has produced hundreds of teachers to carry on our Scottish Arts and Traditions.

FLORENCE HART

FLORENCE HART started highland dancing lessons in Scotland when she was 5years old. She became a Cowal medalist and Fife champion. At 15, she won a scholarship to the Celtic Ballet School of Theatre Dance and studied there for 3years in Glasgow. Florence danced in Britain until the age of 23. She arrived in the United States in 1961 where she started teaching highland dancing. She began her SOBHD judging career in 1967. Florence has a fellowship in SDTA and is a member of UKAPTD. She has trained many champion dancers and has had representatives from the Midwest at the U.S.I.R. for the last 25 years. She taught at Macalester College for 38 years and organized the Macalester Highland Games in 1965.

BETTY LAWRENCE

Betty Lawrence, originally from Ayr, Scotland now lives in Oklahoma City with her husband Matt. She has taught highland dancing for over 50 years and is a Member of SDTA. She is a Fellow and Examiner Emeritus of the BATD and is on the SOBHD Judges Panel. Betty has taught at the Ohio School of Scottish Arts for numerous years and has mentored many dancers. She is an advocate of dancers continuing their education to become teachers and judges. Betty continues to foster a love of highland dancing and shares her knowledge with many students and teachers.

SHEILA MITTIG

Sheila Mittig Born in Balloch, Scotland, Sheila studied all forms of dance at the Stewart School, Alexandria. Sheila emigrated to Dearborn, Michigan in 1964 and immediately began teaching Highland Dancing. She is a Life Member of the B.A.T.D. and has been on the S.O.B.H.D. Judges' Panel for many years. Sheila has judged and taught workshops all over the world and has taught two World Champions. Sheila now lives in Novi, Michigan where she still teaches along with her daughter, Alison. A former student of Sheila's, Alison is a four time U.S. Highland Dance Champion.

VERA MILLER PATTERSON'S

Vera Miller Patterson's love of Dance began in Scotland at an early age. Studying with the best teachers she became well versed in the disciplines of Highland, Ballet, Tap and Character, winning many prizes in local competitions. Following the war, Vera emigrated to the US with her husband and young daughter and began teaching Highland and Ballet in Lorain, Ohio. Her students won numerous awards and Championships in the US and Canada including the Eastern US, Adult World and Junior World Titles. With her friends and colleagues, Vera was one of the founders of the USHDA – the forerunner of FUSTA - and was active in the BATD and SOBHD. Many active teachers, judges and dancers were recipients of her generous knowledge, sharing, her uncanny gift of timing and her deep and abiding love of Scotland and the art of Highland Dancing. (d. 2005).

MARGUERITE REID

Marguerite Reid was born in Philadelphia, PA on March 19, 1933. Her parents, Sam and Isabel Watson, emigrated here from Scotland. As a young child she went to Scotland where her love of Highland Dancing was born. She began dancing when she was five in Trenton, NJ with Wilma Buick. Marguerite began teaching at an early age by teaching her cousins, Helen Magee and Judy Magee Hackett. The Daughters of Scotia also provided her with dance students, one of those being Catherine Davidson Fisher. She was a pioneer in the field of highland dancing in a number of ways. She was one of the first teachers to embrace the new philosophy of the SOBHD. She was one of the first SOBHD judges in the US. She served as the fourth President of FUSTA and paved the way to FUSTA's becoming an Affiliated Member of the SOBHD. Her willingness to try new methods or approaches is what kept her teaching inspirational. (d. 2004).

MARY STEWART

Mary Stewart came to Kearny from Glasgow, Scotland in December 1951. In 1953, she started teaching Scottish Highland Dancing at the Masonic Temple on Kearny Avenue. In 1968, she moved her school to a small studio in the basement of a two-family home, a short walk from her Devon Street home. In 2000, Mrs. Stewart retired after nearly 50 years of teaching. In those years, she taught hundreds of dancers and trained 6 current FUSTA members. Mrs. Stewart was a past Grand Chief of the Daughters of Scotia Bonnie Doon Lodge 10, a member of the Siloam Shrine 17, the Order of the Eastern Star Kelvin Chapter 69, and the Order of the Eastern Star Arlington Chapter 66. Mrs. Stewart was a long-time member of FUSTA and its predecessor, USHDA. She judged all over Scotland, Canada, and the United States and was a BATD examiner and life member. (d. 2001).

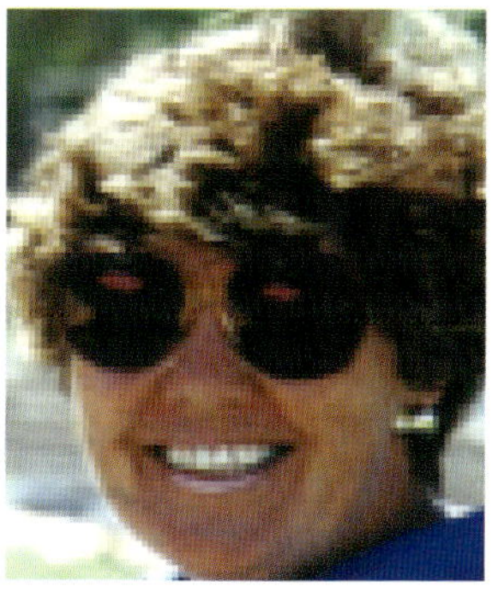

NORINE HARMON

Norine Harmon grew up in Western Canada where she was a competitive highland dancer from the time she was very young, winning many awards including Championships in Canada. After her family moved to California when she was in her late teens, Norine competed as a professional roller skater. When she came back to highland dance, it was as a certified Highland Dance instructor with the SDTA in 1965. Norine and her husband settled in San Jose, CA where she started the San Jose School of Highland Dance. In addition to being a successful highland dance instructor, Norine contributed to highland dance through many other avenues. She was the highland dance coordinator for the Caledonian Club of San Francisco and for many other highland games, including the first Monterey Highland Games since it was first held in Pebble Beach. Norine also judged throughout the United States and Canada. She was a Life Member of the SDTA. Norine inspired many highland dancers. She was one of a kind, and we are all fortunate to have shared her enthusiasm for highland dance and Scottish culture. (d. 2007).

CATHY HYND

Cathy Hynd began Highland lessons at an early age in St. Catharines, Ontario, spending most of her competitive years with Shirley Ashdown. She had a very successful career as a competitor at all the major competitions in the Eastern United States and Ontario. Cathy was the co-founder of the United States Highland Dancing Association (USHDA) and was influential in organizing the first SOBHD sanctioned Championship in the U.S. in the early 1960's. She married John Hynd and moved to California. Cathy and John were amongst the first American members of the Worldwide SOBHD Judges Panel. Cathy was part of a group who organized FUSTA in Las Vegas in 1980. From its inception, she has continued to be committed to the goals and success of FUSTA and has actively participated to the present day. Cathy has produced 12 USIR champions, a Junior World Champion and a 1st runner up. Some of her former pupils are current members of FUSTA and several are on the SOBHD World. wide Judges Panel. Over a 50-plus year span, Cathy remains committed to the goals of FUSTA and the SOBHD, and to excellence in competitive Highland Dancing. She is currently a Life Member of the BATD and a Member and Examiner of the UKA.

UNITED STATES WORLD CHAMPIONS

COWAL GATHERING - DUNOON, SCOTLAND

Noreen Keros, Michigan
1967 Junior World Champion
Teacher: Sheila Mittig

Lynne Erbrick, Pennsylvania
1967 Junior World Champion
Teacher: Marguerite Reid

Hugh Bigney, Ohio
1973 Adult World Champion
Teacher: Vera Miller

Mary Beth Miller, Missouri
1976 Juvenile World Champion
1977Junior World Champion
Teacher: Sheila Mittig

Fiona Nash, California
1980 Junior World Champion
Teacher: Cathy Hynd

Sandra Scafate, Ohio
1970 Junior World Champion
Teacher: Vera Miller
(No Photo Available)

Michelle Cumagan, Texas 1997
Juvenile World Champion
Teachers: Donna Cusack and Diane Krugh

USIR 1995 Champions
Bree Brownlee, Ashley Knox and Kimberly Capitani with Sharon Capitani

Ashley Knox, Michigan 1999
Juvenile World Champion
Teacher: Jill Fuller

Left: FUSTA Head Delegate Aileen Robertson, Rhona Lawrence and Jacqueline Aird - Scottish Judges at USIR 2007.

USIR 2009 Champions
Kaylee Finnegan, Jean Stein, Mikhaila Markham, Lauren Cooper and Kari MacNaughton

USIR 1999 Champions
Michelle Cumagan and Chrissy Taft with Teachers Donna Cusack and Diane Krugh

The Official Board of Highland Dancing South Africa

THE OFFICIAL BOARD OF HIGHLAND DANCING SOUTH AFRICA

The Republic of South Africa is located at the southern tip of the African continent. It borders the countries of Namibia, Botswana, Zimbabwe, Mozambique and Swaziland. Lesotho is an enclave entirely surrounded by South African territory.

South Africa has experienced a significantly different evolution from other nations in Africa as a result of two facts. Firstly, immigration from Europe reached levels not experienced in other African communities. Secondly, the strategic importance of the Cape Sea Route. As a result of the former, South Africa is a very racially diverse nation, often referred to as The Rainbow Nation - a term coined by Archbishop Desmond Tutu and later elaborated upon by then President Nelson Mandela as a metaphor to describe the country's newly-developing multicultural diversity in the wake of segregationist apartheid ideology. There are 11 official languages.

South Africa is an all year destination so when you visit depends on what you intend and prefer to do. Winters are mild except in the highest country, where there are frosts and occasional snowfalls. Holidaymakers stream out of the cities from mid December to late January and resorts and national parks are heavily booked during these times.

The vegetation varies dramatically - from the Wild Coast, the inland Game parks and Nature reserves or farms to the hot dry open spaces of the interior. Apart from the abundance of wildlife there is an abundance of rock art sites left by the Bushmen, for one to explore. South Africa is quite justly proud of its rich natural heritage, which is being diligently protected in the many nature reserves and wildlife parks. South Africa is the third most biologically diverse country in the world.

SHORT HISTORY OF THE OBHD(SA)

Historically, Highland Dancing in the country has been in evidence as far back as the 1920's with the first recorded South African Championships having been held in 1932. Originally, highland dancing activities in the country were governed by the Federated Caledonian Society of Southern Africa, but documentary evidence points to the OBHD(SA) being formed during the period 1961 to 1963, from which time it became the recognised governing body of Highland Dancing in South Africa. The OBHD(SA) is proud to be an Affiliated Member of the Scottish Official Board of Highland Dancing.

Politically, South Africa was severely ostracised and increasingly isolated from the rest of the world in the seventies and eighties, and it is thanks to the support of the SDTA and annual visits from the likes of Shendl Russell and Helen Fitzpatrick that South African teachers and dancers were able to be kept up to date with technique and prevailing standards. The collapse of apartheid and the 1994 democratic elections heralded a new era of hope and reconciliation for the country.

The Official Board of Highland Dancing South Africa

In 1999, for a variety of reasons, "a new-look" OBHD(SA) was structured, negotiated by all parties in the community and offering members from all around the country, equal and fair representation. Meetings are shared equally amongst the four regions ensuring all areas have the opportunity to share in all business.

Despite our small numbers, registered dancers in the country over the past 2 years show a steady, if slight, increase. Some reasons for this increase may be accredited to the ever-increasing accessibility of overseas travel, which has resulted in teams of dancers, as well as individuals, travelling to compete and perform in Scotland and elsewhere. The positive effects of the resulting exposure to International Competition is possibly best demonstrated by the achievements of Gillian O'Leary, who in recent years twice won the Juvenile World Championship – an extremely proud moment for Highland Dancing in South Africa.

The Official Board of Highland Dancing is structured as follows:

MEMBERS

EXECUTIVE
Elected annually
Current executive

4 Regional Committees Each having 3 delegates

Honorary Members

Mrs.S.Robinson

ECHO (E.Cape) & East London sub-committee	GHDA (Gauteng)	WCHDA (W.Cape)	HDTAN (Kwa-Zulu Natal)
All persons holding a professional dancing qualification	All persons holding a professional dancing qualification	All persons holding a professional dancing qualification	All persons holding a professional dancing qualification

REMINISCENCES OF THE BOARD

Sue (Driver) and I became members of the Board in the early 1970s. The membership at that stage comprised teachers and judges but was headed by a chairman who by default was also chairman of the Federated Caledonian Society and, as such, brought with him the proud Scots traditions but generally had little expertise in the world of Highland Dance.

The secretary at the time was Les Gilbert and she was eventually succeeded by Heather Williamson and then Sue Hicks (Driver). The Board was steered by the secretaries, all of whom were highly knowledgeable about dance matters and upon whom the chairmen relied heavily.

There was also a Treasurer, a position which I held for several years. The Treasurer was, obviously, in control of all finances and also acted as registrar when the dancer registration system was adopted worldwide. The Board was, of course, affiliated to and ultimately controlled by the SOBHD, but in those days operated in a much more independent way. Meetings were usually held monthly and were always well attended and very lively.

Both Sue and I retired from the Board when we relocated back to our hometown, Port Elizabeth, in 1978. The Board went from strength to strength, under the chairmanship of Shonah Robinson who held the position for many years, and Agnes Nugent who was the chairman from 1994 until 1998. As a result of a lack of communication and a good deal of misunderstanding, the OBHD(SA) began to drift slightly off course during the 1980s. After a visit to South Africa by Shendl Russell and Billy Forsyth MBE in May 1999, a special meeting of the SOBHD was called where the South Africa Board was allowed the opportunity to state its case. I was called upon to address the members of the SOBHD at a special general meeting held in Edinburgh, a daunting but ultimately rewarding task. Misunderstandings were resolved and, after the negotiating of an entirely new and approved Constitution by all members of the dancing community in South Africa, the OBHD(SA) was once again recognised as the Official Governing Body in South Africa.

The committee was reformed and I was appointed Chairman, a position which I held with a great deal of pride until my departure from South Africa in 2001. I was supported by hard working and highly knowledgeable persons, the like of Mel Smith, Beverley Leahy, Agnes Nugent and Shonah Robinson (to name but a few), under whose guidance, expertise, dedication and hard work, the OBHD has flourished and gone from strength to strength to once again become a highly respected body of Highland Dancing worldwide.

The Board is currently under the chairmanship of Mrs Bev Leahy, who has held the position since March 2006. Mrs Mel Smith has been the secretary since 1998 whilst the finances have been in the able hands of Miss Roslyn Kruuse since 2005.

Trevor Hicks, past Chairman

THE SCOTTISH DANCE TEACHERS' ALLIANCE

No article on Highland Dancing in South Africa would be complete without reference to the Alliance. The SDTA has, without any doubt, been the most influential overseas body in the history and development of Highland Dancing in South Africa. J.L. McKenzie, that great pioneer of Highland Dancing in South Africa, made his first visit to SA as a representative of the Alliance in the 1950s and to this day all teachers in S.A. have qualified through this body.

We would all look forward to the visit of the Scottish Examiners (initially every second year) and would hang on their every word (well, those we understood!) to gain as much information as we could. The female examiners were usually accompanied on their coastal trips by a local lady (who acted as a tour guide and companion). We would usually have time set aside after the exam sessions for a class or just an informal get-together. The Alliance continued to support our dancers and teachers right through the dark years in SA's history when the rest of the world had turned their backs on us and cultural embargoes were the order of the day. We all remember, with the greatest respect and affection, visits from examiners and the wonderful spirit they brought with them. Lasting friendships were forged and we were kept right up to date by the Alliance. The "girls in the office" (currently Magda and Dianne) have always been helpful and efficient and are always pleased to see members whenever we travel to Scotland and the Alliance continues to support SA with exam sessions being held usually annually.

South African Highland Teachers and Dancers will be eternally grateful to the Alliance for their ongoing encouragement and support.
Trevor Hicks

HIGHLAND DANCING IN SOUTH AFRICA TODAY

SOUTH AFRICAN CHAMPIONSHIPS

2010 sees the holding of the 79th South African Championships. Held since its inception under the auspices of the Federated Caledonian Society of Southern Africa, when it was called the Royal Scottish Gathering, this event has since 2003 fallen under the direction of the OBHD(SA) and is organised by a committee of members of the Highland Dancing community. The South African Championships were traditionally held in September until 2003, when it was decided to change the date to the 4th or last weekend in July to accommodate the increasing number of Pipe Bands and dancers wishing to travel to Scotland to compete. The list of past South African Champions is representative of some of the well-known personalities in the history of Highland Dancing in the country, many of whom are still actively involved today.

LEFT

Beverley Drennan
(current chairman of the the OBHD(SA),
Felicity Watson (SA Champion 1966), Shirley Webb

RIGHT

2006 Mrs.Shonah Robinson presents Webster Cup to
Gillian O'Leary, winner of the
S.A. Adult Championship

THE ROLL OF HONOUR

SHLESINGER CUP
S.A. CHAMPION ADULT
Pre Webster Cup

1932 Bessie Reid
1933 Jenny McKean
1934 Jean Kellas
1935 Bessie Reid
1936 Hilda Watson
1937 B.Ramsay
1938 Nettie Dean
1945 Beryl Clarkson
1946 Beryl Clarkson
1947 A.Sinclair
1948 J.Hall
1949 S.Harcourt
1950 Tommy Kidson
1951 Margeret McKenzie
1952 Sheila McDonald
1953 Sheila McDonald
1954 Shonah Jamieson
1955 Sheila McDonald

WEBSTER CUP

1956 Shonah Jamieson
1957 Shonah Jamieson
1958 Morag Campbell
1959 Joan Dowie
1960 Joan Dowie
1961 Morag Campbell
1962 Barbara Kinghorn
1963 Hilary MacLeod
1964 Heather Parry
1965 Creena Harcourt
1966 Felicity Watson
1967 Judy Moir
1968 Cheryl McMillan
1969 Janet Robertson
1970 Janet Robertson
1971 Beverley McMillan
1972 Dianne McKenzie
1973 Beverley McMillan
1974 Trevor Hicks
1975 Merryl Shaw-Butler
1976 Merryl Shaw-Butler
1977 Brenda Gilbert
1978 Elaine Lambert
1979 Elinor Robinson
1980 Elinor Robinson
1981 Elinor Robinson
1982 Elinor Robinson
1983 Elinor Robinson
1984 Elinor Robinson
1985 Fiona Voss
1986 Linda Richmond
1987 Linda Richmond
1988 Linda Richmond
1989 Linda Richmond
1990 Linda Richmond
1991 Sally Lucas
1992 Sally Lucas
1993 Sally Lucas
1994 Bronwyn Gray
1995 Leigh-Ann McKelvie
1996 Jennifer McWilliams
1997 Leanne Gaffney
1998 Merody Campbell
1999 Allison Conchie
2000 Dana Gamache
2001 Hayley Foulds
2002 Merody Campbell
2003 Merody Campbell
2004 Gillian O'Leary
2005 Lisa Linton
2006 Gillian O'Leary
2007 Gillian O'Leary
2008 Caitlin Boyes/
Kearsney Smith
2009 Caylee O'Leary

THE SHENDL RUSSELL CHALLENGE

S.A.CHAMPION 16 & 17

1994	Allison Conchie
1995	Lesley Marwick
1997	Kate Stalker
1998	Katherine McLaren
1999	Kate Hellig
2000	Kate Hellig
2001	NicoletteVoordecker
2002	Shannon Leahy
2003	Gillian O'Leary
2004	Kearsney Smith
2005	Genevieve Boyes
2006	-
2007	-
2008	Caylee O'Leary
2009	CourtneyPearce

DONALD MCKINTOSH TROPHY

S.A.CHAMPION 13 – 16

1974	Karen Maxted
1975	Elinor Robinson
1976	S.Voss/E.Lambert
1977	Elaine Lambert
1978	Elinor Robinson
1979	Lauren Lambert
1980	Fiona Voss
1981	Fiona Voss
1982	Fiona Voss
1983	Linda Richmond
1984	Lee-Ann Atkinson
1985	Lee-Ann Atkinson
1986	Lee-Ann Atkinson
1987	Tracy McLeod
1988	Carolyn Munks
1989	Leanne Gaffney
1990	Kim Howat
1991	Allison Conchie
1992	Allison Conchie
1993	Kate Stalker
1995	Kate Stalker
1996	Kate Hellig
1998	Nicolette Voordecker
1999	Gillian O'Leary
2000	Gillian O'Leary
2001	Gillian O'Leary
2002	Genevieve Boyes
2003	Kearsney Smith
2004	Caylee O'Leary
2005	Caitlin Boyes
2006	CayleeO'Leary Courtney Pearce
2007	Courtney Pearce
2008	Cendra Williams
2009	Sharne Hein

AUCHENBLAE TROPHY
S.A.CHAMPION UNDER 13

1964	Felicity Watson
1965	Janet Robertson
1966	Janet Robertson
1967	J.Murray-Rogers/ A.Moralee
1968	Elizabeth Scott
1969	Karen Maxted
1970	Bernadine Nay
1971	Bernadine Nay
1972	Sheena Voss
1973	Helen Osborne
1974	Elinor Robinson
1975	Lauren Lambert
1976	Fiona Voss
1977	Fiona Voss
1978	Fiona Mitchelson
1979	Fiona Voss
1980	Linda Richmond
1981	Paula Simmonds
1982	Lee-Ann Atkinson
1983	Cindy Hazelhurst
1984	Candy Edmundsen
1985	Leanne.Gaffney
1986	Leanne.Gaffney
1987	Leigh-Ann McKelvie
1988	Kerry Melville
1989	Allison Conchie
1990	-
1991	Shanna Parker
1992	Shanna Parker/ K.Stalker
1993	Michelle Bean
1994	Kate Hellig
1995	Kate Hellig
1996	Gillian O'Leary
1997	Gillian O'Leary
1998	Gillian O'Leary
1999	Kearsney Smith
2000	Kearsney Smith
2001	Caitlin Boyes
2002	Caitlin Boyes
2003	Caitlin Boyes
2004	Courtney Pearce
2005	Megan McRobert
2006	Shannon van Gool
2007	Shannon van Gool
2008	-
2009	-

R.S.A. INTER-PROVS

This event is held bi-annually and was introduced in 2000. Each region has an opportunity to host the event, in rotation. The event includes all dancers, pre-premier, premier and Championship and incorporates a choreography competition. The 2010 event will be held on the Sunday following S.A. Championships, 8th August, in Benoni and will be hosted by the Gauteng province.

OSCAR AWARDS

This competition was introduced in 1992 with trophies, donated by the daughters of Shonah Robinson and Jean Voss, being presented. Since then a formal set of rules has been adopted and additional age groups included in order to ensure that this competition recognises the best overall dancers over the course of the dancing year. The rules as they stand at present are as follows.

There are 4 Oscar Championships per region, per year, plus S.A. Champs, being allocated as follows : 3 Oscar Championships awarded to the E.Cape and W.Cape and 3 to Gauteng and Natal. There is 1 additional floating Championship per region per year, by mutual agreement of the twinned regions. Only these 9 Championships are included in the points table for the awards. Each region nominates annually the Championships which they wish to hold Oscar status for that year.

Left – The 2006 Oscar Winners, Caitlin Boyes, Cendra Williams, Gillian O'Leary and Caylee O'Leary pictured with the secretary of the OBHD(SA), Mrs Mel Smith and the Chairman, Mrs Bev Leahy

There are 4 age group categories viz. 7 – 12 yrs, 13 – 15 yrs, 16 – 17 yrs and 18 yrs and older. Age groups at Oscar Championships MUST conform to these age groups. If there are insufficient entries for all 4 age groups, they may be split 7 – 15 yrs and 16 yrs and over.

Dancers who change age categories during the year, thereby obtaining points in two different categories, MAY be nominated in both categories should the points they have accumulated place them in the top 6 of the various age categories.

Dancers must have competed in a minimum of 3 Oscar Championships, irrespective of age group, in order to be nominated. Points are awarded to the dancers who finish amongst the final 6 placings of an Oscar Championship as per the recognised SOBHD points allocation for 1st, 2nd, etc.

The Oscar Awards Presentation is held on a rotating basis around the country during the first quarter of the year.

ACCOLADES

Accolades have recently been introduced as a way of recognising those individuals who put so much into Highland Dancing and without whom our jobs would be so much more difficult. As the awards rotate, the host region proposes those in their community who they would like to honour. Presentations to these persons also take place at the Awards Function

A LOOK AT THE HISTORY OF DANCE THROUGHOUT THE PROVINCES OF SOUTH AFRICA

EASTERN CAPE

In 1820, a strong contingent of Settlers from Britain arrived in Port Elizabeth, Eastern Cape. There were many Scottish families amongst them. These families settled initially in the area between Port Elizabeth and Grahamstown.

In 1883, the Port Elizabeth Scottish Association was formed - the very first Caledonian Society to be formed in South Africa. In those early years the culture of the Scots was practised at their functions.

The military history of this region in the mid-1800's also included the presence of various Scottish Regiments who served here from time to time at garrisons throughout the Eastern Cape, namely at Port Elizabeth, Grahamstown, East London, Queenstown and Fort Beaufort, with many smaller forts between these towns. Many of the Scottish Regiments had pipers and regimental dancers.

As schools of dancing were established in all the cities and bigger towns, some of the ballet teachers were also teaching Highland Flings and Sword Dances as well.

PORT ELIZABETH

In the 1930s Mary Dring from Scotland, taught Highland Dancing in Port Elizabeth. When she moved to Cape Town, her school was taken over by Olwen Strachan (Mrs Perridge). Following Olwen's retirement from teaching, Trevor Hicks opened a studio, and amongst his very first pupils were Gwen-Mary Wells and Sue Donald (who later became his wife). When the couple moved to Johannesburg, Beryl Hendriks took over Trevor's studio and later handed over to Barbara Mayhead. Ruth Vance was another prominent teacher at the time as was Gwen Mary Wells who for some years taught Highland Dancing pupils until her ballet school became too big for her to manage both types of dance. Trevor and Sue returned to Port Elizabeth and taught from 1978 until 1990, after which Highland Dance was in the capable hands of Jennifer McWilliams. Avril O'Leary now teaches in Port Elizabeth and since 1992 Barbara Freeborn has also taught Highland Dancing in the city.

EAST LONDON

Also in the 1930s a lady called Mrs Hanbury taught Highland Dancing in East London assisted by her daughter Maureen. The Walker sisters, Kate, Helen and Iris also had a dancing school, but Kate Walker went to Australia after a while where she became involved in Highland Dancing there.

Her Highland Dancing classes were taken over by Stella Siebert. Stella Logan (Mrs Hammond) also had a large dancing school from the 1940s onwards, teaching Highland Dancing as well as other forms of dance. In 1970, Gwen Mary Wells taught Ballet and Highland Dancing in East London and later she moved to Grahamstown and then to Port Elizabeth. After she left, her pupils in East London were taught by Jillian Seaman. In the late 1970's Jeanette Hubbard, who had been a pupil of Stella Siebert, started to teach in East London. Julie Angus & Jeanette Hubbard currently teach the dancers of East London.

QUEENSTOWN

A Ballet teacher in Queenstown in the 1940s used to perform Highland Dancing at socials at the Presbyterian Church. However, it was not until 1949 that Highland Dancing was brought to Queenstown when Stella Heugh opened a dancing studio. She had grown up in Port Elizabeth. She was assisted in her studio by Mrs Helen Preller and we had a very enthusiastic class of Highland Dancers in one of the local halls. When Stella Heugh moved to Cape Town in the early 1960s, Ruth Fletcher taught in Queenstown and a Highland Dancing Club, called the "White Heather Club", was formed by Mrs Heugh's pupils who did not want to go to Ruth's classes. The White Heather Club consisted of unqualified dancers who kept their skills going. Ruth Fletcher married a farmer and moved to the small farming town of Stutterheim (situated between East London and Queenstown), where she had a fairly big dancing school in the local school hall. Barbara Promnitz (Mrs Freeborn), Jackie Wells (Mrs Littleford) and Heather Mundell (Mrs Kittel) all had Highland Dancing schools in Queenstown at that time and we had a lot of pupils and used to hold a couple of competitions in various centres in our area every year. After Ruth Fletcher (Mrs Field) lost her husband, she remarried and moved to Port Elizabeth and her Highland Dancing pupils in Stutterheim were taken over by Cynthia Salzwedel.

GRAHAMSTOWN

Gwen Mary Wells taught in Grahamstown for a short while during the 1970's. Thereafter Barbara Mayhead used to travel to Grahamstown regularly (weekly or fortnightly) to teach.

The Caledonian Societies in Port Elizabeth and East London have for many years held Highland Gatherings which alternate between the two cities, with one being held every third year in Cape Town to complete a cycle of three years.

Initially there was not much communication between the various dancing schools and competition was very fierce. In 1970, the teachers started to get together at one of the towns each year for "refresher classes". This became an annual event. On 22nd April 2000 in East London, during lunch at the Eastern Cape Highland Gathering, the East Cape Highland Organisation was established under the auspices of the Official Board of Highland Dancing (SA).

GAUTENG

Originally known as Transvaal (literally "across the Vaal") you felt a sense of enormous excitement when you crossed that mighty river bound for the bright lights of the richest city in South Africa, Johannesburg. This was the home of everything important. Major companies all had their head offices in Johannesburg. Theatre, Opera and Ballet thrived in this part of the world and Highland teachers and dancers countrywide acknowledged that this was the place where it all happened.

It was the highlight of a dancer's year to dance at the Royal Scottish Gathering (RSG), now known as the South African Championships, the patron of which was Her Majesty, Queen Elizabeth the Queen Mother. This was before the days when dancers travelled to Scotland to spend many months taking classes and competing in the world's most prestigious competitions – to the majority of South African dancers, RSG was what you strove for throughout our career. It was here that the less experienced dancers would watch in wonder and amazement while the South African Champions were selected from large sections in which the best of the best dancers from throughout the country competed.

Sheer numbers dictated that this was the strongest area in the country and many of our most talented teachers and judges were to be found here. RSG was not the only exciting competition. There were competitions all over the Province held regularly throughout the year, many of them outdoors, due to the favourable climate in the Transvaal which follows the pattern of hot, wet summers and dry winters. Even in winter, you would be blessed with the most beautiful highveld day, sometimes very cold in the mornings and late afternoon but generally very pleasant during the run of the competition.

The majority of S.A. dancers and competitions are still to be found in Gauteng. Until 2000 it was also the home of the OBHD (SA) although respected members of the dance community throughout the country now serve on the Board in various capacities as it moves around the country.

Trevor Hicks

NATAL

In the early 1950's it was not surprising that the Scottish culture was alive and well in the Province of Natal, especially as Natal was also known then as the "Last British outpost". After the 2nd World War the desire to keep the Scottish heritage of families in the province was strong.

I can only comment on Highland Dancing in this province since the 1950s. The teachers who were the rock and core of nurturing the dance form and culture in the Durban and coastal areas were Molly Simpson, Mary Rae, Mr McIver and Marjory Pullen. In the midlands and Pietermaritzburg, Mrs Mina Towns, a tiny Scottish-born lady, taught in Pietermaritzburg. I can still in my mind's eye, see her sitting on her low stool and hear her "diddling" the tunes for us to dance to. There were no tape recorders or CD players then.

Because of the firm foundation these teachers set, further generations of teachers have risen from those original studios. The names of teachers that followed included Shonah Robinson, Wilma MacLeod-Smith, Avril O'Leary and Bronwyn Parker (Gray), who presently teaches in the area.

Most of our competitions were held outside in the open air and we were so privileged to dance to "live pipers". Today our pupils are more accustomed to dancing in a hall and the music coming from speakers on the sides of the stage. How times have changed and I am not sure if they are always for the better.

As a competitor in the 50's and 60's we were automatically given forms to complete to become members of the local Caledonian Societies and this membership was a prerequisite to be able to enter a competition. It was not unusual for us to get up at 6.30am to travel an hour and a half on the old main road in order to get to Durban in time to compete at 8am.

The dance costumes have also changed a lot. As a beginner in 1955 my first costume was a Grant clan kilt and hose with a boy's long sleeved shirt and my mother made me a matching Grant clan tie. My sister and I then progressed to kilts with long-sleeved green velvet jackets with all the lace at the sleeve and around our necks. The sporrans, plaids and green velvet feather bonnets were very proudly worn. As a South African you had to order your dance pumps from Scotland as there was just no manufacturer here to meet that need. These would take weeks to arrive and were treated as a very special item. Since then those cumbersome but beautiful costumes have changed, with crisp dress tartans replacing the traditional family ones.

The opportunity to share the joy of Highland Dancing took the form of displays in the Local Botanical Gardens together with the Pipe Bands. Dancing the Reels and jumping over the large old oak tree roots was the norm. The most beautiful time to dance there was in the autumn when the avenue was thick with bronzed oak leaves. Besides dancing at local school fetes we had our monthly display at the Caledonian Society functions.

Our adjudicators were all ladies, with the exception of Mr Alfie Dunn who was "the regular strict judge". In the 50's and 60's we had a number of male dancers, enough to host a boys' section which was often hotly contested by Trevor Hicks, Phillip Coleman, Hamish and Alistair Fynn, to name a few.

Today the Province of Natal is known as Kwa Zulu Natal and as time moves on, dancers come and go but the Scottish Heritage we pass on will never fade. There is nothing as strong as one's roots.

Heather Booysen

WESTERN CAPE

The earliest record of Highland Dancing in Cape Town is a photograph taken in the 1930s of a dance class.

Jean McPherson (Clark) started teaching for the Cape Town Caledonian Society in the late 1940s. She qualified as a teacher in 1951 when J.L. McKenzie first visited Cape Town (by sea). Her brother, Leslie, joined her as a teacher when he stopped competing in the late 50's. The Clark family played a significant part in promoting dancing in those early years. Leslie eventually left Cape Town for the UK in 1965.

In 1949, after the 2nd World War, the Cape Town Highlanders brought Pipe Major Jimmie Marwick to South Africa. Jimmie Marwick also taught dancing to the band members and others. His great nieces Lesley and Andrea Marwick are still involved in dancing today.

Mary Smith (Dring) moved to Cape Town from Port Elizabeth in the late 50s and opened a dance school in 1960. She was a formidable lady and continued to teach until her sudden death in 1976. Three of her senior pupils continued teaching her classes and eventually Margaret Kuus (Brebner) became the sole teacher.

Rose MacMillan began teaching at the Stewarts Club in 1953 and received her qualifications in 1962. She left the Stewarts and opened her own dance school, continuing to teach until 1998 when ill health forced her to close her dance school. Ina Langlands taught the Stewarts for many years before retiring.

Rose was instrumental in the formation of the Highland Teachers' Association of the Western Cape in 1977. The aim of the Association was to help and encourage the 'new teachers' and for our region to speak with one voice.

She was the W. Cape representative to the OBHD (SA). In those days, one could only 'serve' on the board if you lived in Johannesburg or were prepared to travel to Johannesburg for meetings. Acting as our rep meant that she communicated with the Board on our behalf.

Judy Lucas (Moir) & Jeanette Moulder (Brebner) both opened dance schools in 1975 and along with Margaret became the 'young teachers' in Cape Town. Those were the days of large dance schools, big competitions and fun travelling away to competitions. Judy is still teaching and is now the 'old teacher' with Hayley Johnston and Taryn Behr as the young enthusiastic teachers.

WORKSHOPS

The style of the Cape Town dancers was different from Johannesburg, the hub of Highland Dancing, and the rest of the country. The newly-formed Teachers' Association invited Trevor Hicks to hold our first dancing workshop. This was the start of many exciting years of tuition for both dancers and teachers. Trevor was eventually joined by Sue, Shonah and Elinor. It is thanks to these teachers that dancing here in Cape Town has continued to flourish.

Trevor Hicks, Wilma McLeod-Smith & Heather Booysen all eventually moved to Cape Town. Trevor opened a dance school which was taken over by Hayley and Taryn when sadly he left us for the UK. Both Wilma and Heather served us well as Judges. Wilma has now retired while Heather continues to teach and judge.

Mention must be made of Gordon and Beryl Guthrie who worked tirelessly for Highland Dancing for many years. The Easter Gathering every 3 years was as a result of their hard work, the first one being held after World War 2. Their daughter, Pattie taught in the Fish Hoek area for many years.

Emily Tolson a newly married dancer from Cape Town, arrived in Bermuda 2 years ago with her husband. She was delighted to find a Pipe Band and Highland Dancing. At her first lesson she discovered that the 'teachers' had only basic knowledge of the dances from their youth. Emily soon found herself teaching the classes and they now they have close to 50 pupils. Through the OBHD (SA) and Mel Smith, Sandra Bald-Jones was contacted. Sandra conducted a workshop in Bermuda last year and has encouraged Emily to take her professional exams this year and then put pupils in for their first exams.

Judy Lucas

INFLUENTIAL PERSONALITIES IN SOUTH AFRICAN HIGHLAND DANCING

The early history of Highland Dancing in the country was largely moulded by two well-known families, the Kinghorns and the Jamiesons.

Jean Voss (Kinghorn)

I had the pleasure of meeting Jean Voss in the very early 1970s. My wife, Sue (Driver) and I had moved from our home town of Port Elizabeth to start our married life in the great metropolis of Johannesburg. Both champion dancers throughout the Cape Province, we were generally unknown in the Transvaal. We'd been given Jean's name and number and wasted no time in contacting her. It wasn't easy. Jean was protected by her loyal family who vetted all her calls. After a week or two of trying, we eventually got to speak to the great lady herself and, it has to be said, had a bit of a cold reception! I told her that my wife and I had recently moved to Johannesburg and were anxious to come to her classes. "Aren't you a little old?", she enquired in a tone reserved for members of the over-60s Scottish Country Dancing Club who'd decided that they'd like to brush up on some Highland steps!

Being a mere 25, I was mortified. We'd not realised that standard practice in those days was to retire at the age of 18!

Anyway, we managed to enrol in her classes and set out anxiously for the Parktown Convent Hall where she taught at the time. I was uncertain of the required class apparel and decided to err on the side of safety, so I arrived in a kilt. First surprise was that all her pupils danced barefoot. We soon worked out the reason why as we slid and slipped our way around in Highland pumps which simply refused to allow one even to walk on the floor. Her class was astonished and sat on the sides in amazed silence when Sue and I took to the floor. I don't think they'd ever seen such old dancers – or a male dancer – least of all kilted and barefooted!

That was the start for us of a wonderful time in our lives. Jean was a superb technician and believed strongly that "if a job was worth doing, it was worth doing well". There were no short cuts, no compromises. There was just one way to do something and that was the right way. She was a perfectionist in every sense of the word. Her classes were stimulating, challenging, technically perfect and exciting but above all, thoroughly enjoyable. She was aided by her pianist, dear old "Auntie" – a woman at that stage in, I would imagine her 70's. A formidable lady, she would sit at the piano and beat out a rhythm that nobody could (or dared) mistake.

Although an expert in her field, Jean was always keen to learn whatever she could, and use her knowledge to improve her dancers. She herself had been trained only in Highland (and Irish) dance, but was open to input from all other dance disciplines where she felt there would be benefit to her dancers. She was word perfect in her knowledge of the Highland textbook, but she was always willing to discuss various different approaches and put them into practice provided that they didn't in any way violate the prescribed technique.

Jean was not only a very fine teacher and judge, but she was also instrumental in the administration of Highland Dance in South Africa. Sue and I also became heavily involved in all matters Highland, and that's how we met up with those great and wonderful doyennes of the Highland world, mother and daughter - Jenny Jamieson and Shonah Robinson.

Obviously, there were many people involved and it would be remiss of me to imply that we were the only ones. Quite the contrary, names that spring to mind are those of Barbara Beales, Margaret Horn and Hazel Davis, to name but a few. But Jean, Jenny, Shonah, Sue and I seemed to spend a great deal of time in one another's company. The five of us would meet up a couple of times a week at least, one night under the guise of the technical committee, another as members of the OBHD(SA), then we'd be setting judge's exam papers, marking them, planning workshops, having judges' meetings – a very busy and productive time. Jenny (she was always known as Mrs Jamieson to Jean, Sue and myself – and of course "mommy" to Shonah) miraculously managed to knit throughout the proceedings. Those needles would move at the speed of light, but somehow she managed to contribute fully to the dance business whilst producing countless knitted articles. An early example of "multi-tasking"!

We'd all have fun – screeches of laughter would fill the air, but we remained professional throughout and got through a great deal of work, always respecting one another's opinions. It was a wonderful time, without which the Highland World in South Africa would have been a lot less developed.

On top of all this, Jean remained a devoted mother and wife. It couldn't have been easy running a family as well as training Champion dancers and devoting so much time and expertise to ensure that the fine tradition of Highland Dancing would thrive and blossom to give future generations the opportunity to enjoy this wonderful art form. Jean was also a woman of great faith, and it was this faith that gave her the courage and fortitude to fight the dreadful disease which eventually claimed her life. She soldiered bravely right to the end and stolidly refused medication until eventually the pain became so unbearable that she was forced to succumb.

Jean, we salute you. The legacy you left for us has continued to strengthen and help shape Highland Dancing in South Africa into the world champion standard that we see today.

Trevor Hicks

FOUR GENERATIONS OF HIGHLAND DANCING CHAMPIONS

Jenny R. McKean (Jamieson)

Jenny started Highland Dancing in 1921 at the age of 12. She was taught by Helen McLaren and Edyth McCurdie. During her dancing career she was the second South African Adult Champion in 1933 and was presented with the Schlesinger Cup. She obtained her SDTA Fellowship and her Adjudicators qualification. During her long teaching career she taught classes across the West and East Rand and in the Southern Johannesburg areas. Jenny served on the then South African Highland Dancing Governing Body which became the OBHD(SA). Her parents, Dave and Janet McKean were founder members of the Johannesburg Caledonian Society and Jenny also served on the Southern Johannesburg Caledonian Society wherein she actively promoted Highland Dance. Jenny ended her teaching career at the age of 72.

Shonah J. Jamieson (Robinson) followed in her mother's footsteps and started dancing from the age of 4. She was taught by her mother, Jenny. Highlights during Shonah's dancing career include qualifying for the finals at the 1958 World Championships at Cowal. She was also the first winner of the British Overseas Championships together with John Hynd of the United States of America. Shonah won the Adult South African Highland Dancing Championships in 1954, 1956 and 1957. During her dancing career she organised many "camp workshops" attended by dancers and teachers from all over South Africa. The notable overseas instructors included JL McKenzie. Elspeth Strathern, Shendl Russell, Linda Rankin and Helen Fitzpatrick. Shonah is a Fellow of the SDTA and an SOBHD qualified Adjudicator. She chaired the OBHD(SA) for a number of years and convened the Royal Scottish Gathering (Highland Dancing) and S.A. Highland Championships during her career. Shonah celebrated her 50th year of teaching in 2008 and is still "going strong".

Elinor Robinson (Boyes) followed the "family tradition" and danced from the age of six, being taught by her mother. Like Shonah, Elinor danced at Cowal in the 1982, 1983 and 1984 World Highland Dancing Championships. Her most notable success was an overall 6th placing in the 1983 Worlds and qualifying for the finals in 1984. Her success in the South African Adult Championships includes a yet unsurpassed record of six consecutive wins from 1979 to 1984. Elinor is also a Fellow of the SDTA and a SOBHD qualified Adjudicator. Elinor was invited to adjudicate at the 1998 Australian National Championships held in Newcastle. Elinor has been involved with organising various competitions and workshops, and teaches together with Shonah.

Genevieve and Caitlin Boyes are, as far as we know, the first fourth generation Highland Dancing National Champions worldwide. Both girls commenced their dancing careers from the age of four, being taught by Elinor. Genevieve is a Member while Caitlin is an Associate of the SDTA. Genevieve and Caitlin danced at Cowal in 2003. Caitlin also danced at Cowal in 2006 and 2008 where she qualified for the finals. Caitlin became the first "second generation" winner of the British Overseas Championship, her grandmother Shonah being the first South African winner.

The studios have had tremendous success over the years, highlighted by the number of South African Champions they have produced. The "Roll of Honour" which appears elsewhere in this article contains names, many of whom are from this studio.

The studios do not function without the dedicated support of the dancers themselves, and their parents. Many of the organisers of competitions and who have held office in the various organisations started their dancing careers at the Mckean/Robinson/Boyes studios, namely Agnes Nugent, Bev Leahy (current chair of OBHD(SA), Melaney Smith, Carol Jones, Shelly van Gool, Brenda Gilbert and Hillary Webber. Without them and the dedicated parents, Highland Dancing would not function as we know it and their support is sincerely appreciated.

Rob Boyes

LESLIE CLARK (DANCER / TEACHER / JUDGE) CAPE TOWN 1928 - 1984

Leslie was born in Cape Town in 1928 into a family heavily involved in the Scottish Culture. As soon as he was old enough he joined his sister Jean, two years his senior, at dancing classes. They were taught by a teacher known as 'Garvey'. It is unclear as to whether this was a first name or a surname.

The Clark family travelled round South Africa competing in various competitions in Port Elizabeth, East London and Johannesburg, even travelling as far as Bulawayo in what was known as Southern Rhodesia. Leslie also learnt to play the pipes along with his two brothers and joined his dad, Nobby, in the Caledonian Pipe Band.

One of the highlights of his dancing career was dancing at the City Hall, along with other Cape Town dancers, for the Royal Family during their visit to Cape Town in 1947. Another was dancing in the Liberty Cavalcade in 1952 on the newly reclaimed 'Foreshore'.

In 1950, J.L. McKenzie visited Cape Town to hold the first exam sessions. This visit was organised by Mary Smith (Dring). J.L. apparently stayed on board ship for the 3 days conducting exams in a hall in town. This was the first time dancers could officially qualify as teachers.

In 1956 Jean, his sister, opened a dancing class in Pinelands for the Caledonian Society. Leslie, who was still competing, used to sometimes assist her. Another Cape Town teacher reported him to Scotland and he was declared a 'professional'. The definition of an amateur in those days was "one who has never been employed or engaged or accepted remuneration, either in money or kind, as a dancer, a teacher of dancing or as an assistant teacher of dancing or who has never taken part in a competition for which a money prize is offered, or as an organiser or judge of a competition for personal profit." That was the end of his competing career.

In 1961 Leslie and Jean formed the Leslie Clark and Jean MacPherson School of Highland Dancing. At this time the only competition held in Cape Town was the Western Cape Highland Gathering. This was held every three years alternating with Port Elizabeth and East London over the Easter weekend. Dancers in Cape Town took part in the Eisteddfod each year. Unfortunately this was judged by Ballet Teachers and I can remember altering our style of dancing to please the 'judge.'

Leslie decided to start an annual competition in Cape Town and judging from the correspondence I have read this was well received by the other teachers. At this stage there were no 'qualified judges'. From what I understand J.L. McKenzie conducted a verbal test with teachers and they were appointed as judges. Leslie was not allowed to start a competition unless it fell under a Caledonian Society. Again there is an enormous amount of correspondence regarding this first competition and he was eventually given permission by the Governing Body of Highland Dancing (which fell under the Central Council of Federation) to go ahead with 'local judges.'

In 1962, this governing body was disbanded by the Federation and a steering committee was appointed to reform this body in co-operation with the Scottish Association of the Transvaal. This new body was to become the Official Board of Highland Dancing South Africa. An application was made to Scotland for judges papers. And so in 1963 (as far as I can ascertain) the first judges exams were held. Leslie, along with others in Cape Town, took this exam. Acting judges were to remain until the results were available. Leslie had for many years been invited to judge at competitions around the country.

In 1964 Leslie attended a special meeting in Johannesburg. At this meeting it was decided to re-introduce the step–sequence as set by the OBHD(SA). It was also agreed that each Province appoint a proxy to represent them at Board meetings (which according to minutes I have from 64 / 65 were held almost every month)

Unfortunately Leslie left Cape Town in 1966 to settle in London. There he continued to teach Highland in his flat as well as judging at various competitions in the area, until arthritis in the hips made movement difficult. Sadly, he died in London in 1984 at the age of 56.

As a young dancer, Leslie filled me with a love of dancing that has remained with me all these years and I am sure that he is one of the reasons that I am still involved today. Judy Lucas with Jean Mac Pherson (Clark), Rose MacMillan, Wilma Mc Leod-Smith (Gillespie), Noreen Wannacott (Loveland) & Rosemary Watt

TREVOR HICKS

Trevor was born in Port Elizabeth. He began his career in Highland Dancing at the age of 12 when he tagged along to a class with the children next door. It didn't take too long before he had his shoes off and was joining at the back of the class.

His first teachers in Durban were Mrs Pullen and Mr McIver, and thereafter Olwen Strachan in Port Elizabeth through whom he qualified as a teacher and started his own dancing studio. Following a move to Johannesburg, he studied Highland with Jean Voss.

He won all the Championships of the time throughout South Africa, including the South African title in 1974.

His competitive career saw him compete not only at home but also in Scotland in 1976 where he was third overall in the British Championship in Edinburgh and fourth overall at the World Championships at Cowal. He and his wife Sue travelled around Scotland from competition to competition (400 miles in all) on bicycles with their kilts in backpacks. Oh those hills!!

Trevor is Fellow, Examiner and Life Member of the SDTA as well as an SOBHD adjudicator.

His experience in the field of dance extends to Ballet, Theatre, Classical Mime & Dance Drama as well as Irish dancing which he taught in Cape Town as an Associate Teacher for the Irish Dance Commission. In all these fields he has accumulated many awards and accolades. Apart from his own studios, he has also taught workshops throughout South Africa as well as Rhodesia, England and USA. A past Chairman of the OBHD(SA), Trevor now lives in London.

RECOLLECTIONS OF HIGHLAND DANCING IN SOUTH AFRICA IN THE 1930's

In January 1935 I started highland dancing at the age of 7 years with Hazel Black in Benoni, a small town in the eastern Transvaal, South Africa. Our dance classes were held in the Presbyterian Church Hall. Later on I was taught by Jenny Jameison who remained my teacher until I was 21years old. She held her classes at her home in Boksburg. We danced in her lounge and entrance hall. I remember her shouting "I need more elevation" as a result I collided with her lampshade. We wore the full highland outfit, long sleeved jacket, plaid, sporran, Balmoral with a feather, shoulder brooch and a kilt pin. While dancing the Sean Triubhas we wore tartan trews.

In those days we had very few competitions, but the ones we did have were organised on a large scale. There were athletics, tossing of the caber, tug o' war and lots of other forms of entertainment. The Highland Gatherings were organised by the Caledonian Society. At one of the competitions where we danced the Washerwoman Jig, the adjudicator sat under the platform, so she could listen to our beats. Mrs McCurdy played the piano, with great gusto.

I learnt that Highland Dancing teaches one determination and dedication, as well the enjoyment of every moment of what you are doing. These qualities will stand you in good stead for the rest of your life.

I feel very proud today that my daughter Beverley Leahy (Drennan) is now the current chairperson of the OBHD(SA) and that my two granddaughters Shendl and Shannon Leahy are both current Championship Highland Dancers.

Doreen Brown (Drennan)

The Drennan Family
Mrs Bev Leahy and her 2 daughters

Doreen Brown (Drennan)

ScotDance Canada

LETTER FROM PRESIDENT PETER ARCHIBALD OF SCOTDANCE CANADA

On behalf of the membership of ScotDance Canada, I would like to congratulate The Scottish Official Board of Highland Dancing on the celebration of their first sixty years!

ScotDance Canada, a young organization in comparison to the SOBHD, shares a common path with "the Board" - the pursuit of excellence and fairness in competition by all participants from dancers and judges to the countless volunteers who keep each event running smoothly. Over the past two decades, we have been witness to the role we and the other overseas bodies have played in upholding SOBHD rules and fostering better communication within what has evolved into a truly Worldwide Organization.

ScotDance Canada would not be the organization it is today without the vision of our founding members: Heather Jolley, Irene Baird, Sandra Bald Jones, Donna Jean Ostrander, Gail Danysk, Loree Vellner and the late Adeline Duncan, who in consultation with Billy Forsyth MBE and the SOBHD were able to lay the groundwork for the increasingly collaborative relationship we currently share. We are grateful for the guidance we have received from Marjory Rowan, Shendl Russell and Christine Lacey and cannot express enough how extremely fortunate we have been to have Miss Linda Rankin as our Head Delegate, giving ScotDance Canada a strong and fair voice at SOBHD meetings.

Peter Archibald, President

HISTORY OF SCOTDANCE CANADA

Recognizing the need for a national body to oversee the continuity of the "Canadian Inter-Provincial Championships", ScotDance Canada (Scottish Cultural Organization for Traditional Dance in Canada) was formed in July 1987 in Regina, Saskatchewan with its Constitution receiving formal acceptance in Hamilton, Ontario in July 1988. Since November 1990, ScotDance Canada has been an Affiliated Member of the Scottish Official Board of Highland Dancing (SOBHD) and has acted as the Registration Agent for Canadian dancers and competition organizers participating in the Worldwide Registration System since January 1994. In January 1996 the SOBHD recognized ScotDance Canada as the principal organization and means of communication with the SOBHD in Canada.

ScotDance Canada

ScotDance Canada

ScotDance Canada has a vibrant dance community. ScotDance Canada now registers annually over 4,000 dancers, approximately 400 professional members and over 170 events of which 28 are Championships. We have a dynamic executive who communicate through email practically on a daily basis. Our nine Provincial Executive Committee Members are supported by four Office Bearers. ScotDance Canada has honoured 7 founding members. We have nine Independent Members. Our specific mandates are carried out by 12 currently active committees. We are a busy group of Highland Dance enthusiasts.

We have been fortunate with our leadership. A group of people with diverse talents and skills laid the original foundation. They were followed by others who subsequently expanded our thinking and our perception of what was possible. They all have brought us to where we are today. It is interesting and coincidental that the SOBHD is looking back over their 60 years at the very same time that ScotDance Canada is reflecting on where we are and where we want to point our compass for our future travels. At our recent Mid-winter Meeting, we spent much time looking at not only our current position but also how we started and evolved from a group of very forward-thinking people.

ScotDance Canada has prospered under the leadership of seven Presidents: Irene Baird (Manitoba), Loree Martin Vellner (Alberta), Heather Jolley (British Columbia), Anne Sutherland (Ontario), Christa Mackie (Ontario), Marilynn Wright (Ontario) and Peter Archibald (British Columbia). Being at the helm of more than twenty very opinionated Executive and Committee Chairs is not an easy task but these Presidents have managed to bring the voices of our vast country together on the floor of the Annual General Meeting. It is here that our Board of Directors discuss, votes and ultimately changes our course.

ScotDance Conferences provide an excellent opportunity for the exchange of knowledge and ideas amongst its membership. The first National ScotDance Canada Conference was held in Toronto, Ontario in October 1991. In 1994 a Western ScotDance Canada Conference was held in Kelowna, British Columbia and an Eastern ScotDance Canada Conference was held in Toronto, Ontario. The second National Conference was held in Toronto, Ontario in October 1996. ScotDance Canada's National Conferences have continued to be held every other year in October: 1998 – Montreal, QC; 2000 – Halifax, NS; 2002 – Calgary, AB; 2004 – Etobicoke, ON. In 2006 ScotDance Canada supported and participated in the "World of Highland Dancing Conference" in Las Vegas, NV in lieu of a National Conference. Montreal, QC was the location of the 2008 ScotDance Canada National Conference. Plans are underway for the 2010 ScotDance Canada National Conference, which will be held in the Fall in Vancouver, BC. Provided that numbers warrant, an SOBHD Judges' Exam is scheduled in conjunction with the National Conferences. In addition to the regularly scheduled National Conferences, many of the ScotDance Provincial Affiliates hold Provincial Conferences on a regular basis.

In October 1992 a joint ScotDance/FUSTA (Federation of United States Teachers and Adjudicators of Highland Dancing) Conference was held in Las Vegas, Nevada. ScotDance Canada has participated in "The World of Highland Dancing", an International Conference, held in Las Vegas, Nevada in October 1999, 2003 and 2006. The conference in 2006 paid tribute to the "Men of Dance".

Back Row: John Hynd (U.S.): Colin Naismith (U.S.) Fred DeMarse (U.S.) Gregor Bowman (SCOT): Bruce Farrar (U.S.):Steven MacRae (U.S.): Douglas MacFarland (AUS): Terry Lee (CAN) David Tague (U.S.):

Middle Row: Peter Archibald (CAN); Bill Weaver (U.S.): Deryck Mitchelson (SCOT): Victor Wesley (SCOT): Kevin Desereaux (AUS): Mark Forshaw (NZ): Ian MacLean (SCOT): Angus MacKenzie (CAN): Bill Troock (CAN):

Front Row: David Wilton (SCOT): Tony Cargill (SCOT/CAN): Robert Clark (SCOT): Ritchie Gibson (SCOT); Joe Wallin (CAN): Reid McLain (U.S.)

JAMES L. MCKENZIE AWARD

James L. McKenzie, began dancing in a poorly lit barn loft to the scraping of a violin, grew to be the Champion who danced for the Queen, and shared his love of Highland Dancing with the world.

ScotDance Canada established the James L. McKenzie Memorial Fund in honor of Mr. McKenzie following his death in 1992. Monies for this fund are realized through donations, either provincial or personal. In addition, 1% of all of ScotDance Canada's portion of dancer registration fees are allocated to this fund.

The intent of the fund is to keep Mr. McKenzie's memory alive by assisting financially in the development of a dancer who displays not only competitive spirit, but community spirit, as well as a love and enjoyment of, and dedication to Highland Dance and, to this end, the James L. McKenzie Award will be given annually by ScotDance Canada

RECIPIENTS OF THE JAMES L. MCKENZIE AWARD

1996	Genevieve Collis NS	1999	J.George Hamilton MB	2003	Kayleigh Macdonald ON
	Chantal Watt ON		Katie Goldie SK	2004	Kaylee Campbell MB
	Adrienne Petzold BC	2000	Georgina Muir ON		Isaac Lisisk BC
1997	Jessica Imeson AB		Courtney Allen AB	2005	Kirsten Henry MB
	Michael Tucker ON		Emily Cripps NB	2006	Samantha Beach BC
	Natalie Quick ON	2001	Award not given		
1998	Stacey Allen AB	2002	Jacqueline Henderson BC		
	Tara Christie MB		Reagan Robertson MB		
	Adam MacKinnon NS		Emily Fox NB		

Recipients of the James L McKenzie Award perform the Tribute at the 2004 Opening Ceremonies Winnipeg Manitoba.

SPECIAL MEMBERS

Independent Membership has been awarded to seven of the founding members of ScotDance Canada: Mrs. Adeline Duncan of Victoria, British Columbia (1991); Mrs. Irene Baird of Winnipeg, Manitoba (1993); Mrs. Gail Danysk of Calgary, Alberta (1994); and, Mrs. Heather Jolley of Burnaby, British Columbia, Mrs. Sandra Bald Jones of Hamilton, Ontario, and Mrs. Donna Jean Ostrander of Ottawa, Ontario (1995). Loree Vellner of Red Deer, Alberta was made an Independent Member in 1998. 2008 saw the addition of Anne Sutherland of London, Ontario and Bill Troock of Edmonton, Alberta as Independent Members. They are influential ScotDance Canada Members whose one common trait, besides a passion for and deep knowledge of Highland Dancing, is that they are mavericks who don't take the path of least resistance. They forge new ones despite the hardships and struggles. They are not intimidated by a challenge but motivated. In short they inspire us.

Above: Anne Sutherland, Donna Jean Ostrander, Bill Troock, Irene Baird
Below: Sandra Bald Jones, Loree Vellner, Heather Jolley, Gail Danysk

Sadly, 2009 marked the passing of Mrs. Adeline Duncan, Scot-Dance Canada's first Independent (Honorary) Member. An opinionated, non-conformist, she was the original ScotDance Canada maverick. A maverick of a different sort is our Head Delegate Linda Rankin. Since ScotDance Canada gained a voice at the SOBHD Meetings, Linda's quiet eloquence has been heard. Her sophistication, grace and brilliance are evident every time she speaks on our behalf. We have been more than fortunate these past twenty years to have partnered with such a well-respected Lady of Highland Dancing.

Adeline Duncan

COMMUNICATIONS

ScotDance Canada moved rapidly forward into the electronic age during the Presidency of Christa Mackie (2001-2005). Under Christa's leadership, SCOR (ScotDance Canada On-line Registration system) - an electronic program handling the complete administration of a competition from entry form to final results - was developed. Unfortunately, a change in service provider resulted in the loss of this program and considerable time is now being put into the development of a similar program. Pierie Danysk, SDC Communication Chairperson, and Kathy Ramesar, Winnipeg, MB, have dedicated countless hours of work to this project. The new and improved ScotDance Canada website (www.scotdancecanada.ca), under the careful management of Pierie Danysk, is now considered to be ScotDance Canada's main source of communication with its membership and the Canadian Highland Dance community in general. As well, ScotDance Canada operates a site dedicated to the "ScotDance Canada Championship Series".

Kathy Ramesar

The first edition of the ScotDance Canada Newsletter was issued in July 1991. Avril Wood, Rothesay, NB, served as the Newsletter Editor from 1991-1992. Donna Jean Ostrander, Ottawa, ON, filled this position from 1993 1999. Heather Jolley, Burnaby, BC, became the next Newsletter Editor serving from 2000-2004. Peter Archibald, Vancouver, BC, took over the Newsletter Editor responsibilities in 2005 and distribution became electronic. Over the next few years, the ScotDance Canada website became our primary means of communication and the Newsletter seemed to become an unnecessary tool. However, recently there has been a renewed interest in having a ScotDance Canada Newsletter. A Canadian Events List outlining dates and contacts for the majority of the competitions in Canada is compiled and issued annually by ScotDance Canada. Originally, this informative list was distributed by mail accompanying the Newsletter. It is now prepared by the National Competition Organizer Registrar and appears on the ScotDance Canada website.

Christa Mackie

In 2003 a commemorative book entitled "Canadian Highland Dance Experience – Past,
Present and Future" edited by Deborah Wardrope was published by ScotDance Canada. This limited edition book details the history of Highland Dancing in Canada, and also illustrates Canada's place in the worldwide community of Highland dance.

SCOTDANCE CANADA SPECIAL PROJECTS

Sheryl Joyner Fraser

The "ScotDance Canada Suite", undertaken as a Millennium project, was choreographed by Sheryl Joyner, Chairperson of the National Choreography Committee, from steps provided by ScotDance Canada members from across the country. The choreography committee members in each Province were asked to choreograph a part of the dance.

The Suite had its inaugural performance at the 2003 ScotDance Canada Championship Series in St. Catharines, ON and was performed again at the Opening Ceremonies of the 2004 SDCCS in Winnipeg, MB, marking the 30th Anniversary of the "Canadian Inter-Provincial Championships".

Opening Ceremonies SDCCS 2004 Winnipeg - Performing the ScotDance Canada Suite

Best Wishes with your dancing Deborah

Deborah Wardrope

ScotDance Canada's latest innovative project is the introduction of an online Judges' Exam Preparation Course developed and conducted by Deborah Wardrope, the current Secretary of ScotDance Canada. The course is proving to be a much needed study tool for candidates preparing for the SOBHD Judges' Exam.

Spearheaded by Deborah Wardrope, the 2008-2009 year has seen the development of an Education Centre on the ScotDance Canada website. This comes at a time when professional development is very much to the forefront. Plans are to continue to develop the Education Centre to serve as a much needed reference library for professionals.

The 'Canadian Inter-Provincial Championships' and ScotDance Canada Championship Series

The 'Canadian Inter-Provincial Championships', sanctioned by the Scottish Official Board of Highland Dancing, had their origin at the City of Ottawa Highland Games, where they were staged in 1974, 1975 and 1976. The concept of holding a National Highland Games was the idea of Pipe Major A.M. Cairns. Events were held on an Inter-Provincial level, with each Province eligible to send representatives in the areas of pipe bands, solo pipers, solo drummers, drum majors, dancers, caber tossers and tug-of-war teams. In addition, the Inter-Provincial representatives could enter competitions in their related areas open to all-comers. The Highland Dancing events were organized by Coordinators, Heather Jolley of Burnaby, BC and Donna Jean (Ritchie) Ostrander of Ottawa, ON.

Dr McLaren then President of S.O.B.H.D. presenting Baby Class Trophy to Allison Milne & Lisa Ann Morrison

Heather MacKinnon 1974 & 1975

Cheryl Rafter 1974 & 1976

Donna Cove (Cram)
1975, 1978, 1979 & 1981

Kathleen MacKenzie
1974 & 1976

Fiona Nash (Champagne) 1976

Jan Sandles (Oakes) 1976

Debbie Clarke 1974

Shona Smith (AB), Debbie Rozell (ON), Donna Cove (MB), Jill Young (AB), Ann Milne (ON)
1978 Canadian Champions - Winnipeg MB

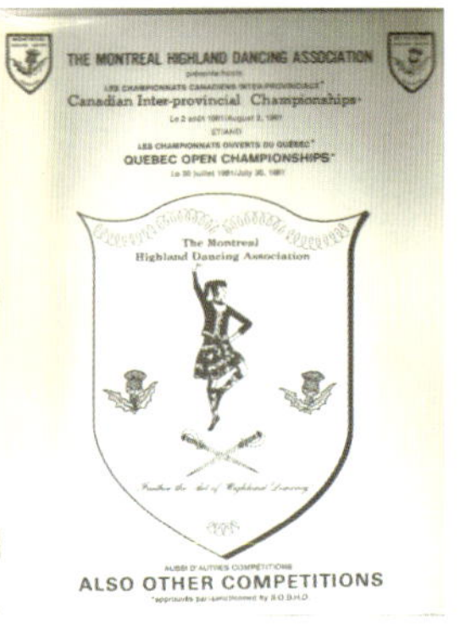

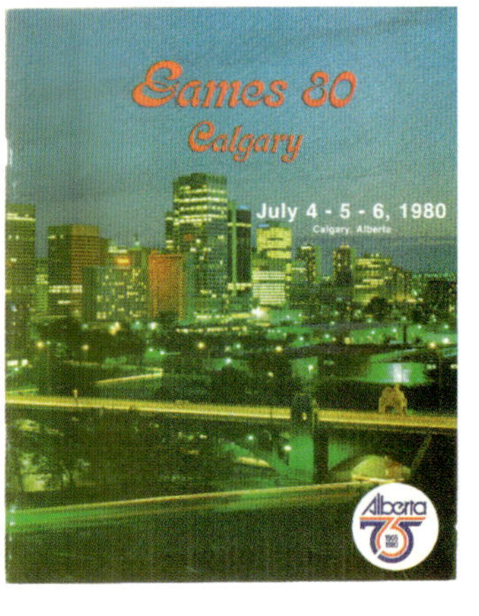

Anne Milne (ON), Mary Munro (BC), Michelle Baird (MB),
Dove Cove (MB), Jill Young (AB)
1979 Canadian Champions - Antigonish

1982 Canadian Champions - Burnaby British Columbia
Lisa Nickle (ON), Ann Milne (ON), Natalie Gray (ON),
Jennifer Lindsay (BC), Mary Munro (BC)

1983 Canadian Champions - Cambridge Ontario
Sandy Couper (ON), Fiona McGillivary (ON)

1984 Canadian Champions - Winnipeg Manitoba
Suzanne Neilson (BC), Adeline Duncan,
Jennifer Lindsay (BC), Jeanette Tikhane (BC)

In 1977, the City of Ottawa withdrew its financial assistance from these National Highland Games; however, the 'Canadian Inter-Provincial Championships' in Highland Dancing had become such a popular event that plans were put in place to ensure the continuance of these Championships. Since 1978, when the 'Canadian Inter-Provincial Championships' were held in Winnipeg, Manitoba, the Championships have moved on an east-west rotation and have been held in Antigonish, Nova Scotia (1979, 1985), Calgary, Alberta (1980, 1994), Montreal, Quebec (1981, 1993), Burnaby, British Columbia (1982), Cambridge, Ontario (1983), again in Winnipeg, Manitoba (1984, 1992), Edmonton, Alberta (1986), Regina, Saskatchewan (1987), Hamilton, Ontario (1988), Saint John, New Brunswick (1989), Whistler, British Columbia (1990), Halifax, Nova Scotia (1991), London, Ontario (1995), Kelowna, British Columbia (1996), Sydney, Nova Scotia (1997), and Regina, Saskatchewan (1998). The 'Canadian Inter-Provincial Championships' returned to Ottawa, ON for its 25th Anniversary in 1999. Edmonton, AB hosted the 2000 'Canadian Inter-Provincial Championships' followed by Montreal, QC in 2001 and Vancouver, BC in 2002.

1986 Canadian Champions - Edmonton Alberta
Jennifer Lindsay (BC), Krista Tronnes (AB), Tied with Ann Milne (ON) pictured separately, Christa Mackie (SK), Danielle Gallant (AB), Kelly Ann Carey (ON)

1985 Canadian Champions - Antigonish NS
Sherri-Lynn Murray (NS), Tracey Barker (AB)

1987 Canadian Champions - Regina Saskatchewan
Carleigh Leighton (ON), Rachelle Wilson (ON), Jacqueline Smith (ON), Ann Milne (ON), Jennifer Lindsay (BC)

1988 Canadian Champions-Hamilton Ontario
Jennifer Lindsay (BC), Jillian Currie (MB), Jacqueline Smith (ON), Estelle Clewes (AB), Heather Martin (ON)

1989 Canadian Champions - Saint John, NB
Ann Milne (ON), Rachelle Wilson (ON)
Dawn Brennan (ON)

1990 Canadian Champions– Whistler British Columbia
Colleen Rintamaki (ON), Natalie Quick (ON), Sabrina Quick (ON),
Dawn Brennan (ON), Ann Milne (ON)

First time 2 sisters had won National Championship titles in the same year. Sabrina and Natalie pictured with their teacher Delma.

1991 Canadian Champions - Halifax Nova Scotia
Natalie Quick (ON), Estelle Clewes (BC), Colleen Rintamaki (ON),
Christina Watts (BC), Ann Milne (ON)

1993 Canadian Champions - Montreal Quebec
Dawn Brennan (ON), Estelle Clewes (BC), Natalie Quick (ON), Colleen Rintamaki (ON), Laura Hester (ON), Amy Turpin (ON)

1994 Canadian Champions - Calgary Alberta
Jacqueline Smith (ON), Colleen Rintamaki (ON), Stephanie Grant (NS), Natalie Quick (ON), Laura Hester (ON), Amy Turpin (ON)

INTERPROV 1995
LONDON ONTARIO

1995 Canadian Champions - London Ontario
Jacqueline Smith (ON), Natalie Quick (ON), Colleen Rintamaki (ON), Sonya Doucette (NS), Laura Hester (ON), Jacqueline McKeown (ON)

1996 Canadian Champions - Kelowna British Columbia
Laura Hester (ON), Erin Welk (BC), Stephanie Grant (NS), Colleen Rintamaki (ON), Jacqueline Smith (ON), Jacqueline McKeown (ON)

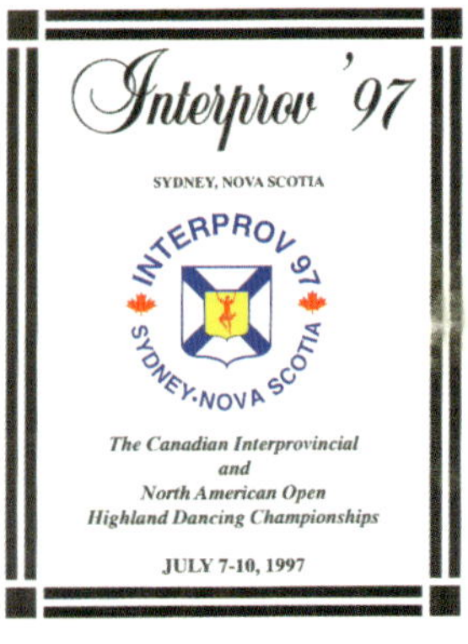

1997 Canadian Champions– Sydney Nova Scotia
Catherine Maitland (ON), Chantal Watt (ON), Ashley Stowkowy (AB), Erin Welk (BC), Colleen Rintamaki (ON)
Missing from picture Adult Canadian Champion Estelle Clewes (BC)

1998 Canadian Champions - Regina Saskatchewan
Estelle Clewes (BC), Chantal Watt (ON),
Colleen Rintamaki (ON), Erin Welk (BC), Stephanie Wilson (BC), Michael Tucker (ON)

2000 Canadian Champions— Edmonton Alberta

2000 Canadian Champions— Edmonton Alberta
Mary McKeever (ON), Stephanie Wilson (BC) Chantal Watt (ON), Georgina Muir (ON), Amy Turpin (ON), Colleen Rintamaki (ON)

It is an amazing accomplishment that these Championships have continued so successfully over the years, largely due to the enthusiasm and hard work of the dedicated committees who have undertaken the organization of the event each year and to the participation of dancers from coast to coast. The event has grown from a one-day Championship to a multi-day event now known as the 'ScotDance Canada Championship Series' and attended by dancers from around the globe.

David Wilton—Scotland
Millennium Sword Winner
SDCCS 2000

Ellis Hayes—Scotland
Best Overseas Dancer
SDCCS 2009

Kimberlee Couper
Teacher—Betty Sutherland
Millennium Sword Winner
SDCCS 2000

2002 Canadian Champions—Vancouver British Columbia
Colleen Rintamaki (ON), Christine Henderson (BC), Chantal Watt (ON), Stephanie Wilson (BC), Christina Mass (AB), Caitlin Wilson (BC)

In 2003 the parent body of ScotDance Canada undertook responsibility for the hosting of the Championship Series, which was held in St. Catharines, ON that year. The need for a more formal rotation system for the location of future Championship Series was recognized and a rotational schedule for the future was established.

2003 Canadian Champions—St Catharines ON
Michelle Nadeau (ON), Laura Cafferty (ON), Marielle Lesperance (ON), Stephanie Wilson (BC), Courtney-Anne McRitchie (ON), Caitlin Wilson (BC)

2004 marked the 30th Anniversary of the 'Canadian Inter-Provincial Championships' with the 'ScotDance Canada Championship Series' being held in Winnipeg, MB. A project to expand the historical records to include the names of winners of the 'Open' Championships held at the Championship Series was spearheaded by Mrs. Helen Christie, mother of ScotDance Canada member, Tara Christie. The information accumulated has now been added to the official historical records of ScotDance Canada and is updated annually.

1980 Open Championship Title Winners
Fiona Nash, Michelle Baird, Kelly Hall, Krista Tronnes, Jennifer Wilson, Jan Sandles

The ScotDance Canada Championship Series was held in Antigonish, NS in 2005, Calgary, AB in 2006, Saint John, NB in 2007 and in Victoria, BC in 2008 where the "City of Victoria Open Championships – Honoring Adeline Duncan" were held. Marking the 35th anniversary of the 'Canadian Inter-Provincial Championships', the summer of 2009 saw this prestigious event take place at the Metro Toronto Convention Centre in downtown Toronto, ON. In addition to the customary competitions and Championships, a Special Event was held in tribute to the late Mr. James L. McKenzie from Aberdeen, Scotland, a judge at the first 'Canadian Inter-Provincial Championships' in 1974 and a great ambassador of Highland dancing who shared so much of his expertise and love of Highland dancing with Canadians in the early days of the Scottish Official Board of Highland Dancing.

1995 Canadian Champions—Antigonish Nova Scotia
Shannon McLean (AB), Kayleigh Macdonald (ON), Michelle Nadeau (AB), Anne Thomson (ON), Courtney-Anne McRitchie (ON), Bevin Wiley (AB)

2006 Canadian Champions- Calgary Alberta
Shayla Appell (AB), Laura Mack (AB), Shannon McLean (AB), Alana McAdie (AB), Marielle Lesperance (ON), Laura Cafferty (ON)

2007 Canadian Champions—Saint John NB
Marielle Lesperance (ON), Beth Whitfield (ON), Keely McPhee (AB) not pictured, Treyven Robitaille (ON), Laura Mack (AB) not pictured,Mykaela Johnston (ON)

2008 Canadian Champions—Victoria British Columbia
Bevin Wiley (AB), Olivia Freeman-Shaw (ON), Mykaela Johnston (ON), Morgan McDougall (ON), Keely McPhee (AB), Marielle Lesperance (ON)

2009 Canadian Champions—2009
Morgan McDougall (ON), Mykaela Johnston (ON), Bevin Wiley (AB), Katie Lee (AB), Olivia Freeman-Shaw (ON), Marielle Lesperance (ON)

CLOSING REMARKS

The introduction and acceptance of the standardized technique of the SOBHD in Canada in the 1960s was no easy task. Starting with only a few Canadian teachers willing to workvery hard to persuade the others that this was a viable idea, thanks to the likes of these teachers and JL McKenzie and Sadie Simpson, Canadian Highland dancers are now amongst the best exponents of 'Board' technique. It is no secret that over the years we have struggled to implement some of the rules & regulations imposed upon us by the SOBHD. ScotDance Canada is now very grateful for the more inclusive attitude being taken by the Board in its role as a truly Worldwide Governing Body.

ScotDance New Zealand

IN THE BEGINNING

ScotDance New Zealand began with a powerful conversation between future members, socialising at a Conference in 1999. This would forever change the face of Highland Dancing in New Zealand.

OUR BACKGROUND

For decades, individuals throughout NZ, many of whom are SDNZ members today, had been trying to initiate changes to the structure of NZ dancing with one goal in mind; simply to dance to the same standard as the Worldwide Governing Body, the SOBHD. Qualifications gained within NZ were internal only and the dancing so vastly different in style and technique that it was unrecognisable to the rest of the highland world. Up until ten years ago, there was no alternative for parents who wanted their child to learn Highland Dancing in NZ.

Despite this difference, the Governing Body of NZ (who once held a membership with the Board) and the SOBHD were in constant communication trying to bridge an ever-widening gap. Inevitably communications would always break down with Scotland because NZ would not accede control of Highland Dancing to the International Board, resulting in the membership being withdrawn. Crucial time passed with no progress. This became frustrating for many who knew that NZ dancing was stagnating with no outside stimulus. The world had opened up with travel, technology and communications yet NZ had chosen to remain in isolation.

If change was to happen in our lifetime, and if true freedom of choice was to exist for NZ dancers, the only way forward was to form a breakaway organisation. This was the conversation at the Conference in 1999, which proved to be the turning point.

It may be of interest to fellow SOBHD members to know that the same personal struggle had gone on many years before. New Zealand Author Ewen McCann relates his story... www.highlanddancinghistory.org

THE WINDS OF CHANGE

With a new century fast approaching, the time was right for a fresh start and to formulate a growing exchange of ideas. Overseas travel had given us exposure to SOBHD in other countries, and an appreciation of the technique which to us was more aesthetically pleasing, musically superior and more anatomically correct than what we had experienced in the New Zealand system.

We knew if we were to join the rest of the world that we had to show our commitment. Board textbooks were purchased, opened and studied furiously and self-training began. At this time there were very few qualified people within NZ, so re-training and up-skilling was done by phone calls, emails and supporting one another.

Overseas friends were called upon for their expertise and knowledge. Old habits had to be shed and replaced with new terminologies. Affiliations grew strong and determination never waivered. It was an extraordinary bonding time for everyone.

The United Kingdom Alliance offered us the breakthrough of an Examiner to sit our Highland and National exams so that Memberships could become Qualifications. With new credentials under our belts, it was time to take the next step…

In January 2001, we met and formed an organisation…ScotDance New Zealand was born. We began to pursue and cultivate contacts throughout the world for input to help shape our constitution to present to the SOBHD, including elections of officers, logos, incorporation of our organisation and mission statements.

Whilst creating this new organisation, teachers began to include Board Technique at competitions in NZ. This sent the country into turmoil. Nowhere in the existing rules did it state the type of technique to be performed on the NZ stage, yet former Champions were overlooked and penalised by judges in favour of far inferior dancers. This placed a huge strain on all involved and we once again make reference to many years before in regards to William Sutherland and his tumultuous years. www.highlanddancinghistory.org The same prejudice had reared its ugly head decades later. It became obvious that a split was inevitable and that our dancers needed to belong to a worldwide organisation that would accept their technique. It was now time to contact the Board in Scotland. SDNZ issued an official invitation to the Board's hierarchy to visit NZ. The invitation was accepted; the stage was set.

THAT MAGICAL MOMENT

At our first formal meeting with the SOBHD held in Auckland October 2002, SDNZ made a ground-setting presentation to our guests Miss Shendl Russell and Miss Marjory Rowan. Along with our Constitution we formally applied to the Board to become an Associate Member, to be recognised as the Official Body within our country.

For the integration to be a success, SDNZ also asked for dispensations to the existing SOBHD rules. We pleaded for support to take the necessary steps required to get "On Board" and proposed some internal policies be initiated. This included a two-year dispensation for dancers, teachers and adjudicators known within NZ as the Dual Membership System.

"ScotDance New Zealand brings the world of highland dancing to New Zealand, by joining a worldwide organisation of highland dancers; a sharing of knowledge and friendships in an international forum, and competing on international stage."

This meant dancers and teachers could remain in the existing NZ system and still be SOBHD without incurring penalty, for a period of two years. To enable our country to begin its growth, NZ qualified judges were able to judge SOBHD competitions within NZ only. The importance of this time allocation was to give us a chance to strengthen internal structures. SOBHD Competition Organisers were created and teachers and dancers gained confidence in the new technique.

The National dances were completely new to NZ and the Jigs and Hornpipes vastly different. Correct uniforms were required. The lack of NZ SOBHD qualified judges meant that the international exam needed to be taken and time given to study. The Board, in its foresight, granted Associate membership and the dispensation and understood the reason for the timeframe. It was a magical moment for SDNZ members, years of thoughts and ideas had finally become a reality. We had persevered and were now truly a part of an International Dancing Arena.

BUILDING BLOCKS

Working the dual system became a very busy and interesting time. Part of the dispensation meant that the Board controlled everything within NZ and approved all administrative matters. All dancers had to be registered via Scotland. For dancers making the changeover to the Board, a full description of their previous achievements had to be forwarded with their registration application. Scotland made all decisions regarding the necessary grade of all dancers based on information supplied. All programmes were sent to Scotland and all monies paid direct to Scotland. It was an intense learning curve, the immense distance between the countries making communication often difficult. For the countries, Day was Night, Winter was Summer, holidays dissimilar and three NZ dollars equalled the Sterling Pound. However knowledge increased and by the time the dual system ended, SDNZ had learnt vast amounts.

Our first NZ registered Board competition was held on 2nd January 2003, at one of the oldest NZ Highland Games, the Waipu Highland Games. Just as a High 'A' across on the Piping Board, was the same as a High 'A' in Scotland, here were our dancers competing on the board performing the same technique as Scotland. Following this momentous occasion, SOBHD competition organisers appeared throughout NZ. The construction of new societies to run competitions became another educational curve for us with committees needing to be formed and constitutionalised. Funds to establish cups and costs needed to be built. SDNZ members made every effort to support all competition areas to help organisers make a success of their day. All competition organisers had to be approved through the Board and a term of three years experience holding competitions had to be completed before organisations could request Championships.

In Easter 2006, the first registered Championship was held in New Plymouth and in 2007 the first SOBHD NZ Championship title was competed for. The standard of NZ dancers has always been commented on by overseas teachers and examiners and NZ prides itself on this knowledge. From the outset it has been our practice to invite and to learn from those International Teachers, Judges and Examiners who have visited our shores. We have always been eager to learn and to listen as they have imparted their wealth of knowledge over the years and to those individuals we thank you sincerely for your assistance and friendship.

HOMEGROWN WORLD CHAMPIONS

For many years before, NZ dancers had trickled into Scotland to face the challenge of converting their style to compete internationally. In 1966, Sandra Wright became the first NZ dancer to win a World Championship title. This set NZ on the map as a country of Highland Dancers. Years later, our own local Kiwi dancer, Morgan Bamford was to follow by becoming one of the youngest dancers ever to win a World Championship title. Her achievement has continued on to date, winning 4 Juvenile World Championships and in 2009 the Junior World Championship.

BECOMING SELF SUFFICIENT

Forever looking to the future, we applied and were approved our own NZ SOBHD Registration Agent in 2005. As mentioned, up to this point our dancers had been registering through Scotland so an active and working Registration Committee had to be formed. This not only created crucial income for SDNZ but also gave us a good understanding of where our dancers were at in terms of growth. The registration form is now available from our website and so dancers and their families became familiar with logging onto our domain:
www.scotdancence.co.nz

In 2007, SDNZ made a proposal to the Board to become an Affiliate Member. When we heard of our achievement we were delighted. From the inception of our organisation this had been our long-term goal and having the privilege of our own delegate has been such a huge benefit to us many, many miles away.

In 2008 New Zealand became responsible for granting our own Competition Registrations and once again, this has enabled SDNZ the advantage of reaching a wider audience and being nationally responsible.

THE JOURNEY

The growth of our organisation has been gradual and controlled. Many times SDNZ had applied to the Board for various things and been turned down. Sometimes it was difficult to understand why, but in hindsight, the Board has been careful to make sure that our growth was at a rate that was manageable to our country and our members and we have appreciated every little step taken. We have also had major support from many people throughout the administration and management of the Board. Each piece of advice has been vigilantly listened to and considered.

To those dancers, teachers, administrators, examiners, judges, parents and friends who have travelled to our country to participate and encourage us, we say thank-you for embracing us – when we made our pact at the Conference of '99 we left behind some longtime friends, but as we travel the road of our new destination we realize our passion for Highland Dancing is worldwide and our friendships forever.

Highland Dancing Teachers Association of England

A BRIEF HISTORY

In the early seventies Highland Dancing teachers would only meet each other at festivals and competitions. These meetings were the only opportunity the teachers had to discuss technical questions and other dance related issues. Scotland seemed far away in those days.

One of these teachers Mrs Valerie Geddes thought it would be a good idea to form an Association of teachers where the issues raised during these informal chats could be openly debated and resolved for the benefit of the whole of the dancing community.

This was put to the teachers of the main dancing schools at the time. They all agreed it was an excellent idea and as a result, a preliminary meeting was arranged at Valerie's home in March 1973. The following teachers attended, Mrs Sophie Reid, Mrs Roseleen Cooper, Mrs Jean Gibson, Mrs Mary Hosker, and Miss Janet Cook. The idea was discussed and all present concluded that forming an Association of teachers was the only direction to go if Highland Dancing was to progress in England.

Office Bearers were elected Mrs Jean Gibson as the Secretary, Mrs Valerie Geddes as the Treasurer with Mrs Sophie Reid, Mrs Rosaleen Cooper, and Miss Janet Cook elected to the Committee, Valerie's husband Mr Allen Geddes was asked to fill the role of Chairman, which he did for many years.

The first meeting of the newly formed committee was held on 1st July 1973 and from that day the Association has never looked back. The committee busied itself with establishing rules and regulations, organising lecturers and devising a name for this new alliance, and so the Highland Dancing Teachers Association of England was founded.

The first Annual General Meeting of the HDTAE was held on the 31st March 1974 with 15 members attending. The Association was found to be a great assistance to both teachers and pupils.

The HDTAE applied for membership- of the Scottish Official Broad of Highland Dancing and this was granted in 1979. Membership of the SOBHD meant that the HDTAE would be up to date on all the latest developments in the World of Highland Dancing.

Miss Janet Cook took over as secretary when Mrs Jean Gibson retired. Miss Patricia Reid took over as Chairman when Mr Allen Geddes retired. Janet Cook while secretary decided that the HDTAE should run a Dancing Festival with choreography one year and then National the next year. Janet Cook still organises the HDTAE Festival which is held at the end of March each year. Mrs Valerie Geddes is still Treasurer. We now have area officers for organising the workshop, and delegates to the SOBHD which means we now have a committee of 12 which is nearly the size of the membership in 1974!

When Janet Cook retired as Secretary in 2004 Helen Buckingham became Secretary for three years and the present Secretary is Amanda Bignell.

Each year two workshops are organised for pupils and teachers. In May/June Championship for Premier dancers ready for All England Championships and basic highland for Pre-premier dancers. In September/October it can be any subject. At these workshops lecturers come not only from current members but lecturers are also brought down from Scotland. In March, in the morning, there is a lecture for HDTAE members (no pupils). The AGM is then held in the afternoon.

Memories
the way we were

721
793

BEA
BEA

Glayva
Drambuie
Baileys
Tia Maria
Midori

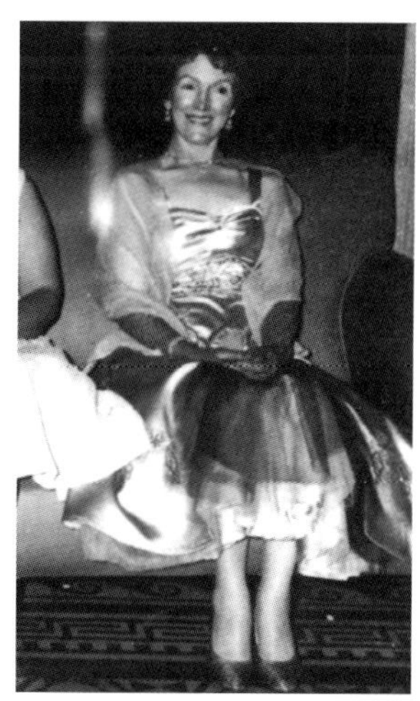